"In our time, traditional liturgies from Christian Churches lack new resources. Diann Neu offers us an alternative. *Stirring Waters* rouses static traditions, enlivening them with new energy. With deep sensibility to the cries for justice, particularly for women's lives, Diann designed creative liturgies which celebrate our women ancestors and invite their stories to speak to our daily joys and pains. Her work inspires us to foster new relations among women around the world, as well as between women and the planet."

—Dr. Ivone Gebara, ecofeminist philosopher and theologian
Brazil

"This book is a gift and an inspiration for women's groups and faith communities seeking to drink from the spiritual well of women's wisdom across time, cultures, and space through liturgical action. Beautifully written by a foremost liturgist, it reclaims the power of rituals as a source of hope, bonding, and imagination for actions to change the world. I recommend it highly."

—Kwok Pui-lan, William F. Cole Professor of Christian Theology and Spirituality, emerita, Episcopal Divinity School

"*Stirring Waters* is exactly what the church needs right now: an inclusive, creative, thoughtful resource that draws deeply from the wells of women, past and present. Neu does a masterful job of bringing the feminist spirit to life through prayers, poems, and hymns. I can't wait to host these liturgies in my community."

—Jessie Bazan, M.Div., editor and co-author of *Dear Joan Chittister: Conversations with Women in the Church*

"What an amazing resource of female wisdom and lived experience. Through ritual celebration, women all around the world can unite on those issues that matter most for the well-being of all life forms and the future of our planet. Pioneering WATER pioneers again."

—Miriam Therese Winter, Ph.D., Medical Mission Sister

"*Stirring Waters: Feminist Liturgies for Justice,* Diann Neu's new contribution to the development of contemporary spirituality, does more than simply write a chain of liturgies. It brings the art of meaning to the depth of reflection. If anything affects the growth of the faith as well as the spiritual life of the faithful, it is liturgy that touches the heart, expands understanding, and stretches the soul. This book will enrich the quality of prayer for group after group, for occasion after occasion, over and over again."

—Joan Chittister, OSB

"For the past 35 years Diann Neu has been teaching people world-wide how to create and celebrate feminist liturgies. *Stirring Waters: Feminist Liturgies for Justice* makes these liturgies available to an international audience. I highly recommend this book in the hope that many will not only read it but also celebrate its feminist liturgies in these wearisome times."

—Dr. Elisabeth Schüssler Fiorenza
Krister Stendahl Professor
Harvard University Divinity School

"Offering an awesome array of rituals, *Stirring Waters* expands our moral imaginations about justice possibilities and inflames our passion for realizing them. Neu's rituals teach us inspiring histories of justice-making women and girls from around the world. Overflowing with ideas for action, study, and communal spiritual practice, it is the grounding resource faithful people struggling against social injustice need right now."

—Traci C. West, author of *Solidarity and Defiant Spirituality: Africana Lessons on Racism, Religion, and Ending Gender Violence*

"These powerful and moving liturgies help us form tangible justice-making in community. Neu's fine sense of blending words, music, and reflection touches our souls and comforts our spirits and also provides meaningful ways to live out the call for justice each of these liturgies challenge us to undertake. Once again, Neu gives us a powerful resource for head and heart."

—Emilie M. Townes, Dean and E. Rhodes and Leona B. Carpenter Professor of Womanist Ethics and Society
Vanderbilt University School of Theology

"*Stirring Waters* is a spectacular resource for planning feminist liturgies. For every season, every month, every human need, this collection of liturgies provides forms, words, songs, and actions. Diann Neu offers us the fruits of a lifetime of leading, imagining, and embodying ways of praying, celebrating, remembering, and living justly. On every page there is just the right word, sound, movement to evoke feminist ways of naming what is true and acting upon it. *Stirring Waters* is a long-awaited gift."

—Janet Walton
Professor of Worship at Union Theological Seminary in New York

"This rich collection of liturgies for a range of religious and political occasions does a terrific job centering women's voices. There's much to learn from each chapter about ritual-making inspired by a diverse group of women representing diverse eras and cultures. Readers can adopt particular liturgies in whole, or select from the many songs, readings, invocations, litanies, and gestures to create something that meets a group's specific needs. A terrific resource for anyone interested in feminist spirituality and ritual."

—Judith Plaskow, author of *Standing Again at Sinai: Judaism from a Feminist Perspective*

Stirring WATERS

Feminist Liturgies for Justice

Diann L. Neu

water
Women's Alliance for Theology, Ethics, and Ritual
Silver Spring, Maryland
www.waterwomensalliance.org

LITURGICAL PRESS
Collegeville, Minnesota
www.litpress.org

Cover design by Amy Marc. Art courtesy of Getty Images.

ISBN 978-0-8146-6613-5 (hardcover) ISBN 978-0-8146-6496-4 (e-book)

1 2 3 4 5 6 7 8 9

Library of Congress Cataloging-in-Publication Data

Names: Neu, Diann L., 1948– author. | Women's Alliance for Theology, Ethics, and Ritual.
Title: Stirring Waters : feminist liturgies for justice / Diann L. Neu.
Description: Collegeville : Liturgical Press, 2020. | Includes index. |
Summary: "A collection of fifty-two feminist liturgies for justice from the Women's Alliance for Theology, Ethics, and Ritual (WATER), ready-made to help communities venerate powerful women of faith, develop a richer and deeper spirituality, and take real action for justice"—Provided by publisher.
Identifiers: LCCN 2019032392 (print) | LCCN 2019032393 (ebook) | ISBN 9780814664728 (paperback) | ISBN 9780814664964 (epub) | ISBN 9780814664964 (mobi) | ISBN 9780814664964 (pdf)
Subjects: LCSH: Worship programs. | Women in Christianity—Miscellanea. | Christianity and justice—Miscellanea. | Women in public worship.
Classification: LCC BV199.W6 N48 2020 (print) | LCC BV199.W6 (ebook) | DDC 264.0082—dc23
LC record available at https://lccn.loc.gov/2019032392
LC ebook record available at https://lccn.loc.gov/2019032393

To the WATER community worldwide.
With wondrous gratitude for thirty-five years together
stirring waters and letting justice flow. Be well!

Contents

Section Three: Let Justice Flow like Water

Section Four: Be Well!

Section Five: Ever-Flowing Streams

Introduction

by Mary E. Hunt

What a thrill to have Diann L. Neu's *Stirring Waters: Feminist Liturgies for Justice* available for a global audience. We at the Women's Alliance for Theology, Ethics, and Ritual (WATER) have been privileged to cocreate and celebrate with Diann these fifty-two ways of praying and worshiping, and many others that remain for subsequent publication. The collection is a fitting gift for WATER's thirty-fifth anniversary offered with thanks to the many people who are part of this justice-seeking network. Those who meet WATER for the first time through this collection can imagine a broad and deep array of hearty colleagues, many living, but some already having moved on from this life, lifting voices in praise, hands in work, and hearts in hope.

Most people meet religion through liturgy and ritual. At least more find it there than will ever encounter it in theology or ethics! WATER's liturgy offerings are at once practical and life-saving. Many people, especially women, people of color, and nonbinary folks, feel deeply excluded from their religious traditions of origin or choice. Restrictive language and imagery, male-only celebrants in some traditions, and sheer boredom from often stale prayers and sermons leave people wanting more. Some people fear exposing our children to such uninspiring celebrations, yet we want them to have a rich spirituality. These celebrations are ways to address such dilemmas.

At WATER, people are encouraged to shape their own ways of being religious. We do not do it alone, but in concert with other seekers who want their faith expressions to cohere with their inclusive, Earth-loving politics. The two are not mutually exclusive as this book proves. Everyone experiences the illness of a child or loved one, the death of a parent, the need for role models who look like us, and so many other exigencies for which these creative, empowering, nurturing liturgies and rituals are a necessary balm.

We gather, as in the first section "Drink from the Well," to nourish one another when traditional fonts are simply not adequate. This set of a dozen liturgies draws on historical figures like Miriam, Hildegard of Bingen, Sojourner Truth, Julian of Norwich, and Mary Magdalene. They invite us to the edges of our own wells where we drink gratefully.

Over WATER's first thirty-five years, we have spent the privilege that accrues to white, US-based, cisgender, well-educated, economically comfortable people to overcome oppression. That is our work, to change the conditions of inequality and exclusion. WATER includes many people of color, folks from all over the world speaking many languages, trans people, elderly persons, those living with disabilities, immigrants, and those made poor by global capitalism and greed. Together, we take every opportunity to "Step into the Pool" as the second section is named. We push the parameters of our knowledge and our comfort zones, learning from women around the globe (and one in space!). They are our guides and resources, our inspiration and our role models. Invoking their names—Malala Yousafzai, Sally Ride, as well as feminist ministers, among so many—reinforces our activism and helps to frame the parameters of our commitments.

Contemporary problems come into focus in the third section, "Let Justice Flow like Water." Human trafficking, racism, the need for peace, domestic violence, and HIV/AIDS are just a sample of contemporary challenges. These liturgies are designed to demonstrate how useful prayer can be for people who are deeply engaged in social change work. At the same time, Diann wisely weaves in celebrations of friendship, mother-daughter bonds, and fun to help communities balance struggles and hopes, what feminist songwriter Carolyn McDade terms "Trouble and Beauty." Many groups use these popular prayers, or similar rituals modeled on them, as they engage in civil disobedience, ecclesial resistance, and organized persistence.

Over the years, we at WATER have learned to embrace the need for healing and the power of imagination. We know the wisdom of honoring everyday life, including the seasons, the New Year, Thanksgiving, and Earth Day. We take time to set a simple, lovely table, to gather friends, colleagues, and family, always including any who might be left aside. We believe in the human right to a safe, enjoyable common life lived with intention and according to the local culture. Far from being the stuff of privilege, this is simply the birthright of all. The rituals in this fourth section, "Be Well!" are good examples of how to live it.

Violence, especially against women, children, and Earth, is ubiquitous. But empowering resources are needed to reclaim and refocus our voices as we strive to change this common aspect of the human condition. The closing section, titled "Ever-Flowing Streams," underscores the power of feminist liturgies to inspire and animate future generations.

WATER includes more than ninety interns who have graced the office in the first three decades. Virtually all of them have had a hand in a ritual, helping to plan, execute, and evaluate. For many of them, the very notion of creating ways to be religious that are not sexist and racist, that aim to reinforce social justice is novel and welcome. Many have taken their new skills to their countries, cities, and universities of origin to be used there.

Diann Neu insists that rituals are simple prototypes. Make them over as you need to in your community. Add your own touches; leave out what does not fit or work in your setting. The book is replete with concrete information, especially the section "How to Create a Feminist Liturgy for Justice." Use the resources to enlarge your scope in this rapidly developing field. Check out the wonderful music, especially from feminist musicians whose work inspires, solidifies, indeed sings our commitments.

The rush to the doors of many mainline religious institutions does not mean postmodern people are not religious. To the contrary. For many, it means that they take their spirituality too seriously to waste time in worship that is not commensurate with the depth of their commitments and the urgency of Earth's needs. Diann Neu's liturgies and her encouragement to all of us to be proactive, to be agents of our own spirits, are a big step in a useful direction. So "Stir the Waters" where you are, knowing that you are well accompanied by people over millennia who have done and will do the same.

Overview

Every day I go to the water. Presently my water is a pond with a fountain that sits on the deck at my home. Throughout my life the water has been a lake: Lake Manitou in northern Indiana, Lake LaSalle in Brown County, Indiana, and the lakes at St. Mary-of-the-Woods, Indiana. In my childhood the water was a creek flowing beside my family home. During my graduate studies, the water was the San Francisco Bay. Now it is the Atlantic Ocean.

Water: rain, streams, lakes, rivers, oceans, ponds, creeks, pools, wells, waterfalls; and the fluids of most living organisms

According to Cherokee tradition, going to water at the beginning and at the end of each day is good practice. On each visit one asks the water to take what is not needed or what does not belong (like anger, worry, blame, competition, conflict, anxiety) and to bring what one needs (like calm, inspiration, insight, compassion, patience, healing). The Cherokee understand that the waters of our lives and the waters of Earth are intertwined. Throughout my life I have known this too, perhaps beginning with living in the water of my mother's womb.

Stirring: inspiring, moving, impassioned, exciting, moving briskly, electrifying, awakening, motivating, stimulating, provoking, affecting, disturbing, causing commotion, energizing

Throughout the thirty-five years that the Women's Alliance for Theology, Ethics, and Ritual (WATER) has been in operation, I have been creating and teaching people worldwide how to design feminist liturgies for justice to celebrate with their communities.

Stirring Waters: Feminist Liturgies for Justice presents the scripts of those liturgies designed and celebrated with local, national, and international groups: the WATER community; Sisters against Sexism (SAS), the oldest US women-church base community; other women-church groups; house churches; women's religious communities; intentional eucharistic communities; the Providence community of St. Mary-of-the-Woods; ecumenical and interfaith feminist groups; and justice organizations worldwide.

The Creative Process

Every month at WATER, I meet with staff to design, write, and celebrate a liturgy that is appropriate for the needs of that particular month. As seen in the contents of this book, a liturgy may raise up a particular holy person, like

Julian of Norwich, or focus on a universal theme, like Earth Day. It might be created to encourage solidarity with a justice focus, like Domestic Violence Awareness, or focus on wellness for the new year. These liturgies seek to bring feminist insights to the theme of the month.

Use the liturgies in this book as a resource to plan the ones that you and your community need to nourish your souls, focus your passions, and call you to make the world a better place.

The Structure of This Book

Each of the fifty-two liturgies in *Stirring Waters* is a complete ritual focused on a specific theme. The book contains four sections of twelve liturgies each that correspond to one of the months of the year. The pairing of a given liturgy with a specific month offers a suggestion for themes throughout the year. There are four more liturgies to round out the year with fifty-two. The liturgies can be celebrated whenever you and your community need them, and the sections within a given liturgy can be interchanged with another one.

The first section, "Drink from the Well," features twelve liturgies honoring holy women who invite us into their sacred spaces to inspire and awaken us to spiritual insights and practices. They challenge us to be bold and stir the waters!

Like the ancient village well, these women give water to present generations like they did to searching souls of their day. Like many women of the Bible who make their entrances by a well, these women are a source of life-giving water. Rigoberta Menchú, Mayan Quiché-Indian human rights activist from Guatemala who won the Nobel Peace Prize in 1992, speaks for them in *Crossing Borders* (Brooklyn, NY: Verso Books, 1998): "I am like a drop of water on a rock. After drip, drip, dripping in the same place, I begin to leave a mark, and I leave my mark in many people's hearts."

Come to the water and drink from the wells of Sojourner Truth, Brigit, Miriam, Catherine of Siena, Julian of Norwich, Sophia Spirit, Mary Magdalene, Wise Woman, Hildegard of Bingen, Mother Théodore Guérin, *Comadres* and Martyrs of El Salvador, and Mary. They tell their stories, share their wisdom, and challenge us to act justly now.

The second section, "Step into the Pool," presents twelve liturgies that challenge us to electrify, provoke, disturb, and cause commotion like Sojourner Truth, African American abolitionist and women's rights activist who said in 1851 at the Women's Rights Convention in Akron, Ohio: "While the water is stirring, I'll step into the pool."

Come to the water and step into the pool: Recognize Women in Politics; Called to Heal; Come to Waters of Peace for World Water Day; Return to Life for Earth Day; Reach for the Stars with Sally Ride on National Space Day; Praise the Sun for Summer Solstice; Stand with Malala Yousafzai; Keep on Moving in Solidarity; Bless Feminist Ministers; The Faces of Breast Cancer;

Give Thanks for Women of Wisdom; and Bringing the Light of Wisdom for Winter Solstice. These liturgies invite action.

The third section, "Let Justice Flow like Water," consists of twelve liturgies that invite communities to be impassioned, motivated, energized, and stimulated like Wangari Maathai, environmental activist, founder of the Green Belt Movement in Kenya, and Nobel Peace Prize laureate who said in a 2006 speech at the Goldman Awards in San Francisco: "Until you dig a hole, you plant a tree, you water it and make it survive, you haven't done a thing. You are just talking."

Come to the water and let justice flow: Praying to End Human Trafficking; Witnessing Womanist Wisdom during Black History Month; Celebrate International Women's Day; Imagine a Church for Our Daughters and Take Them to Work; Remembering and Letting Go on Mother's Day; Grateful, Proud, and Connected for Pride and Equality Day; The Saving Grace of Fun; Cherishing Friends on Friendship Day; Lift Up Peacemakers for International Day of Peace; Breaking Silence to End Domestic Violence; Becoming Saints of Love and Justice on All Saints' Day; and Telling Love's Story on World AIDS Day. These liturgies call for justice-seeking work that stirs waters!

The fourth section, "Be Well!" includes twelve liturgies for personal meditation to sustain, cleanse, refresh, and rejuvenate drooping spirits. In *The Interior Castle* (Mahwah, NJ: Paulist Press, 1979), Teresa of Avila, Spanish mystic and Doctor of the Catholic Church, reflects: "The tree that is beside the running water is fresher and gives more fruit" (181).

Come to the water and be well: A Cup of Blessings for the New Year; Goodbye Winter, Hello Spring!; Thank ReSisters Worldwide; Earth Day Prayer; You Are the Salt of the Earth; Drawing from Wisdom's Well; Hand in Hand—Imagine!; Bless Me with Creative Hope; Pray for Peace on Earth; Grant Me Healing; Thanksgiving Meal of Gratitude; and You Are Home. These liturgies call us home to ourselves, to breathe again, to replenish ourselves so we are ready to stir the waters, step into the pool, and let justice flow.

The fifth section, "Ever-Flowing Streams," offers four more liturgies for the other four weeks in the year: Listen to the Cries for Justice; Pray with Us; #MeToo: Reclaiming Our Voices in an Age of Violence; and Water Meditation for Wellness.

Each liturgy is preceded by an epigraph that introduces the theme of the service and lists the materials that are needed to prepare for the liturgy. Place the materials needed for the liturgy on a table or in the center of a circle of chairs. The order of each liturgy includes the following:

Call to Gather welcomes participants, focuses the liturgy, states why we are celebrating this theme, and invites people to gather.

Naming the Circle invites participants to create the liturgy circle by speaking their names and saying something specific that focuses the liturgy.

Songs | Prayers | Litanies | Lighting Candles support the theme, establish the mood, transition into readings and blessings, and weave the liturgy together.

Readings can be Scripture passages, poems, stories, and/or excerpts from writings by women or justice leaders to capture the message of the liturgy.

Reflection | Sharing, traditionally the homily, offers time for communal sharing since the Divine speaks to everyone. A few sentences recap the message of the readings, and then one or two questions are posed for quiet reflection before sharing.

Presentation of the Symbol introduces the symbol in relation to the theme of the liturgy. A blesser holds it, presents it to the community, and says why it is being used.

Blessing the Symbol involves prayer, song, gesture, and community response.

Interaction with the Symbol may come before or after the blessing. One gives directions for interacting with the symbol: pass it around the circle, one person offers it to others, participants go to stations/centers to interact with it, several people start passing it to different parts of the circle, groups of people come forward to drink water from the common well, and many other ways.

Sending Forth gathers up the message of the liturgy and challenges people to go forth to act on it.

Greeting of Peace offers a time to bid farewell with handshakes, warm greetings, hugs, embraces, and/or exchanging symbols used in the liturgy.

Closing Song sends people forth empowered to live the message of the liturgy.

Take Action challenges participants to act for justice to make the world a better place for all creation.

Learn More from These Resources offers feminist resources that enhance and expand the theme for each liturgy. They can be books, websites, YouTube videos, organizations, articles, and more. Each liturgy offers an educational opportunity.

After the liturgy, think about what went well, what worked, what could have been different or better. Then incorporate those changes the next time.

Use these liturgies as you will to motivate and deepen your work for justice.

Many blessings, and enjoy your liturgies!

Liturgy of Invitation
Come to the Water

Blessed are you, Divine Wisdom,
for stirring waters and
challenging us to step into the pool.

From time to time we are invited to step into the waters and to even stir the waters. The precious resource of water refreshes, soothes, and heals the parched body and dry Earth. In ancient times, fountains, springs, and wells were traditional gathering places for those who brought the life-sustaining waters back to their homes and communities.

This liturgy invites participants to "Come to the Water," to gather in community to drink from the well of Divine Wisdom, to step into the pool of waters for healing, and to take action that justice may flow like water. Oh, and to be well while acting for justice!

Preparation

Gather and sit beside a body of water. Or pick a favorite bowl, representing a well, and put it in a special place on a table. Pour into a pitcher rose water, ocean water, spring water, or tap water with desired additives: salt, herbs, a few drops of oil, a flower, or vegetable coloring for a seasonal theme. Place three candles, the water representing a well, two green branches, and a bell on the table or central space. Invite people to bring a flask of water from their local area, if appropriate.

Call to Gather

Come to the water today and join water carriers worldwide. Give thanks f the precious resource of water. It is the life-giving element of nature from which all life emerges. Water contains a unique spiritual energy that c nects us to ancient powers.

Fountains, springs, and wells signify traditional meeting places wh eir gh- bors gathered with their water jars, caught up on the daily new n, re- stories, drank healing waters, and connected with the commu waters. plenished on all levels, they returned home to nourish other e world.

Water plays a central role in many religions and beliefs epresents

- Water cleans the body and purifies it. As source (re)birth.

- Water is often perceived as a god, goddess, or divine agency in religions.
- In some religions water is considered to have powers to transform this world, annihilate sins, and create holiness.
- In Buddhism, water is used in funerals.
- In Christianity, water is linked to baptism.
- In Hinduism, water is imbued with powers of spiritual purification. Morning cleansing with water is an everyday obligation.
- In Islam, water is used for purification ablutions after sex, before the Friday prayers, and before touching the Koran.
- In Judaism, water is used for ritual baths, or mikveh, to restore or maintain a state of purity on Fridays and before large celebrations, before a wedding, after giving birth, and after menstruation.
- In Shinto, veneration of the *kami*, which are deities believed to inhabit nature, must always begin by a ritual of purification with water. This act restores order and balance between nature, humans, and the deities. Waterfalls are considered sacred in Shinto.

Let us call upon Divine Wisdom, the Wellspring of Life, the Ever-Flowing Stream, to be with us as we come to the waters. Let us pour our local waters into the well.

Naming the Circle

To create our circle today, let us say our names, and then we will all respond, "Come to the Water."

Song

"Wa Wa Wa Emimimo" ("Come, O Holy Spirit, Come"), Yoruba & Music © The Church of the Lord (Aladura) Worldwide, P.O. Box 71, Shagamu, Ogun State, Nigeria. Transcription as taught by Samuel Solanke & English paraphrase: I-to Loh © 1986 WCC and the Asian Institute for Liturgy and Music. Used with permission.

Come, O Holy Spirit, come.	*Wa wa wa Emimimo.*
[illegible]me, [illegible] Loving Spirit, come.	*Wa wa wa Alagbara.*
Co[illegible], co[illegible]e, come.	*Wao wao, wao.*

[illegible]ghting Candles

[illegible]*der lights a candle, saying:* Blessed are you, Divine Wisdom, for stirring [illegible] and challenging us to step into the pool.

[illegible]"Come, O Holy Spirit, Come"

A yo[illegible]man lights a candle, saying: Blessed are you, Wellspring of Life, for in[illegible] to drink from the well.

Song [illegible] Holy Spirit, Come"

A third person lights a candle, saying: Blessed are you, Ever-Flowing Stream, for calling us to do justice.

Song: *"Come, O Holy Spirit, Come"*

To ensure that the light remains a part of our journey long after the candles burn away, cup your hands in front of these flames and gesture them toward your eyes and body three times as a blessing. *Blessing.*

To ensure that the light sparks justice worldwide, gesture your hands outward to bless the cosmos. *Blessing.*

Song: *"Come, O Holy Spirit, Come"*

Litany of Need

Many people yearn to come to life-sustaining waters for healing and refreshment. We recognize among us these varieties of people by inviting a few to give testimony. Please respond to each by saying, "And there is a healing community."

Two people alternate praying this litany.

1. In my life there are strong women, men, and children,
Response: And there is a healing community.
2. In my life there are liberating struggles,
Response: And there is a healing community.
1. In my life there are closed doors,
Response: And there is a healing community.
2. In my life there is racism, sexism, classism, many -isms,
Response: And there is a healing community.
1. In my life there is homophobia and transphobia,
Response: And there is a healing community.
2. In my life there are oppressive structures,
Response: And there is a healing community.
1. In my life there is domestic violence,
Response: And there is a healing community.
2. In my life there are wounds from clergy sexual abuse,
Response: And there is a healing community.
1. In my life there is joy to be shared,
Response: And there is a healing community.
2. In my life . . . Name others and we will respond.

Song

"Creation of Peace" by Carolyn McDade, We Come with Our Voices *(Surtsey Publishing © 1979, renewed © 1991 Carolyn McDade). Used with permission.*

We'll build a land where we bind up the broken.
We'll build a land where the captives go free,
Where the oil of gladness dissolves all mourning.
Oh, we'll build a promised land that can be.

Chorus:
Come build a land where sisters and brothers
Anointed by God then create peace
Where justice shall roll down like waters
And peace like an ever-flowing stream.

We'll build a land where we bring good tidings
To all the afflicted and those who mourn.
We'll then give them garlands instead of ashes.
Oh, we'll build a land where peace is born. *Chorus.*

We'll be a land building up ancient cities,
Raising up devastations from old,
Restoring ruins of generations.
Oh, we'll be a land of people so bold. *Chorus.*

Come build a land where mantles of praises
Resound from spirits once faint and once weak,
Where like oaks of righteousness stand her people.
Oh, come build the land my people we seek. *Chorus.*

Reading from the Gospel of John

"An angel of God would come down to the pool from time to time, to stir up the water; the first one to step into the water after it had been stirred up would be completely healed."

—John 5:4

Pause.

Reading from Hildegard of Bingen

"The soul that is full of wisdom is saturated with the spray of a bubbling fountain—God [her]self."

—Gabriele Uhlein, *Meditations with Hildegard of Bingen* (Rochester, VT: Bear & Company Publishing, 1983), 63

Pause.

Reading from Sojourner Truth

"While the water is stirring, I'll step into the pool."

—1851 Women's Rights Convention in Akron, Ohio

Pause.

Reading from Wangari Maathai

"Until you dig a hole, you plant a tree, you water it and make it survive, you haven't done a thing. You are just talking."

—2006 speech at the Goldman Awards in San Francisco

Pause.

Reading from Maya Angelou

"A Woman in harmony with her spirit is like a river flowing. She goes where she will without pretense and arrives at her destination prepared to be herself and only herself."

Pause.

Song

"Creation of Peace"

Come build a land where sisters and brothers
Anointed by God then create peace
Where justice shall roll down like waters
And peace like an ever-flowing stream.

Blessing the Waters

Three blessers pray alternately.

All blessers: Come! Let us gather around this well together.

1. You who are thirsty, come to the water.
2. You who need healing, come to the water.
3. You who seek community, come to the water.

1. You who search for spiritual connections, come to the water.
2. You who are healers, come to the water.
3. You who need hospitality, come to the water.

1. Let us bless this water together. Extend your hands.

1. Blessed are you, Divine Wisdom, for stirring waters and challenging us to step into the pool.
2. Blessed are you, Wellspring of Life, for hovering over the waters.
3. Blessed are you, Ever-Flowing Stream, for bringing rain to dry lands.

1. Blessed are you, Miriam, for dancing your people through the waters to promised lands.
2. Blessed are you, Women Water Carriers, for hauling water from sacred wells to thirsty towns.
3. Blessed are you, Compassionate Tear, for weeping with us because of the violence your people experience from churches, synagogues, mosques, and governments.

1. Blessed are you, Risk-Takers, for rolling away stones of injustice so water can flow to quench thirsty souls.
2. Blessed are you, Eternal Spring, for filling our jars with the divine gift of water.
3. Blessed are you, Healing River, for sending amazing grace to your people.

All blessers: Come! Let us receive this water and bless ourselves with it.
The three blessers dip green branches into the water and sprinkle the gathered.

Blessing with Stirring Waters

Touch your heart and say after me:
Bless my heart, that I may be open to the Spirit. *Echo.*
Touch your eyes, saying:
Bless my eyes, that I may see clearly the pain of others. *Echo.*
Touch your ears, saying:
Bless my ears, that I may hear the cries of those pushed to the margins. *Echo.*
Touch your mouth, saying:
Bless my mouth, that I may speak words of wisdom. *Echo.*
Touch your feet, saying:
Bless my feet, that I may step into the waters and walk the path of justice. *Echo.*
Touch your hands, saying:
Bless my hands, that I many touch respectfully with loving grace. *Echo.*
Touch your whole body, saying:
Bless my whole body, that I may be filled with healing grace. *Echo.*
Greet those around you carefully, blessing them in your own words.

Song

"Blessing Song" by M. T. Winter, from Woman Prayer, Woman Song *(Meyer Stone Books © 1987 by Medical Mission Sisters). Used with permission.*

May the blessing of God go before you.
May Her grace and peace abound.
May Her Spirit live within you.
May Her love wrap you 'round.
May Her blessing remain with you always.
May you walk on holy ground.

Take Action

Let us put our prayers into action. Here are some possible ways:

- Discover where the waters are in your neighborhood—rivers, streams, wells, springs, fountains, creeks, pools, lakes, ocean.
- Give a drink of water to plants and animals.
- Write an encouraging note, or give a card to someone who is working for a justice issue like climate change, gun safety, voting rights, farmers, protecting the Affordable Care Act, LGBTQIA+ rights, immigration, raising children, and many others.
- Comfort a child or friend who is crying.
- Gather with a community to celebrate the liturgies in this book.

Sending Forth

Let us go forth refreshed from gathering at the well.
Let us go forth committed to stepping into the pool.
Let us go forth challenged to stir waters for justice.
Let us go forth to engage in wellness.

Learn More from These Resources

Aldredge-Clanton, Jann, with composer Larry E. Schultz. *Inclusive Songs for Resistance & Social Action.* Burnet, TX: Eakin Press, 2018.

Brandt, Cindy Wang. *Parenting Forward: How to Raise Children with Justice, Mercy, and Kindness.* Grand Rapids, MI: Wm. B. Eerdmans Publishing Co., 2019.

Crabtree, Maril. *Sacred Waters: Stories of Healing, Cleansing, and Renewal.* Avon, MA: Adams Media, 2005.

section one

Drink from the Well

The soul that is full of wisdom is saturated
with the spray of a bubbling fountain—God [her]self.

—Hildegard of Bingen, *Meditations with Hildegard of Bingen* by Gabriele Uhlein

The teachings of the wise are a fountain of life.

—Proverbs 13:14

Refresh me with springs of living waters.
Draw me down into your well of rebirth and let my wounds open
and empty into your wonderful compost heap.

—Alla Renée Bozarth, "O Earth, Wrap Me," *The Book of Bliss*

1. January

Step into the Pool with Sojourner Truth

If the first woman God ever made was strong enough to turn the world upside down all alone, these women together ought to be able to turn it back, and get it right side up again!
And now they is asking to do it, the men better let them.

—Sojourner Truth, "Ain't I a Woman?"

In January, in keeping with the "I have a dream" theme of Martin Luther King Jr. Day, we raise up a wise African American woman who inspires us to live the dream. Sojourner Truth was a Spirit-led activist for abolition, women's rights, and nonviolence, who continues to inspire us today. She was born into slavery but escaped to freedom with her infant daughter.

This liturgy tells the story of Sojourner Truth, using her own words about women's rights, antiracism, and nonviolence. It challenges participants to step into the pool while the waters are stirring.

Preparation

Set the table with a bowl filled with water; also include on the table pictures, quotes, and books of Sojourner Truth.

Call to Gather

Today we gather to celebrate Sojourner Truth, preacher, abolitionist, and activist. She was born a slave near Kingston, New York, in approximately 1797. After laboring for four masters until 1826, she finally took her freedom and never looked back. She is honored in American history for her speeches against slavery and for women's rights, and for her work on behalf of freed women and men after the Civil War.

Sojourner was renowned in her time for her speaking and singing abilities. As someone who could neither read nor write, she had people read to her, especially the Bible. She was a down-to-earth preacher and a Spirit-led activist. Sojourner stirred the waters of her day and inspires us to do the same in ours.

Our table is set with quotes and pictures of Sojourner and a bowl of water for "stirring the water." Let us come together to reflect on her wise words and powerful impact on the world.

Naming the Circle

Let us begin by introducing ourselves to one another to create our community. Share your name and speak a word that comes to mind when you hear the phrase "step into the pool."

Song

"Come and Go with Me to That Land," African American spiritual.

*Come and go with me to that land, *(3x)*
Where I'm bound, where I'm bound.

*Come and go with me to that land, *(3x)*
Where I'm bound.

*There'll be peace in that land . . .
*No more hatred in that land . . .
*We'll be together in that land . . .
*Come and go with me to that land . . .

Reading

"A Name is Sometimes an Ancestor saying Hi, I'm with You" from LIVING BY THE WORD: Selected Writings 1973–1987 *by Alice Walker.*

"There are always people in history (or herstory) who help us, and whose 'job' it is, in fact, to do this. . . . Now these people—our 'spirit helpers,' as indigenous peoples time after time in all cultures have referred to them—always create opportunities that make a meeting with and recognition of them unavoidable.

"Sojourner Truth is one such figure for me. Even laying aside such obvious resemblances as the fact that we are both as concerned about the rights of women as the rights of men, and that we share a certain 'mystical' bent, Sojourner ('Walker'—in the sense of traveler, journeyer, wanderer) Truth (which 'Alice' means in Old Greek) is also my name. How happy I was when I realized this. . . .

"I get power from this name that Sojourner Truth and I share. And when I walk into a room of strangers who are hostile to the words of women, I do so with her/our cloak of authority—as black women and beloved expressions of the Universe (i.e., children of God)—warm about me.

"She smiles within my smile. That irrepressible great heart rises in my chest. Every experience that roused her passion against injustice in her lifetime shines from my eyes.

"This feeling of being loved and supported by the Universe in general and by certain recognizable spirits in particular is bliss. No other state is remotely like it. And perhaps that is what Jesus tried so hard to teach: that the transformation required of us is not simply to be 'like' Christ, but to *be* Christ.

"The spirit of our helpers incarnates in us, making us more ourselves by extending us far beyond."

The words of Alice Walker.

Song
"Come and Go with Me to That Land"

*Come and go with me to that land, *(3x)*
Where I'm bound, where I'm bound.

*Come and go with me to that land, *(3x)*
Where I'm bound.

The Words of Sojourner Truth

Let the words of Sojourner Truth flow through us. After each quote, as the person who reads stirs the water, we will sing the words written to the tune of "Come and Go with Me."

1851 Women's Rights Convention in Akron, Ohio
". . . while the water is stirring, I'll step into the pool." *Stir the water.*

Song
"Come and Go with Me to That Land"

*We'll be free in that land . . .

1867 First Annual Meeting of the American Equal Rights Association in New York
"There is a great stir about colored men getting their rights, but not a word about the colored women; and if colored men get their rights, and not colored women theirs, you see the colored men will be masters over the women, and it will be just as bad as it was before. So I am for keeping the thing going while things are stirring; because if we wait till it is still, it will take a great while to get going again." *Stir the water.*

Song
"Come and Go with Me to That Land"

*There'll be peace in that land . . .

1851 Women's Rights Convention in Akron, Ohio
"Well, children, where there is so much racket there must be something out of kilter. I think that 'twixt the negroes of the South and the women at the North, all talking about rights, the white men will be in a fix pretty soon. But what's all this here talking about?

"That man over there says that women need to be helped into carriages, and lifted over ditches, and to have the best place everywhere. Nobody ever helps me into carriages, or over mud-puddles, or gives me any best place! And ain't I a woman? Look at me! Look at my arm! I have ploughed and planted, and gathered into barns, and no man could head me! And ain't I a woman? I could work as much and eat as much as a man—when I could get it—and bear the lash as well! And ain't I a woman? I have borne thirteen children, and seen most all sold off to slavery, and when I cried out with my mother's grief, none but Jesus heard me! And ain't I a woman?

"Then they talk about this thing in the head; what's this they call it? [Member of audience whispers, 'intellect.'] That's it, honey. What's that got to do with women's rights or Negroes' rights? If my cup won't hold but a pint, and yours holds a quart, wouldn't you be mean not to let me have my little half measure full?

"Then that little man in black there, he says women can't have as much rights as men, 'cause Christ wasn't a woman! Where did your Christ come from? Where did your Christ come from? From God and a woman! Man had nothing to do with Him.

"If the first woman God ever made was strong enough to turn the world upside down all alone, these women together ought to be able to turn it back, and get it right side up again! And now they is asking to do it, the men better let them." *Stir the water.*

Song
"Come and Go with Me to That Land"

*They'll be singing in that land . . .

Reflection | Sharing

Let us pause to reflect on what we have heard. Let us take a few moments of quiet to reflect on these questions:

What has been stirred up in you? What has Sojourner Truth said to you about women's rights, antiracism, and nonviolence? How and when will you step into the pool?

After a quiet time, I will invite us to share some of our reflections with our community.

Song

"Wade in the Water," African American spiritual.

Wade in the water, wade in the water, children.
Wade in the water, God's gonna trouble the water.

I stepped in the water and the water is cold, God's gonna trouble the water.
It chilled my body but not my soul, God's gonna trouble the water.

I went to the water one day to pray, God's gonna trouble the water.
And my soul got happy and I stayed all day, God's gonna trouble the water.

Blessing with Water

Come to the water. Stir the water. Bless yourself with this water. Touch your whole body saying,

Bless my body, mind, and spirit, that I may sense when the water is stirring and step into the pool.

Song

"Wade in the Water"

Wade in the water, wade in the water, children.
Wade in the water, God's gonna trouble the water.

Sending Forth

Like Sojourner Truth, we are called to stir the waters and step into the pool.

Let us go forth committed to paying attention to every experience that rouses our passion against injustice.

Let us go forth remembering we are loved and supported by recognizable ancestors like Sojourner Truth to act justly.

Let us go forth knowing that we are not alone; we are part of a compassionate community.

Song

"Sojourner Truth Came to Set People Free," words by Jann Aldredge-Clanton; Music Traditional Irish melody SLANE 10.10.10.10 in Inclusive Songs for Resistance & Social Action *(words © 2017 Jann Aldredge-Clanton). Used with permission.*

Sojourner Truth came to set people free,
Claiming her vision of full liberty,
Freeing the slaves held by gender and race,
Guiding us all to create a new place.

Sojourner Truth sang a Spirit-filled song,
Pleading for people who suffered so long;
"Rise up and act so all rights are restored;
Help those who labor without a reward."

Sojourner Truth preached to take down each wall,
Opening doors to new freedom for all,
Helping her race to escape painful plights,
As she urged women to claim equal rights.

Sojourner Truth led the way to new life,
Challenging evil so people can thrive;
With her we follow the Wisdom an ıd Way,
Working for justice and pe sway.

Take Action

Let us put our prayers into action. Here are some poss e! iturgy. death pen- ur community.

- Read more about the life of Sojourner Truth
- Meditate with the quotes from Sojourne
- Take a stand on antiracism, women's r alty, gun control, climate change

Stir the waters!

Greeting of Peace

Let us greet one another with peace and send one another forth with the words of Sojourner Truth, "Step into the pool."

Learn More from These Resources

Cannon, Katie Geneva. *Remembering What We Never Knew: The Epistemology of Womanist Theology.* Richmond, VA: Center for Womanist Leadership Publishing, 2018.

Harris, Melanie. *Ecowomanism: African American Women and Earth-Honoring Faiths.* Maryknoll, NY: Orbis Books, 2017.

Hayes, Diana L. *Forged in the Fiery Furnace: African American Spirituality.* Maryknoll, NY: Orbis, 2012.

Hinga, Teresia Mbari. *African, Christian, Feminist: The Enduring Search for What Matters.* Maryknoll, NY: Orbis Books, 2017.

Morris, Catherine, and Rujeko Hockley, et al. *We Wanted a Revolution: Black Radical Women 1965–85; New Perspectives.* Durham, NC: Duke University Press, 2018.

Vesely-Flad, Rima. *Racial Purity and Dangerous Bodies: Moral Pollution, Black Lives, and the Struggle for Justice.* Minneapolis, MN: Fortress Press, 2017.

West, Traci C. *Disruptive Christian Ethics: When Racism and Women's Lives Matter.* Louisville, KY: Westminster John Knox Press, 2006.

2. February

Embraced by Brigit with a Breath of Spring

God bless the poor, God bless the sick, and bless our human race.
God bless our food, God bless our drink, all homes, O God, embrace.

—"Brigit's Table Grace," St. Brigid's Convent in Kildare, Ireland

February 1 is Brigit's Day, also known as Imbolc, the traditional Gaelic festival marking the beginning of spring. In Celtic spirituality, Brigit was goddess of poetry, healing, and smithwork. In Christian history, she was an abbess and saint. Brigit bridged the worlds between rich and poor, pagan and Christian, slave and free.

This liturgy invites participants to be refreshed with Brigit's welcome, dance, story, fire, threshold, cloak, well, cross, and communion.

Preparation

Set the table or center space with a cloth that represents Brigit's cloak, an unlit candle, a bowl of water, a little milk and honey, Irish soda bread, and sixteen pieces (for each person) of twelve-inch rush, straw, raffia, or half-inch by eleven-inch strips of paper to make Brigit's cross. You will need matches and scissors. Additionally, we will walk across or through a threshold during the liturgy. Participants at WATER use a Brigit's belt (Crios) made by and given to us by Irish colleagues, but you may use a doorway or other representation.

Call to Gather

Today we gather to celebrate Brigit's Day, which marks the beginning of spring. In fact, the whole month of February is called *Mí na Féile Bríde*, Month of the Festival of Brigit. She is the female figure of divinity from Old Europe and was said to "breathe life into the mouth of dead winter."

In Celtic spirituality, women's power was believed to be most manifest in Brigit, the goddess of poetry, healing, and smithwork. In Christianity, Brigit was a revered abbess and saint. She often brought together people from different backgrounds and traditions.

Naming the Circle

Let us form our circle in memory of this wise and holy woman of Ireland. Share your name, a connection you have to Brigit, and a thought you have about spring this year.

Brigit's Welcome

Gatherer: Brigit calls us.
All: Spring into life!

Gatherer: Brigit touches our hearts.
All: Spring into life!

Gatherer: She opens our minds.
All: Spring into life!

Gatherer: And heals our spirits too.
All: Spring into life!

Gatherer: Brigit renews Earth.
All: Spring into life!

Gatherer: She invites us to growth.
All: Spring into life!

Dance Brigit's Circle

"Dancing Brigit's Circle" adapted from "Dancing Sophia's Circle" by Colleen Fulmer, Dancing Sophia's Circle *© 1994, https://www.youtube.com/watch?v=YqDiVZpS8_w. Used with permission.*

Ring us round, O ancient circle,
Great Brigit dancing free.
Beauty, strength, and Holy Wisdom.
Blessing you and blessing me.

A Glimpse into Brigit's Story

Read the story in parts or as a group.

Brigit of Ireland was born in the middle of the fifth century CE into a home where she was in touch with the secrets of the old religion and the emerging Christianity.

Brigit's Fire

Brigit was goddess of hearth and guardian of fire. She founded a famous monastery in Kildare that housed a sacred flame until well into the sixteenth century.

Light Brigit's Fire

Chant by Mary Condren, adapted from the music to Deus Meus *(My God).*

Brigit of the sparkling flame
Be with us now, we call on your name
Be with us now, we call on your name
Brigit of the sparking flame

Virgin Mother and Ancient Crone
Nourish our spirits, flesh and bone
Nourish our spirits flesh and bone
Virgin, mother and Ancient Crone

Brigit of the sparkling flame
Be with us now, we call on your name
Be with us now, we call on your name
Brigit of the sparking flame

Brigit's Threshold

The context of Brigit's birth has great significance. She was born during a transitional time as Ireland was moving from the old religion into an era where St. Patrick and others were bringing the message of Christianity to the people. She was also born in a transitional location, the place of the threshold.

At sunrise, as Brigit's mother crossed the threshold into the house, she gave birth in a place neither in nor out, neither day nor night. In Celtic spirituality, thresholds are sacred places where the veil between heaven and Earth seems especially thin and people feel keenly the presence of the sacred. Even today, many hang Brigit's cross on their threshold or hearth to seek her blessing and remember that the sacred is part of our everyday life.

Walk through Brigit's Threshold
Neither in nor out,
Neither day nor night,
Neither heaven nor Earth,
Shedding the past, walking into the future
We pass through the threshold of Brigit.

Two people hold the Crios (belt) while others walk through it in silence.

Dance Brigit's Circle

"Dancing Brigit's Circle"

Ring us round, O ancient circle,
Great Brigit dancing free.
Beauty, strength, and Holy Wisdom.
Blessing you and blessing me.

Brigit's Cloak

Later in her life, Brigit asked a rich man for land to build a monastery. He offered to give her a site as far as her cloak would reach. When she spread her cloak, it encompassed all of Kildare. This story places Brigit in the long line of female divinities throughout Europe and beyond who used their cloaks to claim the land they needed for their work. Brigit's cloak is the cloak of mercy. This also refers to the Cailleach (Old or Mysterious Woman under many names throughout the world) who created the landscape from their aprons or baskets — metaphors for their wombs. An Old Irish blessing is: *May Brigit's mantle protect you always.*

Spread and Touch Brigit's Cloak for Healing
May Brigit's mantle protect me always.
May Brigit's mantle protect our families and communities always.
May Brigit's mantle protect the cosmos always.

Brigit's Well

As abbess of her vast monastery, Brigit performed many miracles of healing using water. There are hundreds of holy wells in Ireland and Europe dedicated to her with healing qualities for those who invoke her and offer little gifts to her sacred trees.

Wash at Brigit's Well
Put your hands in the bowl of water and let water flow through them. Wash your hands and face and ask Brigit to heal you or a loved one in whatever way you need.

Brigit's Cross

Brigit was a form of the sun goddess, and her symbolism remains attached to the sun in the form of Brigit's crosses. On the eve of Brigit's Day, January 31, people honor her memory by weaving crosses from rushes or straw. These "Brigit's Crosses" are believed to bestow the saint's special blessing on their households. On February 1, the old cross is burned, and the new cross replaces the old one above the door, hung each year to protect the house from fires.

Make a Brigit's Cross
Let us make Brigit's crosses as we reflect on her life. After the crosses are made, we will bless them. We invite you to hang the crosses in a doorway, on the hearth, or on another threshold in your home. *(Instructions can be found: http://fisheaters.com/stbrigidscross.html, written directions, and https://www.youtube.com/watch?v=1eDUXepmNLY, video directions.)*

Reflection | Sharing

As you make a Brigit's Cross, invite Brigit into your heart. Think about what you heard in Brigit's story. Open yourself to newness and to a connection to Divine Wisdom. Take a few moments of quiet to reflect on these questions:

What do you resonate with in these stories of Brigit? What aspects of her life do you relate to in your own?

After a quiet time, I will invite us to share how Brigit is speaking to us this evening.

Hang Brigit's Cross
Hold your cross in one hand, and extend your other hand in blessing:

Holy Brigit, watch over our homes and our communities.
Goddess of hearth and guardian of fire,
Embrace us with your mantle of protection.
Breathe your healing blessing on each one.

Brigit's Communion of Bread, Milk, and Honey

In Brigit's manifestation both as goddess and saint, one of her symbols is that of a cow. She is often depicted carrying a milk pail. The milk of the Sacred Cow was one of the earliest sacred foods throughout the world, equivalent to our present-day communion. Milk represented the ideal form of food for its purity and nourishment. Mother's milk was especially valuable and was believed to have curative powers. Milk from the Sacred Cow was believed to provide an antidote to the poison of enemies' weapons.

Share Brigit's Communion
Take a piece of Irish soda bread; dip it in honey and then in milk. Let us pray "Brigit's Table Grace" from St. Brigid's Convent in Kildare, Ireland.

Translation from Thomas Cahill, How the Irish Saved Civilization (New York: Anchor Books, 1995), 174.

I should like a great lake of finest ale for (all the people).
I should like a table of the choicest foods for the family of heaven.
Let the ale be made from the fruits of faith, and the food be forgiving love.

I should welcome the poor to my feast, for they are God's children.
I should welcome the sick to my feast for they are God's joy.
Let the poor sit with (Sophia) at the highest place
and the sick dance with the angels.

God bless the poor, God bless the sick, and bless our human race.
God bless our food, God bless our drink, all homes,
O God, embrace.

Let us share Brigit's Communion.

Take Action

Let us put our prayers into action. Here are some possible ways:

- Pray "Brigit's Table Grace" from St. Brigid's Convent in Kildare, Ireland, before your evening meal.
- Plan a Brigit's festival. An excellent guide to planning and preparing Brigit's festivals is https://womanspiritireland.wordpress.com/.
- Make and enjoy Irish soda bread with friends. You can search online for a recipe. Be sure to bless the dough by cutting a cross into it!

Sending Forth with Brigit's Blessing

Let us go forth embraced by Brigit with a breath of spring.

May Brigit's flame give you inspiration.
May Brigit's communion give you healing.
May Brigit's creativity guide your way.

Song

"Sacred Spark of Life and Beauty," words by Jann Aldredge-Clanton; Music Traditional French carol PICARDY 8.7.8.7.8.7, in Inclusive Songs for Resistance & Social Action *(words © 2016 Jann Aldredge-Clanton). Used with permission.*

Sacred spark of life and beauty,
  Goddess Brigid brings new birth,
springing forth in fields of flowers,
  giving hope to all on Earth;
while inspiring verse and music,
  she will fill our hearts with mirth.

Sacred well of loving kindness,
  Mother Brigid pours out care,
easing all our pain and sorrow,
  bringing healing everywhere,
spring of Wisdom ever flowing,
  she will guide us all to share.

Sacred queen of Earth and heaven,
  Sister Brigid blesses all,
bringing everyone together
  taking down dividing walls;
peace and unity will flourish
  as we follow her clear call.

Learn More from These Resources

Brigit's Garden, Gairdín Bhríde. Galway, Co. Galway, Ireland. http://www.brigitsgarden.ie/.

Brigit's Wells, Ireland. Search online to learn about them and their fascinating history.

Condren, Mary. *The Serpent and the Goddess: Women, Religion, and Power in Celtic Ireland.* San Francisco: Harper & Row, 1989.

———. Academia. https://tcd.academia.edu/MaryCondren.

Milligan, Bryce. *Brigid's Cloak: An Ancient Irish Story.* Grand Rapids, MI: Eerdmans Books for Young Readers, 2002.

Woman Spirit Ireland. Search online to learn how Irish women are reclaiming suppressed her-stories and exploring indigenous wisdom in a global context. https://womanspiritireland.wordpress.com/.

Special thanks to Dr. Mary Condren, director of Woman Spirit Ireland, for her groundbreaking work on Brigit. I am indebted to Mary for many of the ideas in this liturgy and, most especially, for taking me to Brigit's Wells all over Ireland.

3. March

Rejoice at Miriam's Well for Passover

And the women dancing with their timbrels
Followed Miriam as she sang her song
—Debbie Freidman, "Miriam's Song"

The tenth of Nissan marks the death of Miriam, a prophetess, daughter of Amram and Jochebed, older sister of Aaron and Moses. Passover, the fourteenth day of Nissan, invites the telling of the story of Miriam and Miriam's Well, the most famous well in Jewish lore.

This liturgy invites participants to gather at Miriam's Well to tell her story and focus her ministry as a prophetess whose song of deliverance was divinely inspired.

Preparation

Place a large bowl of water, a towel, and a tambourine on a table or in a central space in the center of a circle of chairs.

Naming the Circle

Let us create our circle by speaking our names and sharing a word about why we are here to rejoice at Miriam's Well.

Call to Gather

Today we gather to rejoice at Miriam's Well and remember her story. Miriam, a wise, God-fearing prophet, was the one who led the Jewish people out of Egypt. She took a tambourine in her hand, and all the women went out after her dancing with tambourines to praise God after the miraculous crossing of the Red Sea (*Yam Suf*).

Due to her merits—her powers of prophecy, her protection of her baby brother Moses, her skillful midwifery among Hebrew slaves, and her victory song at the Sea of Reeds—a mysterious well, later named Miriam's Well (*Be'erah shel Miriam*), miraculously accompanied the Jewish people on their forty years of wandering in the desert. This well was a rolling rock that provided an abundant supply of constantly flowing fresh water for the people, their cattle, and their sheep.

Miriam gets her name from the Hebrew words *mar* and *mari*. *Mar* means "bitter"—it was a bitter time for the Hebrew people in Egypt. We too feel bitter for having had the legends and traditions of our mothers hidden from us. *Mari* means "rebellion"—Miriam rebelled against her oppression as a woman and as a Jew. We follow the rebellious tradition of Miriam as we reclaim her story.

Miriam's life as a prophet and leader in Israel provided encouragement to the women of Israel. Her ministry as a prophet challenges God's people today to understand that women have much to contribute to God's work and that they have much to teach those who are willing to listen.

Shulchan Arukh (Orach Chayim 299:10), the sixteenth-century code of Jewish law, teaches that at the end of Shabbat Miriam's Well fills all waters of the world, imbues them with curative powers, and brings healing to those who are ill and suffering.

Let us Rejoice at Miriam's Well.

Song

"Miriam's Song" by Debbie Friedman, from Songs of the Spirit: The Debbie Friedman Anthology *(Artist Share Music Publishing © 2005), https:/www.ritualwell.org/sites/default/files/imce_uploads/file.2005-06-27.1260090386.mp3. Permission requested.*

Chorus:
And the women dancing with their timbrels
Followed Miriam as she sang her song
Sing a song to the One whom we've exalted.
Miriam and the women danced and danced the whole night long.

And Miriam was a weaver of unique variety.
The tapestry she wove was one which sang our history.
With every thread and every strand she crafted her delight.
A woman touched with spirit, she dances toward the light. *Chorus.*

When Miriam stood upon the shores and gazed across the sea,
The wonder of this miracle she soon came to believe.
Whoever thought the sea would part with an outstretched hand,
And we would pass to freedom, and march to the promised land.
Chorus.

And Miriam the Prophet took her timbrel in her hand,
And all the women followed her just as she had planned.
And Miriam raised her voice with song.
She sang with praise and might,
We've just lived through a miracle, we're going to dance tonight.

And the women dancing with their timbrels
Followed Miriam as she sang her song
Sing a song to the One whom we've exalted.
Miriam and the women danced and danced the whole night long.

Miriam Appears in the Hebrew Scriptures

Miriam was a leader in Israel. The prophet Micah reveals: "For I brought you up from the land of Egypt, and redeemed you from the house of slavery; and I sent Moses to lead you, and Aaron, and Miriam!" (Mic 6:4).

Miriam was a clever girl on the banks of the Nile. Miriam first appears in Exodus 2:4 as the nameless sister who watched over a basket made of bulrushes carrying the infant Moses to see what would happen to him.

Miriam was a gifted prophet at the Red Sea. Miriam is first called by name at the time the Israelites celebrated their victory against Egypt at the Sea. In the song of celebration called "The Song of Miriam" (Exod 15:20-21), Miriam is called a prophet: "Then Aaron's sister, the prophet Miriam, picked up a tambourine, and all the women, followed her, dancing, with tambourines, while Miriam sang: 'Sing to YHWH who has triumphed gloriously, who has flung horse and rider into the sea!' " According to scholars, the Song of Miriam is one of the most ancient of poetic compositions in the Hebrew Bible.

Miriam led the women and the congregation of Israel in a song of celebration. Exodus 15:20 reveals: "all the women, followed her, dancing, with tambourines, while Miriam sang." It also shows Miriam leading the congregation in worship.

Miriam was midwife. Rabbinic lore identifies Miriam and her mother as Hebrew midwives who went by the names of Puah and Shifrah and risked their lives to defy the Pharaoh and save Jewish boys from being killed at birth (Exodus Rabbah 1:13, Babylonian Talmud, Sotah 12a).

Song

"Miriam's Song"

And the women dancing with their timbrels
Followed Miriam as she sang her song
Sing a song to the One whom we've exalted.
Miriam and the women danced and danced the whole night long.

Jewish Feminists Speak about Miriam

The Feminist Miriam

Judith Plaskow, Standing Again at Sinai: Judaism from a Feminist Perspective *(San Francisco: Harper & Row Publishers, 1990), 54, quoting the poem "Miriam: The Red Sea" by Muriel Rukeyser, in* Breaking Open *(New York: Random House, 1973), 22.*

"The feminist Miriam is the woman we glimpse through the gaps in the biblical story, the one who refuses to be 'a forgotten flute, a broken harp.' This is the Miriam who 'dared be like a man, a prophet,' who stands on the shores of the Red Sea singing forever 'until the lands / sing to each other.' This is the Miriam who knows the validity of her own revelation. It is the Miriam who insists to her brother, 'We have both been chosen. / What you witness on the mountain / cannot live without the miracles / below.' "

Miriam as My Great, Great . . . Great Aunt?

Marjorie Feldman, from Open Heart, Open Hands, *March 2015, https://open-heart-open-hands.com/2015/03/.*

"Miriam, as Moses' sister, could have been my great, great, great . . . great Aunt. I claim her as family and mentor. Miriam was a prophetess, a leader of her tribe. She was the one who encouraged and nudged her brother Moses to take his place and do the job he needed to do. She was a community activist and agitator. She was fierce and strong. She led the women in prayer and song and dance. She was responsible for water flowing from the desert to the people. As long as she lived, the wandering Jewish tribes had access to water. When she died, there was no more magical spring that bubbled up at her command. Moses, confronted by the thirsty and complaining throngs, in the midst of his grieving, gets water for the people, but he does so the wrong way causing him to not be able to enter the 'promised land.'

"The wrong way is the violent way of hitting the Earth and rock way, versus the Miriam way of calling up the water from the underground spring, of singing to and with the Earth."

Miriam's Cup at the Seder

Tamar Cohen, Jewish Women's Archive, *"In the Case of Miriam's Cups," https://jwa.org/feminism/cohen-tamara-2.*

"In the case of Miriam's Cups, Ma'yan did not invent the ritual object; we simply set out to bring it from the fringes into the mainstream. Born out of a meditation on the midrash of Miriam's Well in a Rosh Hodesh group in a suburb of Boston, the idea of a ritual goblet filled with water which would symbolize the mythic healing waters of Miriam's Well immediately struck the members of the group as something that 'already existed and was just waiting to be discovered.' In 1992, *Lilith* magazine began spreading news of the new ritual object more widely when it first commissioned a Miriam's Cup. Then in 1998, Ma'yan invited 80 artists from around the world to participate in an exhibition and sale entitled *Drawing From the Source: Miriam, Women's Creativity and New Ritual.* Artists were invited to make usable original Miriam's Cups. Many, for whom the exhibition was their first discovery of the Miriam's Well story and/or Jewish feminist ritual, have continued to produce Miriam's Cups which have become part of more and more *seders* and other rituals across the country and indeed the world."

Miriam's Tambourine

Sandy Eisenberg Sasso, interview in https://jewishfoodhero.com/jewish-storyteller/.

"As powerful as Miriam's well, was her tambourine. The tambourine seems like a strange choice to carry with you when you are leaving Egypt and facing the prospect of raging sea and arid desert. The seemingly frivolous musical instrument did something that nothing else could have accomplished. It made the sound of hope. She teaches us never to underestimate the power of music, poetry and story. She had no map, but she knew what was needed at the moment."

Song
"Miriam's Song"

And the women dancing with their timbrels
Followed Miriam as she sang her song
Sing a song to the One whom we've exalted.
Miriam and the women danced and danced the whole night long.

Miriam the Healer
Jill Hammer on March 29, 2017 blog, https://feminismandreligion.com/2017/03/29/miriam-the-prophetess-as-guardian-and-healer-by-jill-hammer/. Used with permission.

"The veneration of Miriam is especially deep in Sephardic Jewish traditions—those Jewish traditions stemming from the Spanish Jewish diaspora, which may be found everywhere from North Africa to Holland to Greece and Bulgaria. Sephardic women used incantations along with various rituals involving salt, herbs, and other substances, as healing for various ailments and troubles; women skilled in these practices were called *precanteras* or *precantadoras*. Some of their healing incantations invoke Miriam as the ancestress of all women healers, as in the following prayer:

Viene para sanarte milesinarte
Como Miriam a Levy
Qui sinava y milseinava
Yo todo mal se lo quitava
Y a la mar lo echava

This comes to heal you and bring you medicine
like Miriam the Levite
who would bring medicine and heal
and take all the illness away
and throw it to the bottom of the sea. *(Source: Derya F. Agis, "Beliefs of the American Sephardic Woman Related to the Evil Eye," 2010.)*

"This prayer is written in Ladino, a Jewish language that is a mixture of Hebrew and Spanish. The woman who chants the prayer identifies herself as acting in the tradition of Miriam, healing with water (as Miriam did by means of her sacred well). The healer invokes Miriam as a healer who would cure the people with her medicine. The healer then uses salt water to draw out the illness, and then pours out the salt water into the sea or another body of water, casting the illness away into the watery depths. The word 'yam' in Miriam's name, which means 'sea,' may further identify Miriam with the salt water that the healer uses to cure the illness of the sick person."

Miriam the Well
Barbara Holender, "Miriam's Well," in All the Women Followed Her, *edited by Rebecca Schwartz (Rikudei Miriam Press, 2002), 37.*

"She was the one we followed, who knew each of us by name. Healing rose from her touch as drink from the deep, as song from her throat. She was the well. In our hearts we called her not Miriam, bitter sea, but Mayim, water."

Song
"Miriam's Song"

And the women dancing with their timbrels
Followed Miriam as she sang her song
Sing a song to the One whom we've exalted.
Miriam and the women danced and danced the whole night long.

The Legend of Miriam's Well

From Penina V. Adelman, Miriam's Well: Rituals for Jewish Women Around the Year *(Fresh Meadows, NY: Biblio Press, 1986), 63.*

"At twilight on the second day of Creation, God embedded a precious liquid jewel in the Earth, a miraculous well of pure, sparkling water. From one generation to the next, the well belonged to those who knew how to draw up its water. Filled with *mayim chayim*, living waters, the well was a reminder to all who drank or drew from it, that Torah, the way of the Jewish people, is also a well from which all may drink and be restored."

Guided Meditation on Miriam's Well

Written and read by Rabbi Julie Danan, http://wellspringsofwisdom.com/guided-meditation-miriams-well-desert/.

The imagery in this meditation is based on teachings from the Midrash and ancient Jewish lore about Miriam's Well.

Reflection | Sharing

Let us take a few moments of quiet reflection on the guided meditation and on the words we have heard about Miriam. *Quiet reflection.* After a quiet time, share words of wisdom with this community.

Form a Mikveh

Let us form two lines facing each other as we sit, close our eyes, and imagine that water is flowing through us and around us. *Pause.* Raise your arms and let us form a bridge, a birth canal, through which we will each pass with the help of midwives. When you reach the end of the bridge, sprinkle yourself with water from the bowl. Then the next person takes the journey through the water.

When all have passed through the bridge, gather everyone into a circle and spiral while singing:

Song

"The Water in the Well" by Debbie Friedman, from The Water in the Well *(Sounds Write Productions © 2001), https://www.youtube.com/watch?v=1jJXCpEqO54. Permission requested.*

Spring up a well, and sing ye unto it
Spring up a well, and sing ye unto it

Chorus:
Oh the water in the well and the healing in the well
The women and the water and the hope that's in the well (x2)

When the world was created, there was heaven and dry land
And all the waters gathered, upon hearing God's command
There was a bit of water, that was left or so they tell,
That was the water that became the water from the well *Chorus.*

It was in Miriam's honor that the first well came to be,
To celebrate her music, her dance and prophecy,
The people came to Miriam when their spirits rose and fell
She nourished all their visions with the water from the well *Chorus.*

"Spring up a well!" the twelve tribes sang and the rushing waters flowed
High as pillars, into rivers to the oceans they would go
Surrounded by the trees and fruits so rich and bountiful
The Israelites were nourished by the waters from the well *Chorus.*

When Miriam died, the well dried up, and Moses shed his tears
And God said, "Moses, touch this rock and water will appear"
Well Moses raised his staff in anger and upon the rock it fell
And out came springs of water, it was water from the well *Chorus.*

Bridge:

For the memory of the women, for the memory of the well
For the ones who came before us, their stories we must tell
We are searching for the water, where we wander, where we dwell
For Miriam and all of us, who thirst to find the well *Chorus.*

Take Action

Let us put our prayers into action. Here are some possible ways:

- Tell children that you are close to the story of Miriam's Well.
- Listen again to the guided meditation based on the legends of Miriam's Well, written and read by Rabbi Julie Danan, at http://wellspringsofwisdom.com/guided-meditation-miriams-well-desert/.

Sending Forth

This then is the power of Miriam, which we all need to aspire to become:
The power to banish the bitter with the cleansing power of the living waters.
The ability to sense the prophetic power ensconced within each soul.
The power to sing and dance.
Let us go forth and carry on the legacy of Miriam.

Learn More from These Resources

Adelman, Penina V. *Miriam's Well: Rituals for Jewish Women Around the Year.* Fresh Meadows, NY: Biblio Press, 1986.

Alpert, Rebecca. *Like Bread on the Seder Plate: Jewish Lesbians and the Transformation of Tradition.* New York: Columbia University Press, 1997.

Chesler, Phyllis, and Rivka Haut, eds. *Women of the Wall: Claiming Sacred Ground at Judaism's Holy Site.* Woodstock, VT: Jewish Lights Publishing, 2003.

Christ, Carol P., and Judith Plaskow. *Goddess and God in the World: Conversations in Embodied Theology.* Minneapolis, MN: Fortress Press, 2016.

Danan, Rabbi Julie. Guided Meditation on Miriam's Well written and read by Rabbi Julie Danan at http://wellspringsofwisdom.com/guided-meditation-miriams-well-desert/.

Falk, Marcia. *The Book of Blessings: New Jewish Prayers for Daily Life, The Sabbath, and the New Moon Festival.* San Francisco: HarperSanFrancisco, 1996.

Frankel, Ellen. *The Five Books of Miriam: A Woman's Commentary on the Torah.* San Francisco: HarperSanFrancisco, 1996.

Hammer, Jill. *The Jewish Book of Days: A Companion for All Seasons.* Philadelphia, PA: The Jewish Publication Society, 2006.

———. *Sisters at Sinai: New Tales of Biblical Women.* Philadelphia, PA: The Jewish Publication Society, 2001.

Neu, Diann L., Mindy Shapiro, Barbara A. Cullom, Tobie Hoffman. *Miriam's Sisters Rejoice: A Holy Thursday and Passover Feminist Seder.* Silver Spring, MD: WATERworks Press, 1988.

Pinsky, Dina. *Jewish Feminists: Complex Identities and Activist Lives.* Urbana and Chicago: University of Illinois Press, 2010.

Plaskow, Judith. *The Coming of Lilith: Essays on Feminism, Judaism, and Sex*ual *Ethics, 1972–2003.* Boston, MA: Beason Press, 2005.

———. *Standing Again at Sinai: Judaism from a Feminist Perspective.* San Francisco: Harper & Row Publishers, 1990.

Sasso, Sandy Eisenberg. *But God Remembered: Stories of Women from Creation to the Promised Land.* Woodstock, VT: Jewish Lights Publishing, 1995.

4. April

Set the World on Fire like Catherine of Siena

Be who God meant you to be and you will set the world on fire.

—Catherine of Siena

April 29 is the feast day of St. Catherine of Siena, a fourteenth-century Italian mystic, prophet, and activist. In 1970, Pope Paul VI proclaimed Catherine one of the first women Doctors of the Church.

This liturgy shares the words and works of Catherine of Siena to tell her story. Like Catherine, we are called to be mystics, prophets, and activists who love and serve our neighbors, advocate for justice, challenge abuses of power by church and civil authorities, and work for reform, reconciliation, and healing.

Preparation

Set the table or center space with lilies, books about and pictures of Catherine of Siena, a candle and rock for each participant, matches, bread, and wine/juice/drink.

Call to Gather

We gather today to honor St. Catherine of Siena on her feast day, April 29th, which marks her death in 1380 at the age of thirty-three. We come together to be challenged by Catherine "to set the world on fire." She is a fourteenth-century Italian mystic, prophet, saint, and activist who serves as an example for contemporary justice seekers.

In 1970, Pope Paul VI proclaimed St. Catherine of Siena and St. Teresa of Avila the first women Doctors of the Church. This means Catherine is among the thirty-six major theologians recognized by the church, and her writings are approved teachings for the whole church for all time. Today, we lift up this amazing woman who challenges us to share in her wisdom, knowledge, and love.

Naming the Circle

Let us introduce ourselves. Speak your name and share a word that comes to your mind when you hear the phrase "Set the world on fire."

Pray with Catherine

"Prayer 6," from The Prayers of Catherine of Siena, *2nd ed., trans. and ed. Suzanne Noffke, OP (Lincoln, NE: Authors Choice Press, 2001), 53. Excerpts used with permission.*

"Oh Holy Spirit, come into my heart;
by your power draw it to you, God,
and give me charity with fear.
Guard me, Christ, from every evil thought;
And so warm and enflame me again
with your most gentle love
that every suffering may seem light to me.
My holy Creator [Father] and my gentle Love [Lord],
help me in my every need!
Christ love! Christ love!"

Song

*"As a Fire Is Meant for Burning," text by Ruth Duck © 1992, GIA Publications, Inc. All rights reserved. Used by permission. (*The Faith We Sing *2237, https://www.youtube.com/watch?v=dImpl1CsQOs.)*

As a fire is meant for burning
with a bright and warming flame,
So the church is meant for mission,
giving glory to God's name.
Not to preach our creeds or customs,
but to build a bridge of care,
We join hands across the nations,
finding neighbors everywhere.

Catherine's Story

"Proclaim the truth and do not be silent through fear."
—Catherine of Siena

St. Catherine of Siena is perhaps the most remarkable woman of the fourteenth century. She was born March 25, 1347, and died on April 29, 1380. She cared for the sick, wrote letters to popes, and counseled kings, queens, and her own mother. Filled with joy, compassion, and charm, she attracted disciples, who called her "Mama."

Catherine's works are written in the beautiful Tuscan dialect of her time and rank among the classics of the Italian language. Her writings consist of *The Dialogue*, or *Treatise on Divine Providence*; a collection of nearly four hundred *Letters*; and a series of *Prayers*.

Her words are also recorded in her biography, *Life*, by her friend and confessor, Raymond of Capua.

We use Catherine's words and works in this liturgy to tell the story of how she "set the world on fire."

Catherine the Mystic

"The human heart is always drawn by love."
—Catherine of Siena

From an early age, Catherine experienced visions, ecstasies, and spiritual struggles. She had various visions of Christ and ultimately wrote *The Dialogue*, an imagined conversation between God and herself. Its central message is the unifying power of love through the personal Christ who cares for all.

Listen to Catherine

"Dialogue 85," from Catherine of Siena: The Dialogue, trans. Suzanne Noffke, The Classics of Western Spirituality (Mahwah, NJ: Paulist Press, 1980), 157–58. *Excerpts from* Catherine of Siena: The Dialogue *translated and introduced by Suzanne Noffke, OP, copyright © 1980 by Paulist Press, Inc., New York/Mahwah, NJ. Reprinted by permission of Paulist Press, Inc. www.paulistpress.com.*

"I have told you this, my dearest daughter, to let you know the perfection of this unitive state in which souls are carried off by the fire of my charity. In that charity they receive supernatural light, and in that light they love me. For love follows upon understanding. The more they know, the more they love, and the more they love, the more they know. Thus each nourishes the other. By this light they reach that eternal vision of me in which they see and taste me in truth when soul is separated from body. "

Response: Catherine of Siena, be with us on our journey.

Take Action

Light a candle in Catherine's name. *Each participant lights a candle.*

Pray with Catherine

"Prayer 12," from The Prayers of Catherine of Siena, *117–18.*

"In your nature,
eternal Godhead,
I shall come to know my nature.
And what is my nature, boundless love?
It is fire,
because you are nothing but a fire of love.
And you have given humankind
a share in this nature,
for by the fire of love
you created us.
And so with all other people
and every created thing;
you made them out of love.
Oh ungrateful people!
What nature has your God given you?
His very own nature!
Are you not ashamed
to cut yourself off from such a noble thing
through the guilt of deadly sin?

"Oh eternal Trinity,
my sweet love!
You, Light,
give us light.
You, Wisdom,
give us wisdom.
You, supreme Strength,
strengthen us.
Today, eternal God,
let our cloud be dissipated
so that we may perfectly know
and follow your Truth,
in truth,
with a free and simple heart.

"God, come to our assistance!
[Lord], make haste to help us!
Amen."

Reflect Silently

How are we called to be mystics today? *Pause.*

Song

"Ubi Caritas" by Taizé, music by Jacques Berthier © 1979, Ateliers et Presses de Taizé, France, GIA Publications, Inc., agent.

Ubi caritas et amor. Ubi caritas; Deus ibi est.
Live in charity and steadfast love. Live in charity; God will dwell with you.

Catherine the Prophet

"Be who God meant you to be and you will set the world on fire."
—Catherine of Siena

Catherine was a public voice in the political and ecclesiastical affairs of her time. She advised Pope Urban VI on the reunification of the church during the Great Schism, when two popes claimed legitimacy. She encouraged Pope Gregory XI to return the papacy to Rome in 1377 after seventy years in France, confronting the clergy for their avarice and urging them toward greater holiness. And he did. Though she had public relationships with popes and other national leaders, like other women of the fourteenth century, Catherine experienced sexism. Catherine was vocal about her belief in the unifying power of the Eucharist for all those who crave it.

Listen to Catherine

From Raymond of Capua, Legenda major *1.3, in* The Life of Catherine of Siena, *trans. Conleth Kearns (Wilmington, DE: Michael Glazier, 1980), 217.*

"My very sex, as I need not tell you, puts many obstacles in the way."
Response: Catherine of Siena, be with us on our journey.

"Does it not depend on my own will where I shall pour out my grace? With me, there is no longer male and female, nor lower and upper class. All stand equal in my sight."
Response: Catherine of Siena, be with us on our journey.

"Dialogue 60," from Catherine of Siena: The Dialogue*, 115.*

"Love transforms one into what one loves."

Response: Catherine of Siena, be with us on our journey.

Take Action

Preach the truth and shout out an injustice with your prophetic voice.

Pray with Catherine

"Prayer 12," from The Prayers of Catherine of Siena*, 114.*

"Eternal goodness,
you want me to gaze into you
and see that you love me,
To see that you love me
gratuitously
so that I may love everyone
with the very same love.
You want me, then,
to love and serve my neighbors
gratuitously,
by helping them
spiritually and materially
as much as I can . . .
God, come to our assistance!"

Reflect Silently

How are we called to be prophets today? *Pause.*

Song

"Ubi Caritas"

Ubi caritas et amor. Ubi caritas; Deus ibi est.
Live in charity and steadfast love. Live in charity; God will dwell with you.

Catherine the Activist

"All the way to heaven is heaven."
—Catherine of Siena

Catherine was bold and fearless. After her early visions, she left her solitary life to minister and comfort those with disease, the dying, and those in prison. She did what many others avoided, including digging graves for the deceased with her bare hands and attending to those with aggressive cancers that the doctors would not treat. She exemplified selflessness, mercy, and love. Catherine challenges us to comfort those who are suffering and to act justly.

Listen to Catherine

"Letters 66, Letter to Sister Daniella of Orvieto," in Medieval Women's Visionary Literature*, ed. Elizabeth Alvilda Petroff (New York: Oxford University Press, 1986), 268.*

"I pray you then, you and me and every other servant of God, that we devote ourselves to understanding ourselves perfectly, in order that we may more perfectly recognize the goodwill of God, so that enlightened, we may abandon judging our neighbor, and acquire true compassion."

Response: Catherine of Siena, be with us on our journey.

"Dialogue 95," from Catherine of Siena: The Dialogue, *178.*

"O dearest daughter, this patience is a queen who stands guard upon the rock of courage. She is an invincible victor. She does not stand alone, but with perseverance as her companion."

Response: Catherine of Siena, be with us on our journey.

Take Action

Take a rock. Hold this rock of courage as we reflect.

Reflect Silently

How are we called to be activists today? *Pause.*

Song

"Ubi Caritas"

Ubi caritas et amor. Ubi caritas; Deus ibi est.

Live in charity and steadfast love. Live in charity; God will dwell with you.

Reflection | Sharing

Think about what you have heard Catherine of Siena say and pray. Let us take a few moments of quiet to reflect on this question:

What does it mean for us to be mystics, prophets, and activists today?

After a quiet time, share with one another the wisdom we have gained from Catherine of Siena.

Song

"So Great a Love" by Carolyn McDade, O Beautiful Gaia *(Carolyn McDade © 2000). Used with permission.*

What do we do with so great a love, so great a love? *(3x)*

Catherine and the Eucharist

"With affectionate love."

—Catherine of Siena

The Eucharist was central to Catherine's spirituality. She believed the Eucharist calls us to action, to take responsibility, to apply our faith in all the events of daily life. She explicitly disapproved of priests who believed they controlled the Eucharist and thus denied it to those who crave it.

Let us take bread, drink, and listen to Catherine's words as our eucharistic prayer.

Listen to Catherine
"Dialogue 112," from Catherine of Siena: The Dialogue, *211.*

"Contemplate the marvelous state of the soul who receives this bread of life, this food of angels. . . . When she receives this sacrament she lives in me and I in her. . . . Grace lives in such a soul because, having received this bread of life in grace, she lives in grace. When this appearance of bread has been consumed, I leave behind the imprint of my grace, just as a seal that is pressed into warm wax leaves its imprint when it is lifted off. Thus does the power of the sacrament remain there in the soul; that is, the warmth of my divine charity, the mercy of the Holy Spirit, remains there."

Song
"So Great a Love"

What do we do with so great a love, so great a love? *(3x)*

Share bread and drink.

From "Dialogue 112," 212.
"I in my divine providence gave you this food, my gentle Truth, to help you in your need."

Song
"So Great a Love"

What do we do with so great a love, so great a love? *(3x)*

Share bread and drink.

From "Dialogue 111," 211.
"You must receive this sacrament not only with your bodily senses but with your spiritual sensitivity, by disposing your soul to see and receive and taste this sacrament with affectionate love."

Song
"So Great a Love"

What do we do with so great a love, so great a love? *(3x)*

Share bread and drink.

Pray with Catherine
Catherine's prayer reflects that the Eucharist expresses God's continuing presence among us and strengthens us for our life's journey.

"Prayers 10:24-45," from The Prayers of Catherine of Siena, *114.*

"O boundless charity!
Just as you gave us yourself,
wholly God and wholly human,
so you left us all of yourself as food
so that while we are pilgrims in this life
we might not collapse in our weariness
but be strengthened by you, heavenly food."

Song
"As a Fire Is Meant for Burning"

As a fire is meant for burning
with a bright and warming flame,
So the church is meant for mission,
giving glory to God's name.
Not to preach our creeds or customs,
but to build a bridge of care,
We join hands across the nations,
finding neighbors everywhere.

We are learners; we are teachers;
we are pilgrims on the way.
We are seekers; we are givers;
we are vessels made of clay.
By our gentle, loving actions,
we would show that Christ is light.
In a humble, listening Spirit,
we would live to God's delight.

As a green bud in the springtime
is the sign of life renewed,
so may we be signs of oneness
'mid earth's peoples, many hued.
As a rainbow lights the heavens
when a storm is past and gone,
may our lives reflect the radiance
of God's new and glorious dawn.

Take Action

Let us put our prayers into action. Here are some possible ways:

- On April 29, the feast day of St. Catherine of Siena, focus on love and do something to honor Catherine of Siena.
- Visit someone who is sick. Comfort a child.
- Read about Catherine of Siena. Use the resources listed below or go online to read more.

Sending Forth and Greeting of Peace

Like Catherine, we are called to be mystics, prophets, and activists who love and serve our neighbors, advocate for justice, challenge abuse of power by church authorities, and work for reform, reconciliation, and healing.

Let us greet and send one another forth with the words of Catherine of Siena, "Be who God meant you to be and you will set the world on fire."

Learn More from These Resources

Catherine's Writings

Catherine of Siena: The Dialogue. Translated by Suzanne Noffke, OP. The Classics of Western Spirituality. Mahwah, NJ: Paulist Press, 1980.

The Letters of St. Catherine of Siena. Vol. 1. Translated by Suzanne Noffke, OP. Binghamton, NY: Center for Medieval and Early Renaissance Studies, 1988.

The Prayers of Catherine of Siena. 2nd edition. Translated and edited by Suzanne Noffke, OP. Lincoln, NE: Authors Choice Press, 2001.

Books about Catherine

Dreyer, Elizabeth A. *A Retreat with Catherine of Siena: Living the Truth of Love.* Cincinnati, OH: St. Anthony Messenger Press, 1999.

Jones, Kathleen. *Women Saints: Lives of Faith and Courage.* Maryknoll, NY: Orbis Books, 1999.

King, Ursula. *Christian Mystics: The Spiritual Heart of the Christian Tradition.* New York: Simon & Schuster, 1998.

Madigan, Shawn, ed. *Mystics, Visionaries & Prophets: A Historical Anthology of Women's Spiritual Writings.* Minneapolis, MN: Fortress Press, 1998.

Malone, Mary T. *Four Women Doctors of the Church: Hildegard of Bingen, Catherine of Siena, Teresa of Avila, Therese of Lisieux.* Maryknoll, NY: Orbis Books, 2017.

Meehan, Bridget Mary. "St. Catherine of Siena: 'Cry [out] as if you have a million voices, it is silence that kills the world." *Bridget Mary's Blog.* February 9, 2017. bridgetmarys.blogspot.com/2017/02/st-catherine-of-siena-cry-out-as-if-you.

———. "St. Catherine of Siena, mystic, prophet and activist, walk with us on our journey toward spiritual renewal." *Bridget Mary's Blog.* April 29, 2016. bridgetmarys.blogspot.com/2016/04/st-catherine-of-siena-mystic-prophet.

Noffke, Suzanne, OP. *Catherine of Siena: Vision Through a Distant Eye.* Collegeville, MN: Liturgical Press, 1996.

Raymond of Capua. *The Life of Catherine of Siena.* Translated by Conleth Kearns. Wilmington, DE: Michael Glazier, 1980.

Vardey, Lucinda, ed. *The Flowering of the Soul: A Book of Prayers by Women.* New York: Ballantine Wellspring, 1999.

5. May

Trust All Shall Be Well with Julian of Norwich

All shall be well and all shall be well and all manner of thing shall be well.

—Julian of Norwich, *Revelations of Divine Love*, 27.8–11.209

May 8 is the feast of Julian of Norwich, a fourteenth-century English mystic who had a near-death experience at age thirty, when she received a series of visions known as Revelations of Divine Love *or* The Showings. *She holds the distinction of being the greatest of all the English anchorites of the Middle Ages because of her visions and writings.*

This liturgy invites the gathered to pray and live, through whatever life circumstances, that "All Shall Be Well."

Preparation

Gather hazelnuts, hazelnut chocolates, and a bell. Place them on a table or center space covered with a cloth.

Naming the Circle

Let us create our circle by speaking our names and saying after each, "All shall be well."

Call to Gather

"All shall be well," we pray desperately. We gather tonight at the convergence of three religious holidays: Ramadan, Shavuot, and Pentecost.

The first day of the sacred Muslim month of Ramadan, the month when the Prophet Mohammed began receiving the revelation of the Quran, was (*name the date this year*).

The first day of the Jewish festival of Shavuot, which began in ancient Israel with the celebration of the spring wheat harvest and has become the time to celebrate a spiritual harvest—the revelation of the Torah at Mount Sinai, was (*name the date this year*).

Sunday *(name the date this year)* was the Christian feast of Pentecost, when followers of Jesus gathered to celebrate Shavuot and were imbued with the Holy Spirit, opening them to speak in many languages they had not known—in some ways, opening the path to a multilingual Christianity known as the birth of the church.

"All shall be well," we pray desperately.

Song

"Julian of Norwich." Words and music: Sydney Carter, © 1981 Stainer & Bell, Ltd. (Admin. Hope Publishing Company, Carol Stream, IL 60188). All rights reserved. Used by permission. https://www.youtube.com/watch?v=I-irwWT3oYg.

Ring the bell.

Loud are the bells of Norwich and the people come and go.
Here by the tower of Julian, I tell them what I know.

Chorus:
Ring the bell. Ring out, bells of Norwich,
and let the winter come and go.
All shall be well again, I know.

Love, like the yellow daffodil, is coming through the snow.
Love, like the yellow daffodil, brings joy to all I know. *Chorus.*

Ring for the yellow daffodil, the flower in the snow.
Ring for the yellow daffodil, and tell them what I know. *Chorus.*

All shall be well, I'm telling you, let the winter come and go.
All shall be well again, I know.

The Story of Julian of Norwich

Julian of Norwich (1342–1416) was a fourteenth-century English mystic and theologian who lived as an anchoress outside the walls of St. Julian's Church in Norwich. When she was thirty, she suffered a severe illness and had a near-death experience. At this time, she received a series of visions on May 8, 1373, which she later wrote down as *Revelations of Divine Love* or *The Showings.* Her writings describe her understanding of God's compassion for the world.

Julian witnessed three rounds of the bubonic plague, lost almost everyone she loved, and nearly died herself. She lived in a time of peasant revolts and the Great Schism. She experienced scandal and crisis in the church, with three claimants to the papacy each excommunicating the other.

With injustice all around, Julian was given a glimpse of divine love assuring that "all manner of things will be well."

Her message for us today is simple:

- She reveals God's hope and reminds us that God loves even the smallest creation.
- She proclaims that God is Mother and reminds us that women image the Divine.

- She affirms a God of unconditional love.
- She believes all shall be well.

Song

"Julian of Norwich"

Ring the bell. Ring out, bells of Norwich
and let the winter come and go.
All shall be well again, I know.

Julian's Words from Revelations of Divine Love

The Hazelnut

Julian of Norwich: Selections from Revelations of Divine Love—Annotated & Explained, *ann. Mary C. Earle (Woodstock, VT: SkyLight Paths Publishing, 2013), 21.*

"[God] showed me a little thing,
the size of a hazelnut in the palm of my hand,
and it was as round as a ball.
I looked at it with my mind's eye and thought,
'What can this be?'

"And the answer came to me: 'It is all that is made.'

"I wondered how it could last,
for it was so small I thought it might suddenly have disappeared.
And the answer in my mind was,
'It lasts and will last forever
because God loves it;
and everything exists in the same way by the love of God.'"

Reflection | Sharing

Take a hazelnut in your hand. (This can be a real hazelnut or anything small and round like a marble, a small stone, or a balled-up piece of paper.)

Like Jesus' parable of the mustard seed, Julian's hazelnut is a little thing. Yet, God shows it to Julian as a sign of God's love for creation. The least of things can yield a mystical vision. God is totally here, now. The fullness of God bursts forth in a humble hazelnut.

Eat the chocolate hazelnut candy and taste the fullness and sweetness of God.

The hazelnut is the revelation of God whether God presents herself (and Julian used "Mother" as well as "Father" to describe God) through a mustard seed, a tongue of fire, or our own daily experience.

For Julian, the hazelnut was a sign of hope, a sign of the love of God that sustains us. What things or events are signs of hope for you? After a quiet time of reflection, share signs of hope with this community. *Sharing.*

Pray with Julian

Think of what brings you hope. Let us write a list of reasons for being hopeful. Start with "Because . . . " and end with "I hope in you, O God [or the name you call the Divine]."

For example:
"Because flowers bloom each spring, I hope in you, Loving Creator."
"Because of the love of my family and friends, I hope in you, Divine Love."
"Because of beautiful sunrises, I hope in you, O God."
Let us pray with our hopes, in the form of a litany with the refrain, "I hope in you, O God."

Ring the bell.

Song

"Holy as a Day Is Spent" by Carrie Newcomer, The Gathering of Spirits *(New Rounder © 2002), https://www.youtube.com/watch?v=2qZyoRiBteI. Used with permission.*

Carrie Newcomer captures the spirit of the hazelnut in her song, "Holy as a Day Is Spent." In Newcomer's song, she invites us to experience the holiness of whizzing cars, dogs running in their sleep, a simple breakfast, and doing our daily tasks.

Holy is the dish and drain
The soap and sink, and the cup and plate
And the warm wool socks, the cold white tile
Showerheads and good dry towels

And frying eggs sound like psalms
With bits of salt measured in my palm
It's all a part of a sacrament
As holy as a day is spent

Holy is the busy street
And cars that boom with passion's beat
And the check out girl, counting change
And hands that shook my hands today

And hymns of geese fly overhead
And spread their wings like their parents did
Blessed be the dog that runs in her sleep
To chase some wild and elusive thing

Holy is the familiar room
And the quiet moments in the afternoon
And folding sheets like folding hands
To pray as only laundry can

I'm letting go of all my fear
Like autumn leaves of Earth and air
For summer came and summer went
As holy as a day is spent

Holy is the place I stand
To give whatever small good I can
The empty page, and the open book
Redemption everywhere I look

Unknowingly we slow our pace
In the shade of unexpected grace
With grateful smiles and sad lament
As holy as a day is spent

And morning light sings "providence"
As holy as a day is spent

The Maker, Lover, and Carer

Julian of Norwich, Revelations of Divine Love—Annotated & Explained, *ann. Mary C. Earle, 23.*

"In this little thing [the hazelnut] I saw three properties:
the first is that God made it,
the second is that God loves it,
the third is that God cares for it.

"But what the maker, the carer and the lover really is to me, I cannot tell;
For until I become one substance with [God],
I can never have complete rest or true happiness;
that is to say, until I am so bound to [God]
that there is no created thing between God and me."

Song

"Julian of Norwich"

Ring the bell.

Ring out, bells of Norwich
and let the winter come and go.
All shall be well again, I know.

Reflection | Sharing

Julian affirms a God of unconditional love—the Maker, Lover, and Carer of all—who delights in holding each created thing and being and whose love works to make all things well. Eat another hazelnut or hazelnut candy as you reflect quietly on this question:

What do you think of Julian's idea of the Trinity: God as Maker, Lover, and Carer?

After a quiet time, I will invite us to share our reflections on Julian's Trinity.

Pray with Julian

Look at your list of reasons for being hopeful and create an affirmation, a message of self-love or love for others that reminds you that God is Maker, Lover, and Carer. Start your affirmation with "I . . . "

For example: "I see God in flowers that bloom each spring."
"I am an expression of God's love for my family and my friends."
"I am strong like the beautiful rising sun."

Ring the bell.

God as Mother

"14th Showing," in Julian of Norwich, Showings, *trans. Edmund Colledge and James Walsh, The Classics of Western Spirituality (Mahwah, NJ: Paulist Press, 1978), 293–99.*

"And so in our creation God almighty is our loving Father,
and God of all wisdom is our loving Mother,
with the love and goodness of the Holy Spirit,
which is all one God.

"As truly as God is our Father, so truly is God our Mother.
To the property of Motherhood belong nature, love, wisdom and knowledge,
and this is God."

Song

"Julian of Norwich"

Ring the bell.

Ring out, bells of Norwich
and let the winter come and go.
All shall be well again, I know.

Reflection | Sharing

The image of God as Mother is ancient. Isaiah sings of God who comforts us as a mother comforts her child (66:13). Luke's gospel offers the image of God as a mother hen gathering her young (13:34). The thirteenth-century mystic Mechtilde of Magdeburg uses the image of God as a great mother who bends and takes the child from the floor to her bosom. In our time, feminist theologians and ministers alike challenge us to think, as Mary Daly did, *Beyond God the Father* to embrace God the Mother, and beyond God the Mother to Divine Wisdom and more. Eat another hazelnut or chocolate and pause to reflect on this question:

How does Julian's understanding of God as Mother broaden your understanding of the Divine?

After a quiet time, share thoughts on God as Mother.

Pray with Julian

From Bridget Mary Meehan, Praying with Visionary Women *(Lanham, MD: Sheed & Ward, 1999), 51–52.*

"O Nurturing, Nourishing, Mothering God,
with you and through you I journey back to the womb that gave me birth. . . .
May you continue to delight in me. . . .
Heal the hurts that come from the difference between the love I needed and the love I received. . . .
Reach deep within me as I rest in your womb. . . .
You, who loved me into existence and soothe away any pain or fear from my past, fill me with your life-giving force and creativity in my relationships with my parents, children, and all those I am called to nurture. . . .
I belong to you. . . . I love you. . . .
I celebrate your birthing power within me that accepts me . . . that forgives me . . . that liberates me . . . in peace and joy forever."

Ring the bell.

Blessing Bread

One person takes the bread and says:

This bread symbolizes for us wonder and surprise, letting go and delight in God. Let us extend our hands and bless this bread, listening to the words of Julian of Norwich.

Our Soul Must Perform Two Duties

From Meditations with Julian of Norwich *by Brendan Doyle (Santa Fe, NM: Bear & Company Publishing © 1983), 78.*

"Our soul must perform two duties.
The one is we must reverently wonder and be surprised;
The other is we must gently let go and let be always taking pleasure in God.
Seeing God in this life cannot be a continuous experience.
We often fail to see God and then we fall into ourselves
And feel there is something wrong with us—that we are perverse
And responsible for the entrance of sin into the world and all subsequent sins.
These feelings affect us mentally and physically.
But the Holy Spirit, the endless life living within us,
Makes us peaceful and at ease, harmonious and flexible."

Blessed are you, Holy One of Joy, for giving us this bread of wonder and surprise.

The blesser puts the bread on the table.

Blessing Wine and Juice

Another person takes the drinks and says:

This fruit of the vine symbolizes the fullness of joy. Let us extend our hands and bless it, listening to the words of our sister Julian of Norwich.

The Fullness of Joy Is to Behold God

From Meditations with Julian of Norwich *by Brendan Doyle, 60.*

"God is the ground, the substance,
the teaching, the teacher,
the purpose, and the reward
for which every soul labors.
The fullness of joy is
to behold God
in everything."

Blessed are you, Holy One of Joy, for giving us this cup of life.

The blesser puts the drinks on the table and continues:

In the spirit of our foremothers, let us eat, drink, and be joyful as we work for justice. *The blessers pass the bread and wine/juice around the community to share.*

Communion Song

"This Day Is My Daily Bread" by Kathy Sherman, CSJ, from Singing My Soul *(LaGrange Park, IL: Sisters of St. Joseph © 1996). Used with permission.*

This day is my daily bread. Take it, bless it, break it, give it
To all I meet this day.

Take Action

Let us put our prayers into action. Here are some possible ways:

- This month, begin every day with a short meditation or affirmation on what gives you hope, what symbolizes God's love, and what reminds you that all shall be well.
- Write a letter to someone you love, someone you have nurtured, or someone who has nurtured you and tell them why they are special to you.
- Spend time in nature as a reminder that God loves all creation.
- Keep the hope alive that all shall be well while you continue to work for justice!
  - Get out and vote during the primary season and every election!
  - Join a local community action group that helps women and people who are pushed to the margins run for local office.
  - Attend the next Black Lives Matter march in your area.
  - Learn more about or get involved in the Sanctuary Movement to see how your neighborhood or congregation can support immigrants, refugees, and families being broken apart by deportation.

Sending Forth

Let us go forth remembering Julian's message:

As Julian reveals the hazelnut story as a sign of hope,
let us go forth and be hopeful.

As Julian proclaims that God is Mother,
let us go forth and call God Mother.

As Julian affirms a God of unconditional love,
let us go forth and show God's love and compassion.

As Julian believes All Shall Be Well,
let us go forth praying desperately, All Shall Be Well Again.

Song

"Julian of Norwich Reveals Wisdom's Way," words by Jann Aldredge-Clanton; music Traditional Irish melody SLANE 10.10.10.10, in Inclusive Songs for Resistance & Social Action *(words © 2017 Jann Aldredge-Clanton). Used with permission.*

Julian of Norwich reveals Wisdom's way,
Showing us visions for our current day,
Visions of love bringing all into one,
Beauty from dawning to setting of sun.

Julian sees Wisdom, Great Mother of all,
Sending us power to take down each wall,
Changing the world with Her kindness and grace,
Opening all doors for each gender and race.

Now Sister Julian inspires us to grow,
Reaching our fullness of creative flow;
Joined with Sophia, our Wisdom and Friend,
We claim our wholeness, our life without end.

Still Sister Julian reveals mystic dreams,
Well-springs of healing from Earth's sacred streams.
All shall be well and all things shall be well;
Justice and peace shall forever prevail.

Learn More from These Resources

Julian's Writings

Julian of Norwich. *Showings*. Translated by Edmund Colledge and James Walsh. The Classics of Western Spirituality. Mahwah, NJ: Paulist Press, 1978.

Julian of Norwich: Showing of Love. Edited and translated by Julia Bolton Holloway. Collegeville, MN: Liturgical Press, 2003.

Julian of Norwich. *Revelations of Divine Love*. The British Library, 1670.

Books about Julian

Dickens, Andrea Janelle. *The Female Mystic: Great Women Thinkers of the Middle Ages*. New York, NY: I.B. Tauris & Co, 2009.

Doyle, Brendan. *Meditations with Julian of Norwich*. Santa Fe, NM: Bear & Company Publishing, 1983.

Earle, Mary C. *Julian of Norwich: Selections from* Revelations of Divine Love*—Annotated & Explained*. Woodstock, VT: SkyLight Paths Publishing, 2013.

Jantzen, Grace. *Julian of Norwich: Mystic and Theologian*. Mahwah, NJ: Paulist Press, 2000.

Meehan, Bridget Mary. *Praying with Visionary Women*. Lanham, MD: Sheed & Ward, 1999.

Rolf, Veronica Mary. *Julian of Norwich*. Downers Grove, IN: Intervarsity Press, 2018.

——. *Julian's Gospel: Illuminating the Life & Revelations of Julian of Norwich*. Maryknoll, NY: Orbis Books, 2013.

Ruether, Rosemary Radford. *Visionary Women: Three Medieval Mystics*. Minneapolis, MN: Fortress Press, 2002.

6. June

Come, Sophia Spirit, at Pentecost

Sing lo! Sing, O Sophia! Wisdom come to widen my heart.
Sing lo! Sing, O Sophia! Wisdom, come abide in my heart.

—Miriam Theresa Winter, *Songlines*

Pentecost, fifty days after Easter, signals the coming of the Holy Spirit to the apostles and other disciples of Jesus to empower them to witness to all nations. It is the birthday of the Christian church.

This Pentecost liturgy recognizes the presence of Divine Wisdom, Sophia Spirit within various communities. Invite local communities to come together for this celebration.

Preparation

Choose a space outside, if possible, for this liturgy. Hang colored cloths from tree branches. Form a circle of chairs under the trees. Place cloths for sitting on the grass in front of the chairs.

Place three tables with red woven cloths in the center: one holds three baskets filled with three different breads, six goblets of juice and wine, and six red napkins; another holds an oil lamp; and the third has chimes, pinwheels, and bubbles for the children. Invite three women to be bread blessers, four to read, and several to dance wearing flowing red skirts.

Call to Gather

Welcome to our Pentecost Liturgy, "Come, Sophia Spirit." Today is Pentecost, the birthday of the church. This day signifies the coming of the Holy Spirit to her people. Sophia is her Greek name; Wisdom is her English name; *Chokmah* is her Hebrew name; *Sapientia* is her Latin name. She is the life force energy that flows through the universe. She is the divine presence that embraces everything in the cosmos. Have you met her?

Who is Sophia? Why do we speak about Sophia Spirit today?

Jewish Wisdom theology talks about God as Sophia, Divine Woman Wisdom, who appears as God's own being. In the writings of the early Christian community Sophia seems to disappear, yet a deeper reading shows that Sophia assumes the functions of the Spirit. Spirit Sophia's presence is God's Spirit. Early Jesus traditions called Jesus Sophia's prophet and Christ-Sophia.

Divine Woman Wisdom, Sophia Spirit, God with us, continues her call for the liberation of all from patriarchy and kyriarchy. This is what we celebrate today. Please echo after me:

May Sophia Spirit rise inside me like a rushing wind. *Echo.*
May Sophia Spirit leap within us like a revolutionary fire. *Echo.*
May Sophia Spirit flow through the world like a life-giving breath. *Echo.*
Let us share and receive her spirit. *One woman lights the oil lamp.*

Song

"Sing Lo! Sing, O Sophia," African American spiritual, Music: Swing Low. Words adapted by Miriam Therese Winter, from Songlines: Hymns, Songs, Rounds, and Refrains for Prayer and Praise *(New York: The Crossroad Publishing Company © 1996). Used with permission.*

Refrain:
Sing lo! Sing, O Sophia! Wisdom come to widen my heart.
Sing lo! Sing, O Sophia! Wisdom, come abide in my heart.

I looked deep within me. Oh, how can this be?
Wisdom come to widen my heart.
I saw Sophia looking back at me.
Wisdom, come abide in my heart.

I looked to Sophia for setting me free.
Wisdom come to widen my heart.
A deep, dark Presence liberating me.
Wisdom, come abide in my heart.

Naming the Circle

Why are we gathering as many communities together on a day like Pentecost? Many of us meet regularly in our small communities. Sometimes we need to feel the energy when people from various prayer circles, base communities, eucharistic communities, women-church liturgy groups, and peace and justice organizations join together. This is that time.

We come from a variety of communities today. Let us hear the names of the communities represented here. Someone call out the name of your group and then add, "Sophia Spirit is here."

Look around. Notice the faces among us. Turn to those around you and introduce yourself by saying, "Hi! I'm *Name*. Sophia-Spirit is here."

Song

"Sing Lo! Sing, O Sophia"

Refrain: Sing lo! Sing, O Sophia! Wisdom come to widen my heart.
Sing lo! Sing, O Sophia! Wisdom, come abide in my heart.

I looked to my neighbor, now what did I see?
Wisdom come to widen my heart.
A sweet, sweet Spirit beckoning to me.
Wisdom, come abide in my heart.

Setting Sophia's Table of Solidarity

Six women set the table using symbols similar to these.

1. Let us call upon Sophia Spirit who dwells on each continent to feast with us at our table today. We set our table in solidarity with women, men, and children worldwide.

This cloth is a gift from the Philippines. Come, Sophia Spirit, Kwan-Yin of Asia, from the Middle East to Beijing, from the Islands of Japan to the Philippines. Come feast with us.

Response: We are in solidarity with you.

2. This cloth comes from the UN Decade for Women Conference that took place July 1985 in Nairobi, Kenya. Come, Sophia Spirit, Womb of the Universe of Africa, from the land of the Nile in Egypt to the land of freedom in South Africa. Come feast with us.

Response: We are in solidarity with you.

3. This bowl is a gift from a feminist liturgy study group in Germany. Come, Sophia Spirit, Earth Mother of Europe, from the land of the former Berlin Wall to the islands of Greece. Come feast with us.

Response: We are in solidarity with you.

4. This basket was made by the Acama Native American women in New Mexico for the 1993 Women-Church Conference. Come, Sophia Spirit, Grandmother of North America, from the tip of Mexico to the Arctic Ocean. Come feast with us.

Response: We are in solidarity with you.

5. This serape is from Bolivia. Come, Sophia Spirit, Pacha Mama of South America, from the highlands of Guatemala to the rim of Antarctica. Come feast with us.

Response: We are in solidarity with you.

6. This silk cloth was a gift from dear friends in Australia. Come, Sophia Spirit, Sun Woman of Australia, from the outback to the seaside. Come feast with us.

Response: We are in solidarity with you.

Prayer for Peace and Justice

Come, Sophia Spirit, breathe your gifts into us as we struggle for justice.
Come, Spirit of Courage, enlighten our resistance, our insistence, our persistence.
Come, Spirit of Peace, unite races and nations to stop wars and violence.

When we are fearful, challenge us to act bravely.
When we are lonely, bless us with communities of love and compassion.
When we are weary, replenish us with bold dreams.

Spirit of Understanding, open our hearts to those who are pushed to the margins.
Spirit of Wonder, open our beings to the magnificence of creation.
Spirit of Wisdom, spark in us a new fire.
Amen. Blessed be. Let it be so.

Song

"Veni, Sancte Spiritus," by Taizé, music by Jacques Berthier © 1979, Ateliers et Presses de Taizé, France, GIA Publications, Inc., agent. All rights reserved. Used with permission.

Veni, Sancte Spiritus.

Reading

The Pentecost Story, Acts 2:1-21 and 1 Corinthians 12:4-14 (adapted).

Setting: Readers and dancers kneel together in the center of the circle, praying aloud quietly, "Sophia Spirit, come." The singers chant "Veni, Sancte Spiritus." The narrator stands and begins:

N: When the day of Pentecost arrived, they all met in one room. They came from many communities and regions, young and older, speaking many languages of different professions, religious people who practiced their faith in various ways. They came from all corners of the land *(name the places of those gathered).* Suddenly they heard what sounded like a violent, rushing wind from heaven; the noise filled the entire house in which they were sitting. Something appeared to them that seemed like tongues of fire; these separated and came to rest on the head of each one.

The dancers whirl toward the three disciples, trailing red cloths that they swirl over the heads of the kneelers, who then stand.

N: They were all—women, men, and children—filled with the Holy Spirit, Sophia Spirit. *Dancers swirl cloths around all participants.* They began to speak in other languages as she enabled them.

Song

"Veni, Sancte Spiritus"

Verse: Come, Sophia Spirit, from heaven
move forth with your glorious dance.

The dancers move spontaneously.

N: Now there were devout people living in Jerusalem from every nation under heaven, and at this sound they all assembled from every continent known on Earth: Africa, Asia, Europe, South America, North America, Antarctica, Australia. But they were bewildered to hear their native languages being spoken.

2: Why, they're speaking Chinese! *Xiè-Xie!*

3: They speak Serbian! It's a miracle—as though there had never been a Tower of Babel.

4: I hear them speaking Swahili! *Karibu!* What does this mean?

3: Sie sprechen Deutsch!

2: Se hablan espanol!

4: On parle français.

N: What other languages do we speak here? Tell us in that language. *People speak in their own languages.*

N: Whether the pilgrims were from large cities or country villages, they heard the disciples proclaiming in their own language the wonderful works of the Spirit.

2: These words of the prophet have come to pass: "In the days to come—it is our God who speaks—I will pour out my Spirit on all humankind. Your daughters and sons will prophesy, your young people will see visions, your elders will dream dreams. Even on the most insignificant of my people, both women and men, I will pour out my Spirit in those days, and they will prophesy."

Song

"Veni, Sancte Spiritus"

Verses: Come from the four winds, Sophia.
Come, breath of God. Come blow your power through us.
Renew and strengthen your people.

N: Sophia Spirit was given not only to the early community but to us as well. To each person the Spirit gives gifts.

2: There is a variety of gifts, but always the same Spirit.

3: There is a variety of ministries, but we serve the same One. To each person is given the manifestation of the Spirit for the common good.

4: To one, Sophia Spirit gives wisdom in discourse, to another, the word of knowledge through the same Spirit.

2: Through the Spirit, one person receives faith; through the same Spirit, another is given the gift of healing; and still another, miraculous powers.

3: Prophecy is given to one; to another, power to distinguish one spirit from another.

4: One receives the gift of tongues; another, that of interpreting tongues.

2: But it is one and the same Spirit who produces all these gifts and distributes them as she wills.

N: The body is one, even though it has many parts; the body of Sophia-Christ. It was by one Spirit that all of us, whether we are Jews or Greeks, slaves or citizens, female or male, gay, straight, trans, black, brown, yellow, red, white, differently abled or able bodied, poor or rich, were baptized into one body.

All of us have been given to drink of the one Spirit. And that Body is not one part; it is many.

2: And that Spirit calls us to proclaim the good news to all people.

3: Whether in known or unknown languages.

4: Whether in the language of the child or the adult, of the haves or have-nots.

N: We are all called to proclaim that Sophia Spirit is rising in all creation. To her be all glory forever and ever.

All: Amen. Blessed be. May it be so.

Song

"Veni, Sancte Spiritus"

Verses: Kindle in our hearts the flame of your love
That it may spark and bring new life.
May it glow and reach to all forever.

A Pentecost Response

Filled with the gifts and power of Sophia Spirit,
We honor and act on the power of justice. Please repeat:

All: We honor and act on the power of justice.

We honor and act on the power of antiracism, antisexism, antihomophobia, anti all -isms.

All: We honor and act on the power of antiracism, antisexism, antihomophobia, anti all -isms.

We honor and act on the power of forgiveness.

All: We honor and act on the power of forgiveness.

We honor and act on the power of hospitality.

All: We honor and act on the power of hospitality.

We honor and act on the power of Tears . . . Integrity . . . Affection . . . Sexuality . . . Work . . . Struggle . . . Friendship . . . Truth . . . Prayer . . . Peace.

All: Respond after each: We honor and act on the power of . . .

Reflection | Sharing

Sophia Spirit shares her gifts with each of us and with our communities. Children, come around the altar. These chimes, pinwheels, and bubbles are symbols of Sophia Spirit. Sophia Spirit is another name for God. She is our friend. Have fun now playing with these gifts of Sophia Spirit. *Children play in a nearby area.*

Let us take a few moments of quiet to reflect on these questions:

What Sophia Spirit gifts do you bring and what Sophia Spirit gifts do you see in your community? What does it mean to see ourselves as part of something far bigger than we are? How will you use your gifts?

After a quiet time, let us share with three or four people around us. Singing will bring us back to the whole group. *Sharing.*

Song
"Veni, Sancte Spiritus"

Prayers of the People

Let us pray together. Our response is "Sophia Spirit, flow through your people."

We pray for the people fleeing war-torn lands, especially for the women who have been raped and the families who have lost their loved ones.
Response: Sophia Spirit, flow through your people.

We pray for the end to violence, for an end to gun use and the fear that inspires it, for an end to domestic abuse and the unsafe homes it creates, for an end to sexual abuse and the innocence it robs.
Response: Sophia Spirit, flow through your people.

We pray for economic justice, for the equitable sharing of Earth's abundance.
Response: Sophia Spirit, flow through your people.

We pray for children, that they may be safe and well, lively and loving, heirs to our faith and shapers of their own.
Response: Sophia Spirit, flow through your people.

We pause to remember those who have died. Please call out the name of any person you would like to include. *Naming.* They are present with us today. May we remember them.
Response: Sophia Spirit, flow through your people.

Song
"Veni, Sancte Spiritus"

Eucharistic Prayer of Divine Wisdom

Three blessers come to three different places in the center, face the gathered, and pray in turn:

1. Lift up your hearts.
All: We lift them up to Sophia Spirit.
Let us give thanks to our gracious and loving God, Divine Wisdom,
Spirit Sophia.
All: It is right to give her thanks and praise.

Blessed are you, Loving and Challenging Holy Spirit Sophia.
With joy we give you thanks and praise for creating a diverse world
and for creating women in your image.
You call us to share your story,
so we join all creation in singing your praises:

Sung Acclamation
"In Your Presence" by Colleen Fulmer, from Dancing Sophia's Circle © *1994. Used with permission.*

O Wisdom Sophia, Wisdom Sophia,
The power and presence of God.

2. Blessed are you, Womb of All Creation, Spirit Sophia.
You create women, men, and children in your image.
From age to age you form us from your womb;
You breathe your breath of life into us.
And you call us to share your story,
so we join all creation in singing your praises:

Sung Acclamation
O Wisdom Sophia, Wisdom Sophia,
The power and presence of God.

3. Blessed are you, God of our Mothers, Spirit Sophia.
You call diverse women to participate in salvation history:
Eve, Lilith, Sarah, Hagar, Miriam, Naomi, and Ruth,
Mary, Mary Magdalene, Thecla, Phoebe, Hildegard of Bingen,
Sor Juana Inez de la Cruz, Sojourner Truth, Joan of Arc,
Maura, Ita, Dorothy, Jean, Mother Théodore Guérin, and countless others. *Name others.*
And you call us to share our stories,
so we join all creation in singing your praises:

Sung Acclamation
O Wisdom Sophia, Wisdom Sophia,
The power and presence of God.

1. Blessed are you, Creator of all seasons and all peoples, Spirit Sophia.
You call us each by name to be prophets,
teachers, house-church leaders, ministers, saints,
and to image your loving and challenging presence.
And you call us to share their stories,
so we join all creation in singing your praises:

Sung Acclamation
O Wisdom Sophia, Wisdom Sophia,
The power and presence of God.

2. Blessed are you, Companion on the Journey, Spirit Sophia.
You have built your house,
You have set up seven pillars,
You have prepared a rich banquet for us.
And you call us to share your story,
so we join all creation in singing your praises:

Sung Acclamation
O Wisdom Sophia, Wisdom Sophia,
The power and presence of God.

Each blesser puts her script on the table, picks up a bread, drink, and small paper with these words, and the three pray together.

Blessers in unison: Extend your hands toward the bread.

Blessed are you, Divine Wisdom, Spirit Sophia.
In your abundant love you welcome all to come to the table and dine.
You proclaim from the rooftops,
"Come, eat my bread and drink the wine which I have prepared for you."
And you call us to share your story,
so we join all creation in singing your praises:

Sung Acclamation
O Wisdom Sophia, Wisdom Sophia,
The power and presence of God.

Blessers put the bread and drink back on the table and face into the circle.

3. Come, Divine Wisdom, Spirit Sophia, upon this bread, wine, juice, and food.
Come as breath and breathe your life anew into our aching bones.
Come as wind and refresh our weary souls.
Come as fire and purge us and our communities of sexism, racism, classism, heterosexism, ageism, all -isms, and all evils.
You call us to share your story,
so we join all creation in singing your praises:

Sung Acclamation
O Wisdom Sophia, Wisdom Sophia,
The power and presence of God.

1. Come, Soul Sister, Spirit Sophia,
and bring the new creation:
the breaking of bread,
the raising of the cup,
the doing of justice.
You call us to share your story,
so we join all creation in singing your praises:

Sung Acclamation
O Wisdom Sophia, Wisdom Sophia,
The power and presence of God.

2. Let us eat, drink, and partake of the banquet of life.
Receive the love, healing, and nourishment of Spirit Sophia.

Blessers pass bread and goblets around the community.

Communion Song

"Spirit Movin' Where She Will" by Colleen Fulmer, from Her Wings Unfurled © *1989. Used with permission.*

We're seein' how a mighty wind sweeps the surgin' waters.
Spirit movin' where she will, birthin' the light from darkness.

Refrain: O Spirit movin', O Spirit moving,
O Spirit movin', movin' within your daughters.

We're seein' how creation breaths, woven by this artist,
Tapestries of pain and grace, fire, flesh, and stardust. *Refrain.*

We're seein' how our sister pain makes us strong in wisdom;
broken bread that feeds our world, claimin' our faith and vision. *Refrain.*

We're seein' how that leaven grows, long silent voices speakin',
tellin' a story never told the nations to justice leadin'. *Refrain.*

We're seein' a compassion born, the circle's growin' stronger;
lettin' our children live in peace; copin' with wars no longer. *Refrain.*

Take Action

- Meditate on the gifts that you have been given. Use one of them today.
- Thank someone in your community for a gift that you notice they have.
- Read about Sophia Spirit, Divine Wisdom in one of the resources listed below.

Sending Forth

The bread blessers pray:

1. Friends of Sophia, let us go forth with courage, for Sophia Spirit is with us.
Response: Sophia Spirit is with us.

2. Let us go forth to liberate all people and the universe from war and violence, for Sophia Spirit is with us.
Response: Sophia Spirit is with us.

3. May Sophia Spirit rise inside us like a rushing wind.
May Sophia Spirit leap within us like a revolutionary fire.
May Sophia Spirit flow through the world like a life-giving breath.
Response: Sophia Spirit is with us.

Greeting of Peace

Let us share and receive Sophia's Spirit by offering one another a greeting of peace. Blow into your hand. Feel Sophia's breath within you. Blow this greeting to Earth and to the world. Let us offer one another a Pentecost Greeting of Peace.

Song

"Praise Ruah, Spirit Who Gives Birth," Words Jann Aldredge-Clanton; Music Geistliche Kirchengesäng, 1623 LASST UNS ERFREUEN in Inclusive Hymns for Liberating Christians *(words © 1996 Jann Aldredge-Clanton). Used with permission.*

Praise Ruah, Spirit who gives birth
To worlds unknown and life on Earth;
O praise Her! Hallelujah!
Stars dancing mystery through the night
Show forth her joy and endless light.
Praise Ruah! Hallelujah!
Praise the great creative Spirit!
Come and praise Her!

Day dawns at sound of Ruah's voice;
Wake all creation to rejoice;
O praise Her! Hallelujah!
Sun gleams like diamonds on the dew;
Birds join to sing the hymn anew.
Praise Ruah! Hallelujah!
Praise the great creative Spirit!
Come and praise Her!

Learn More from These Resources

Aldredge-Clanton, Jann. *She Lives! Sophia Wisdom Works in the World.* Woodstock, VT: SkyLight Paths Publishing, 2014.

Aquino, María Pilar, and Elisabeth Schüssler Fiorenza, eds. *In the Power of Wisdom. Concilium.* Vol. 5. London: SCM Press, 2000.

Berger, Teresa, ed. *Dissident Daughters: Feminist Liturgies in Global Context.* Louisville, KY: Westminster John Knox Press, 2001.

———. *Gender Differences and the Making of Liturgical History: Lifting the Veil on Liturgy's Past.* Burlington, VT: Ashgate Publishing, 2011.

Chittister, Joan. *Welcome to the Wisdom of the World and Its Meaning for You.* Grand Rapids, MI: Eerdmans Publishing, 2007.

Choi Hee An. *Korean Women and God: Experiencing God in a Multi-religious Colonial Context.* Maryknoll, NY: Orbis Books, 2005.

Grey, Mary. *Introducing Feminist Images of God: Introductions in Feminist Theology.* Cleveland, OH: The Pilgrim Press, 2001.

Johnson, Elizabeth A. *She Who Is: The Mystery of God in Feminist Theological Discourse.* New York: Crossroad, 1993.

Rupp, Joyce. *Prayers to Sophia: Deepening Our Relationship with Holy Wisdom.* Notre Dame, IN: Sorin Books, 2003.

Schroer, Silvia. *Wisdom Has Built Her House: Studies on the Figure of Sophia in the Bible.* Collegeville, MN: Liturgical Press, 2000.

Schüssler Fiorenza, Elisabeth. *In Memory of Her: A Feminist Theological Reconstruction of Christian Origins.* New York: Crossroad, 1983. (See especially pp. 130–40, "The Sophia-God of Jesus and the Discipleship of Women.")

———. *Jesus: Miriam's Child, Sophia's Prophet.* New York: Continuum, 2004.

———. *Wisdom Ways: Introducing Feminist Biblical Interpretation.* Maryknoll, NY: Orbis Books, 2001.

7. July

Witness with Mary Magdalene

If God has made her worthy, who are we to reject her?

—The Gospel of Mary Magdalene 9:8

July 22 is the feast day of Mary Magdalene. Christian feminists also honor her during Holy Week. She was the first to proclaim Jesus' resurrection to the apostles, and she is the foundation of women-church. Yet, she has also been spoken of as a prostitute, the lover of Jesus, and a symbol of lust and repentance.

This liturgy raises up Mary Magdalene on her feast in July and also during Holy Week as a witness to Jesus' resurrection. Using a reader's theatre, women witnesses to the Divine give testimony.

Preparation

Cover a table or center space with a cloth. Place on it oil in a jar or bowl for anointing and symbols of faith.

Call to Gather

Today we gather to honor Mary Magdalene and other women who witness to their faith.

If on July 22 Feast Day: Mary Magdalene is known as the apostle to the apostles. She was the first to proclaim Jesus' resurrection to her brothers. Let us restore her to her rightful place in Christianity as a disciple and leader in the early community of Jesus' followers.

If during Holy Week: This week, Christian feminists celebrate Holy Week and Easter, the movement from death and mourning to life and hope, and tell the stories of how women witness to the journeys from oppression to liberation.

Today, we raise up women who have been faithful witnesses to faith that resists and does justice. The phrase found in the Gospel of Mary Magdalene focuses our liturgy, "If God has made her worthy, who are we to reject her?" (9:8).

Naming the Circle through a Litany of Witnesses

Let us share our names, name a woman witness who inspires us, and invite her into our circle now:

I am *Name* and I invite *(a woman witness)* into our circle.
Response: We are faithful witnesses; pray with us *(woman witness).*

Song

"You Shall Be My Witnesses" by Miriam Therese Winter, from Woman Prayer, Woman Song *(Medical Mission Sisters © 1987). Used with permission.*

Refrain:
You shall be my witnesses through all the Earth,
Telling of all you have heard and received,
For I arose and am with you and you have believed.

Women leave your tombs.
Roll the stones aside.
Do not despair, though so many dreams have died.
Do not be fearful of the vision that you see.
Believe in miracles again.
Believe in me.

Reader's Theater of Women Witnesses

Today we center our readings around the phrase found in the Gospel of Mary Magdalene, "If God has made her worthy, who are we to reject her?" Listen to the women who witness to the Divine.

Miriam

I am Miriam, a prophet, midwife, and leader in Israel. I saved the life of my little brother Moses. I had hope when those around me did not, yet they prophesied to the power of such hope. Due to my merits, a mysterious well accompanied the Jewish people during forty years of wandering in the desert. I led my people in jubilation as we crossed the Red Sea. The women followed me dancing with tambourines to praise G*d after the miraculous crossing. I witness to faith that brings hope instead of fear, liberation instead of bondage, joy instead of sorrow.

Response: Miriam, if God has made you worthy, who are we to reject you?

Mary Magdalene

I am Mary Magdalene, a successor of Jesus. I traveled with him and supported his ministry financially. My discipleship was equal to that of the male disciples. At the foot of the cross when most fled, I stayed. My spirit fell, but in the garden I found hope and was the first to bear witness to his resurrection. I saw Jesus and had faith and the strength to spread that faith. I ran to tell the others who were still in mourning. Many responded with doubt, yet I responded with courage. My story has been altered throughout history, but do not be mistaken: I was the apostle to the apostles and a witness to the resurrection. I witness to the important role women once held in the church.

Response: Mary Magdelene, if God has made you worthy, who are we to reject you?

Aisha

My name is Aisha, wife to the prophet Muhammad. I am the mother of the believers in Islam and a leading scholar who played a vital role in the establishment of the Islamic civilization. Through my knowledge, I helped teach the Quran and conveyed more than two thousand hadiths to Islam. I also had a considerable knowledge of Arabic poetry, medicine, and genealogy, which led me to advocate for the education of women and children. I was a teacher for forty years. I am an eyewitness of the spread and expansion of Islam. I nurtured it as a woman, a wife, a theologian, a political activist, and a leader.

Response: Aisha, if God has made you worthy, who are we to reject you?

Dorothy Day

I am Dorothy Day, cofounder of the Catholic Worker Movement. I have witnessed the abject conditions of those in poverty, the mistreatment of workers at the hands of greedy corporations, the catastrophes of war and violence, and the evil of an economic system that prioritizes profit over people. I have written against these injustices in my newspaper, *The Catholic Worker*. Drawing on my deep religious commitments, I along with many others have created a movement that embodies hospitality, pacifism, equal distribution of resources, and radical faith.

Response: Dorothy, if God has made you worthy, who are we to reject you?

Women of the Wall

I am a Woman of the Wall and I speak out with Jewish women from around the world who believe it is our right to pray freely at our holy site, the Western Wall in Jerusalem. We encounter verbal and physical violence, we risk arrest, and we fight legal battles to empower Jewish women to embrace religion freely. We will not keep quiet until women are able to wear prayer shawls, pray, and read from the Torah at the Western Wall.

Response: Women of the Wall, if God has made you worthy, who are we to reject you?

Ssenfuka Joanita Warry

My name is Ssenfuka Joanita Warry. I am a lesbian, born and raised in a country where same-sex relations are punishable by imprisonment and violence against LGBTQIA+ individuals is commonplace. I am a human rights activist fighting to change this, but I have had to leave my home country of Uganda for my own safety. Many other lesbians and other LGBTQIA+ individuals have been imprisoned or killed in Uganda. I am one of the lucky few.

Response: Warry, if God has made you worthy, who are we to reject you?

Bree Newsome

I am Bree Newsome, an activist who climbed the flagpole in front of the South Carolina Capitol Building to remove the Confederate battle flag. For some, my act was viewed as civil disobedience. For others, it was a symbol of resistance and the empowerment of women. The Confederate flag was a symbol of hate. After a white supremacist killed nine African American worshipers at the historic Emanuel African Methodist Episcopal (AME) Church in Charleston, SC, it was time for change. I had no choice but to challenge, renounce, and resist white supremacy and tell the world that Black Lives Matter.

Response: Bree, if God has made you worthy, who are we to reject you?

Fatima Mernissi

My name is Fatima Mernissi. I am a Muslim feminist raised in a haram with my mother and other women in my family. My mother and grandmother did not know how to read or write. I was the first woman in my family to receive an education and am a pioneer in the field of Islamic feminism. I have challenged misogynistic hadith and forged a new, liberating path for Muslim women in my home country of Morocco and abroad.

Response: Fatima, if God has made you worthy, who are we to reject you?

Maria Gomez

Soy Maria. I am an immigrant woman living in sanctuary. I fled El Salvador after facing harassment from machete-carrying farmworkers. After years of annual check-ins with US Immigration and Customs Enforcement (ICE) in Virginia and wearing an ankle monitor for two years, I was ordered by ICE to buy a plane ticket back to El Salvador. I bought the plane ticket but decided not to "self-deport." I once again fled my home and this time took sanctuary in a church in Maryland to avoid being deported and permanently separated from my two US-born children, the youngest with serious medical conditions. I am worried about the welfare of my children and my own safety if I return to El Salvador. Now I am separated from my children as I live in Maryland and they live in Virginia.

Response: Maria, if God has made you worthy, who are we to reject you?

Naomi Wadler

Listen to Naomi's speech from the March for Our Lives 2018: https://www.youtube.com/watch?v=C5ZUDImTIQ8.

Response: Naomi, if God has made you worthy, who are we to reject you?

Song
"You Shall Be My Witnesses"

Refrain: You shall be my witnesses through all the Earth,
Telling of all you have heard and received,
For I arose and am with you and you have believed.

Reflection | Sharing

We have heard powerful stories of amazing women who, like Mary Magdelene, witness to their faith: Miriam, Mary Magdelene, Aisha, Dorothy Day, Women of the Wall, Ssenfuka Joanita Warry, Bree Newsome, Fatima Mernissi, Maria Gomez, and Naomi Wadler. Think about what you heard in their stories. Let us take a few moments of quiet to reflect on these questions:

Which women do you feel connected to and why? How are you a faithful witness to faith that resists violence and does justice?

After a quiet time, we will share our reflections with this community.

Song

"Gather the Cloud of Witnesses," by Susan R. Beehler. Used with permission.

Chorus:
Gather the cloud of witnesses, anoint each other.
Fold the world into your arms.
Reach out and speak out, share the joy and gently call our sisters home.

Open the alabaster jar of care.
Wash the feet of those named unacceptable.
Dry their tears with your hair.
Though wounded all are acceptable.
Chorus.

Blessing Oil and Anointing

Oil is a sacramental symbol used for anointing. We bless this oil and anoint one another to be witnesses to faith that resists violence and does justice.

Blessed are you, God of our foremothers and sister witnesses,
For giving us this oil to anoint us to witness in troubled times.
Bless us with your healing graces that we may witness to
faith that resists violence and does justice.
Bless us that we may heal and be healers.

Pass the oil around the circle and anoint the person on your left saying: *"Name,* if God has made you worthy, who are we to reject you?"

Sending Forth

Let us go forth proclaiming that we are connected to women who have been faithful witnesses to faith that resists violence and does justice.

Let us go forth knowing that we too are called to witness to that which we believe.

Let us go forth to be faithful witnesses.

Song

"You Shall Be My Witnesses"

Refrain: You shall be my witnesses through all the Earth,
Telling of all you have heard and received,
For I arose and am with you and you have believed.

Take Action

Let us put our prayers into action. Here are some possible ways:

- Support your daughters, granddaughters, nieces, and other young women in the ways they witness the Divine.
- Learn about feminist and womanist theology.
- Let a woman-identified person in your life know that you see their witness at work.

Greeting of Peace

Let us greet one another with peace and send one another forth by saying, "You are called to be a faithful witness."

Learn More from These Resources

Arnold, Margaret. *The Magdalene in the Reformation.* Cambridge, MA: Harvard University Press, 2019.

Beattie, Tina. *New Catholic Feminism: Theology and Theory.* New York: Routledge, 2006.

Beavis, Maryann, Elaine Guillemin, and Barbara Pell, eds. *Feminist Theology with a Canadian Accent: Canadian Perspectives on Contextual Feminist Theology.* Toronto, Ontario, Canada: Novalis Publishing, 2008.

Brooks, Joanna, Rachel Hunt Steenblik, and Hannah Wheelwright, eds. *Mormon Feminism: Essential Writings.* New York: Oxford University Press, 2016.

Cochran, Pamala D. H. *Evangelical Feminism.* New York: New York University Press, 2005.

Gaines-Cirelli, Ginger. *Sacred Resistance: A Practical Guide to Christian Witness and Dissent.* Nashville, TN: Abingdon Press, 2018.

Hearon, Holly E. *The Mary Magdelene Tradition: Witness and Counter-Witness in Early Christian Communities.* Collegeville, MN: Liturgical Press, 2004.

Hunt, Helen LaKelly. *Faith and Feminism: A Holy Alliance; Five Spirited and Spiritual Women Throughout History.* New York: Atria Books, 2004.

Pui-lan, Kwok, Cecilia González-Andrieu, and Dwight N. Hopkins, eds. *Teaching Global Theologies: Power and Praxis.* Waco, TX: Baylor University Press, 2015.

Ruether, Rosemary Radford. *Women and Redemption: A Theological History.* Minneapolis, MN: Fortress Press, 2012.

Schaberg, Jane. *The Resurrection of Mary Magdalene: Legends, Apocrypha, and the Christian Testament.* New York: Continuum, 2002.

Schaberg, Jane, and Melanie Johnson-DeBaufre. *Mary Magdalene Understood.* New York: Continuum, 2006.

Schneiders, Sandra M. *Written That You May Believe: Encountering Jesus in the Fourth Gospel.* New York: The Crossroad Publishing Company, 1999.

Schüssler Fiorenza, Elisabeth. "The Gospel of Mary Magdalene." In *Searching the Scriptures,* vol. 2, edited by Elisabeth Schüssler Fiorenza, 601–34. New York: Crossroad, 1994.

Weems, Renita. *Just a Sister Away: A Womanist Vision of Women's Relationships in the Bible.* San Diego, CA: LuraMedia, 1988.

8. August

Honor a Wise Woman

May you always bear witness to the love of Divine Wisdom in this world.
Go forth good and faithful one! We thank you!
We call you a Wise Woman.

When a woman completes her time of service to a community, organization, board, or committee, it is appropriate and right to recognize her for her dedicated time, work, and energy. Of course, a woman can be honored at any time for her wisdom.

This liturgy honors a woman for her service that has helped shape the group's work for justice. Her community thanks her, gives her gifts, and calls her to become one of the wise women.

Preparation

Gather gifts that are appropriate to give to the wise woman. For anointing, have oil in a bowl and a towel.

Centering Prayer

Creator of the Universe, Welcome!
Wisdom Sophia, Welcome!
She Who Is and Will Always Be, Welcome!
Divine Wisdom, in you we live and move and have our being.
Embrace our dear friend, *Name*, the way she embraces our community.

Naming the Circle

We are here today to honor *Name.* To create our circle, speak your name and share one word that you think captures the spirit of *Name.*

Call to Gather

With these words, we gather to honor you, *Name*, for your presence with our community. We thank you for your generous and dedicated work during your time at *Name of organization*, and in subsequent years. We honor you for your perseverance and creativity that have shaped this community. We call you into the ranks of the Wise Feminists on whose love-filled work this organization rests. We bless you for the future as you continue your life of service, solidarity, and fun.

Prayer

Gracious and Loving Divine Wisdom, we ask that you bless *Name*. Draw near to her and enfold her in your loving embrace. Keep her in our circle as she continues to share your love, creativity, and wisdom throughout the world. Amen. Blessed be. May it be so.

Song

"Sister Wisdom" by Jan Novotka, from Together in the Great Work *(© 2003 by Jan Novotka's Music LLC [ASCAP]. All rights reserved). Used with permission.*

Refrain:
Sister Wisdom, Spirit of Grace, Arise!
Awake in Me!
Sister Wisdom, Spirit of Grace, Arise!
Awake in Me!

I long for wisdom, for healing vision.
Sister Sophia, be my light. *Refrain.*

Come, listen deeply, to wisdom's
presence within the wind, the fire,
the sea. *Refrain.*

Deep in creation, deep in our being,
the song of wisdom echoes clear.
Refrain.

Readings about Wisdom

"Wisdom has built her house; she has set up her seven pillars. She has prepared her food, decanted her wine, and set her table. She has sent out her household staff to call from a spot overlooking the city. 'Whoever wants enlightenment, step this way!' she says, inviting all who lack common sense. Come, eat my bread and drink the wine which I have prepared for you."
—Prov 9:1-5

Refrain: Sister Wisdom, Spirit of Grace, Arise! Awake in Me!
Sister Wisdom, Spirit of Grace, Arise! Awake in Me!

"Who can find a valiant woman? She is more precious than jewels . . . She brings good—not evil—to her house all the days of her life."
—Prov 31:10, 12

Refrain: Sister Wisdom, Spirit of Grace, Arise! Awake in Me!
Sister Wisdom, Spirit of Grace, Arise! Awake in Me!

"Wisdom is clothed with strength and honor; she rejoices in the future. . . . Many women have done very well, but you excel them all!"
—Prov 31:25, 29

Refrain: Sister Wisdom, Spirit of Grace, Arise! Awake in Me!
Sister Wisdom, Spirit of Grace, Arise! Awake in Me!

Anointing with Oil

Beloved colleague, *Name*, we call you to the center of this circle to honor you for your presence in this community. Come forth, good and faithful wise woman!

The gifts you have given so freely to our community have flourished and borne fruit! As a symbol of our gratitude, we honor you with this gift. *Give a gift that is appropriate for the occasion.*

We now anoint you with oil to symbolize the fullness of your role as a Wise Woman.

With her permission, anoint her with oil on her forehead and hands. Anointing is a symbol of being called and strengthened for an important task. Now that your ministry with this community as *Name role* is complete, we anoint you to go forth as a Wise Woman.

You now number among the Wise Women whose loving work created this organization and others. Your compassionate service, loving leadership, creativity, and joy are now a part of that foundation. You are a Wise Woman!

Blessing a Wise Woman

Let us bless *Name* today. Please raise your hand in blessing as we pray together:

Divine Creator of the Universe, Wisdom-Sophia, She Who Is and Will Always Be,
We ask you to bless *Name* today and every day.

Name, may your heart be filled with loving compassion in the work of justice.
May you be filled with hope, love, and laughter.
May you know the comfort of community, good friends, and family.
May you have strength, courage, and fortitude for the journey ahead.
May you be blessed with good health.
May peace live always in your heart and in your home.
May you always bear witness to the love of Divine Wisdom in this world.
Go forth, good and faithful one! We thank you!
We call you a Wise Woman.

Song

"Blessings of Life to You" by Jan Novotka, Together in the Great Work *(© 2003 by Jan Novotka's Music LLC [ASCAP]. All rights reserved). Used with permission.*

May vision and truth companion you.
May beauty be in your eyes.
May peace fill your being. Love hold you close.
Earth give you guidance. Stars give you hope.
Blessings of Life to you.

Take Action

- Who is a wise woman that you admire?
- What wisdom would you like others to recognize in you?
- List the gifts that you have and think of one that you want to develop.

Learn More from These Resources

Haase, Bridget. *Well Said: Children's Words of Wisdom.* Cincinnati, OH: St. Anthony Messenger Press, 2002.

Pak, Su Yon, and Jung Ha Kin. *Leading Wisdom: Asian and Asian North American Women Leaders.* Louisville, KY: Westminster John Knox Press, 2017.

Schüssler Fiorenza, Elisabeth. *Wisdom Ways: Introducing Feminist Biblical Interpretation.* Maryknoll, NY: Orbis Books, 2001.

Winfrey, Oprah. *The Wisdom of Sundays: Life-Changing Insights from Super Soul Conversations.* New York: Flatiron Books, 2017.

9. September

Return Thanks with Hildegard of Bingen

The rivers give rise to smaller streams
that sustain the Earth by their greening power.

—Hildegard of Bingen, *Divine Works* 4.59

September 17 is the feast day of Hildegard of Bingen (1098–1179), as well as the same day she died. She is one of the most gifted spiritual teachers of all time. She is one of only four women to be named a Doctor of the Church.

This liturgy returns thanks to Hildegard for her visions, her healing powers, and a creation-centered spirituality that feels divine pleasures and does divine justice. It celebrates her concept of viriditas, the vitality and vigor inherent in Creation, which expresses the imagery of divine justice flowing like water.

Preparation

Place on the table or in the center space a pitcher of water, a glass, and a candle or sparkler for each person; also put herb plants like sage, thyme, and mint along with soil and pots for planting. Have music by Hildegard ready to play. Put pictures of Hildegard, her books, her paintings, and her music around the space.

Call to Gather

Today we gather to return thanks with and for Hildegard of Bingen, who lived from 1098 to 1179. She is one of the most fascinating and influential spiritual leaders of the twelfth century. Yet she was wiped out of church consciousness for eight centuries because of her spirituality and theology that saw the interconnection of all creation!

Hildegard is a creation-centered mystic, a holistic health practitioner, a prophet of ecological justice, and a feminist who challenged the institutional church. She is a great renaissance woman—musician and prophet, poet and artist, doctor and physicist, mystic and theologian, abbess and lover of creation. She is a role model for all time.

She was finally named Doctor of the Church on October 7, 2012—an honor that, as of 2019, only four women (and thirty-two men) have received thus far!

Naming the Circle

Let us create our liturgical circle by speaking our names and identifying an environmental crisis that is causing us concern.

Song

"In the Name of All That Is" by Jan Novotka, from In the Name of All That Is *(© 2001 by Jan Novotka's Music LLC [ASCAP]. All rights reserved). Used with permission.*

In the name of all that is we come
together.
In the name of the stars and galaxies;
in the name of the planets, moons and
the sun;
in the name of all that is we come.

In the name of all that is we come
together.
In the name of the ocean and the sea;
in the name of the mountain, desert
and plain;
in the name of all that is we come.

In the name of all that is we come
together.
In the name of the buffalo and bear;
in the name of the turtle, eagle and
whale;
in the name of all that is we come.

In the name of all that is we come
together.
In the name of the cactus and the fern;
in the name of the flower, tree and the
herb;
in the name of all that is we come.

In the name of all that is we come
together.
In the name of the elements of life;
in the name of the soil, water and air;
in the name of all that is we come.

In the name of all that is we come
together.
In the name of the children of Earth;
in the name of the Spirit breathing in
all things;
in the name of all that is we come.

The Life of Hildegard of Bingen

Hildegard of Bingen was born into a noble family of Bermersheim vor der Höhe, Germany, in beautiful Bavaria. She enjoyed the advantages of wealth, family connections, and easy access to political and ecclesiastical power. She was the founder of the Rhineland mystic movement, a healer and composer, administrator and preacher, theologian and artist, visionary and author, and a Benedictine abbess of the famous monastery at Rupertsberg.

Like prophets before her, she spoke out against the corruption and abuses of the church. At the age of eighty-one she was put under interdict (denied the sacraments and the right to sing the Divine Office) for being at odds with the local archbishop of Mainz for burying a man in the monastery cemetery who had been excommunicated by the church. During her last months she wrote furious letters to the bishop to exonerate her name and her abbey and to demand justice. The interdict was lifted only six months before she died.

Song

"Consciousness Waking" by Jan Novotka, from Awakening Consciousness *(© 2006 by Jan Novotka's Music LLC [ASCAP]. All rights reserved). Used with permission.*

Consciousness waking, Holy and
Whole.
Creation stirring, birthing anew.
Now is the time. We are the space
for the Holy to rise in our midst.

Hildegard's Visions, *Scivias*

When Hildegard was forty-two, she had mystical visions that transformed her life. She spent the next ten years writing about these visions in *Scivias, Know the Ways*. The three books focus on her six visions of creation, seven visions of redemption, and thirteen visions of sanctification—an allusion to the Trinity. This great work of religious genius can be viewed as a prophetic call, a book of allegorical visions, an exegetical study, and a theological summa.

Scivias resulted from Hildegard's prophetic call and was addressed to indolent male theologians, monastics, and clerics. In *Scivias* 1.1. Hildegard writes: "Unlock for them the enclosure of mysteries which they, timid as they are, conceal in a hidden and fruitless field. Burst forth into a fountain of abundance, and overflow with mystical knowledge, until they who now think you contemptible because of Eve's transgression are stirred up by the flood of your irrigation."

In her last *Scivias* vision, which is really a concert, Hildegard introduced a body of exquisite music that includes seventy liturgical songs in which she offers praise to Mary, the choirs of angels, and saints who are prophets, apostles, martyrs, confessors, and virgins. Hildegard's music and words inspire.

Listen

Play Hildegard von Bingen - Voices of Angels - Voices of Ascension*, conducted by Dennis Keene, and connect with her healing energy: https://www.youtube.com/watch?v=v6qFCYRQKVA.*

Hildegard of Bingen Says

"All living creatures are, so to speak, sparks from the radiation of God's brilliance, and these sparks emerge from God like the rays of the sun."

—*Divine Works* 4.11

Light a Candle and Ponder

How are you a spark of God's brilliance? Light a candle or sparkler and say: "I am a spark of God's brilliance."

Song
"Consciousness Waking"

Consciousness waking, Holy and Whole.
Creation stirring, birthing anew.
Now is the time. We are the space
for the Holy to rise in our midst.

Hildegard's Greening, Viriditas

Hildegard's concept of *viriditas*, a combination of the Latin words for "green" and "truth," conveys a greening life force, the vitality and vigor, lushness and growth inherent in Creation. It expresses divine justice flowing like water.

Hildegard believed that all creation reveals divine blessings. Cosmic interdependence flows through her works. She saw this life force in the green hills and fruitful Earth that surround the Disibodenberg and Rupertsberg areas where she lived and worked. For Hildegard, the Holy Spirit is "green": "She [blessedness] is also surrounded with many gifts which are green with the greenness of the Holy Spirit" (SC III.6.33).

Hildegard of Bingen Sings
"O nobilissima viriditas, O noblest green viridity" from "Responsory for Virgins" (D 165r-v, R 471rb-va, Scivias 3.13.7b) by Hildegard of Bingen. Latin collated from the transcription of Beverly Lomer and the edition of Barbara Newman; translation by Nathaniel M. Campbell. Permission requested.

R. O nobilissima viriditas,	*R.* O noblest green viridity,
que radicas in sole	you're rooted in the sun
et que in candida	and in the clear
serenitate	bright calm
luces in rota	you shine within a wheel
quam nulla terrena excellentia	no earthly excellence
comprehendit:	can comprehend:
R. Tu circumdata es	*R.* You are surrounded by
amplexibus	the embraces of the service,
divinorum ministeriorum.	the ministries divine.
V. Tu rubes ut aurora et ardes	*V.* As morning's dawn you blush,
ut solis flamma.	as sunny flame you burn.

Drink Water and Ponder

Take a drink of water. How do you connect with green *viridity*/creation-centered spirituality when you drink water and listen to creation-centered music? Let us share our reflections with one another.

Song
"Consciousness Waking"

Consciousness waking, Holy and Whole.
Creation stirring, birthing anew.
Now is the time. We are the space
for the Holy to rise in our midst.

Hildegard the Healer

Hildegard was a healer who was knowledgeable in medical matters and knew the therapeutic plants grown in the monastic gardens. She learned the wisdom of her locality from the traditional folk around her. She used herbs for food, medicine, and good luck. Faith in herbcraft kept Hildegard close to Earth and creation.

Hildegard of Bingen Says
"The rivers give rise to smaller streams that sustain the Earth by their greening power."
—*Divine Works* 4.59

Plant an Herb and Ponder
Pick an herb, plant it, and share a thought about *viriditas* and healing.

Prayer of Thanksgiving
Let us bring our hands near our mouths and blow our breath into them as a prayer of thanks for green power and healing.

Song
"Consciousness Waking"

Consciousness waking, Holy and Whole.
Creation stirring, birthing anew.
Now is the time. We are the space
for the Holy to rise in our midst.

Take Action

Let us put our creation-centered prayers into action. Here are some possible ways:

- Work in a garden.
- Brew a cup of tea, sit outside, preferably near water, and commune with the trees, grass, birds, and creation.
- Scent a bath or season food with the herbs.
- Listen to Hildegard's music: https://www.youtube.com/watch?v=BhrCv0zK3SU.

Sending Forth

Return thanks to Hildegard for creation spirituality that feels divine pleasures and does divine justice.

Return thanks to all healers who value creation-centered spirituality and care for the cosmos.

Return thanks to Hildegard of Bingen for her visions, courage, and boldness.

Song

"Sister Hildegard Shows the Way," words by Jann Aldredge-Clanton; music Allgemeines Katholisches Gesangbuch, ca. 1774 GROSSER GOTT 8.8.7.8.7.7, in Inclusive Songs for Resistance & Social Action *(words © 2016 Jann Aldredge-Clanton). Used with permission.*

Sister Hildegard shows the way,
guiding all with visions glowing,
miracles of healing rays, loving
kindness ever growing.
Daily she inspires rebirth, greening
power filling Earth.

Mother Hildegard gives new life,
opening all confining places,
leading us to end the strife, recreating
peaceful spaces.
Joined in circles, free and fair, we will
spread her loving care.

Poet Hildegard sings of Love,
everlasting, ever giving,
deep within us and above, streams of
beauty ever living.
Joining her creative song, all are
blessed, transformed, and strong.

Still, Saint Hildegard speaks today,
calling out with Holy Wisdom:
"Follow peaceful, healing ways, paths
of justice, love, and freedom.
All reflect divinity, joined in mystic
harmony."

Learn More from These Resources

Hildegard's Writings

Hildegard of Bingen. *The Book of Divine Works.* Translated by Nathaniel M. Campbell. Washington, DC: The Catholic University of America Press, 2018.

———. *Causes and Cures: The Complete English Translation of Hildegardis* Causae et Curae Libri *VI.* Translated by Priscilla Throop. Charlotte, VT: Medieval MS, 2008.

———. *Cause and Cure: Holistic Healing.* Translated by Manfred Pawlik and Patrick Madigan. Collegeville, MN: Liturgical Press, 1994.

———. *Hildegard's Healing Plants from Her Medieval Classic Physica.* Translated by Bruce W. Hozeski. Boston, MA: Beacon Press, 2001.

———. *Mystical Writings.* Edited by Fiona Bowie and Oliver Davies. New York: Crossroads, 1990.

———. *Scivias.* Translated by Mother Columbia Hart and Jane Bishop. Classics of Western Spirituality. Mahwah, NJ: Paulist Press, 1990.

Books about Hildegard

Chicago, Judy. *The Dinner Party: Hildegard von Bingen Place Setting and Runner, 1974–1979.* New York: Brooklyn Museum, Elizabeth A. Sackler Center for Feminist Art, 1979.

Dickens, Andrea Janelle. *The Female Mystic: Great Women Thinkers of the Middle Ages.* New York: I.B. Tauris & Co, 2009.

Durka, Gloria. *Praying with Hildegard of Bingen.* Winona, MN: Saint Mary's Press, 1991.

Fox, Matthew. *Hildegard of Bingen: A Saint for Our Times; Unleashing Her Power in the 21st Century.* Vancouver, BC: Namaste Press, 2012.

Jantzen, Grace. *Power, Gender and Christian Mysticism.* Cambridge: Cambridge University Press, 1995.

Kujawa-Holbrook, Sheryl A. *Hildegard of Bingen: Essential Writings and Chants of a Christian Mystic—Annotated & Explained.* Woodstock, VT: SkyLight Paths Publishing, 2016.

Malone, Mary T. *Four Women Doctors of the Church: Hildegard of Bingen, Catherine of Siena, Teresa of Ávila, Thérésa of Lisieux.* Maryknoll, NY: Orbis Books, 2015.

Meconi, Honey. *Hildegard of Bingen.* Women Composers. Urbana: University of Illinois Press, 2018.

Uhlein, Gabriele. *Meditations with Hildegard of Bingen.* Santa Fe, NM: Bear and Company, 1983.

10. October

Walk in Providence with Mother Théodore Guérin

What have we to do in order to be saints? Nothing extraordinary; nothing more than what we do every day. Only do it for [God's] love.

—Saint Mother Théodore Guérin, *Journals and Letters*

October 3 is the feast day of Saint Mother Théodore Guérin, the eighth American saint and the foundress of the Sisters of Providence at St. Mary-of-the-Woods, Indiana. She was a visionary woman who, in the motto of the Sisters of Providence, broke boundaries and created hope. October 22 is celebrated as the Foundation Day for the community.

This liturgy shares the words and works of Mother Théodore Guérin to tell her story and capture her spirit, to reflect on the source of inspiration and hope she was and still is, and to invite us to walk in Providence with her. She reminds us that we can find in our ordinary, everyday lives all the moments we need to become saints. Like Mother Théodore, we are called to be love, mercy, and justice in the world.

Preparation

Set the table or center space with acorns, pictures of oak trees, bread, wine, juice, pictures of Mother Théodore, and pictures of St. Mary-of-the-Woods, Indiana, the sacred land she walked.

Call to Gather

Welcome to this feast day liturgy celebrating Mother Théodore Guérin, the eighth American saint and the foundress of the Sisters of Providence at St. Mary-of-the-Woods, Indiana. We will hear more of her inspiring story throughout our liturgy today.

We gather to give thanks for this holy and wise, courageous and determined woman, to hear her story, and to be inspired to walk in Providence with her as we face the challenges of our day.

Naming the Circle

When Mother Théodore was a child, she liked to pray among the rocks on the seashore where she could look out upon the vast expanse of water near her home in Brittany, France. For her, the sea was the symbol of eternity and her earthly connection with heaven.

Think about your favorite place to pray. *Pause.* Let us speak our names and share with one another our favorite places to pray.

Song

"Place Yourself Gently" by Jeremy Gallet, SP (© 2016 Sisters of Providence, St. Mary-of-the-Woods, IN). Used with permission.

Place yourself gently; place yourself
gently in the hands of Providence.

Place yourself gently; place yourself
gently in the hands of Providence.

Breathing Prayer

Breathe in Providence . . . Breathe out love . . .
Breathe in Providence . . . Breathe out mercy . . .
Breathe in Providence . . . Breathe out justice . . .

Blessed are you, Breath of Providence,
For you give us life to share.

Breathe in Providence . . . Breathe out love . . .
Breathe in Providence . . . Breathe out mercy . . .
Breathe in Providence . . . Breathe out justice . . .

The Story of Mother Théodore

Growing Up in Brittany, France

"Put yourself gently in the hands of Providence."
—Mother Théodore Guérin

Anne-Thérèse Guérin was born in Etables, France, on October 2, 1798. At birth she was consecrated to the Blessed Virgin Mary and was always dressed in white or blue until she was ten years old, the year she made her First Communion.

She grew up in Brittany, the Celtic part of France. She was homeschooled by her mother.

Her father, an officer in the French navy, was killed by bandits on his way home when she was fifteen years old. She lost two baby brothers, one in a house fire that Anne-Thérèse escaped and the other in a bed fire. All of this left her mother bereft. After these tragic incidents, she took charge of the family home and garden and cared for her sick mother and younger sister.

Anne-Thérèse entered the Sisters of Providence of Ruillé-sur-Loir, France, in 1823 when she was twenty-five years old. She educated children and received a medal of honor for excellence in teaching. She studied medicine so she could care for the sick poor who could not afford a doctor.

Reflection

Mother Théodore teaches us, "Put yourself gently in the hands of Providence." When do you put yourself into the hands of Providence, gently or otherwise? Let us pause to reflect quietly. The song will bring closure to reflection time for now.

Song

"Living Providence" by Jeremy Gallet, SP (© 2015 Sisters of Providence, St. Mary-of-the-Woods, IN). Used with permission.

Living Providence:
deep'ning our relationship with God.

Coming to America

"This is the path traced by Providence and I follow it."
—Mother Théodore Guérin

Mother Théodore was assigned to America in 1840. She was chosen by Mother Mary and the bishop of Le Mans, Jean-Baptiste Bouvier, in Ruillé-sur-Loir, France, to accept the invitation of Bishop de la Hailandière of the Diocese of Vincennes, Indiana, to bring good news to the oppressed by opening missions there. She left her beloved homeland of France with five companion sisters—Sister St. Vincent Ferrer Gage, Sister Basilide Seneschal, Sister Olympiade Boyer, Sister Mary Xavier Leree, and Sister Mary Liguori Tiercin—and traveled by ship, train, steamboat, canal boat, and horse-drawn carriage before finally arriving in the wilderness of Indiana in the United States. After hearing the words, "Come down, Sisters, you have arrived," the six women dedicated their mission to Mary and named it St. Mary-of-the-Woods. A seventh French sister, Sister St. Francis, joined them a year later.

Pioneer life was hard for these French women. Mother Théodore waited for a new home to be built in the forest wilderness. She prepared to establish a community and challenged her sisters to respond to the urgent needs of the times. They set captives free by educating youth, establishing many schools, and founding two orphanages. They healed the brokenhearted and comforted the sick by setting up two pharmacies to dispense free medicines to those who were economically poor. They worked to transform the existing social order of their day by opening an academy for girls and women, now known as Saint Mary-of-the-Woods College. They learned to cherish the woods and its herbs, trees, birds, lakes, and natural life surrounding them.

Reflection

Mother Théodore tells us, "This is the path traced by Providence and I follow it." What journey is ahead for you? Where is Providence leading you to see new life, meet new challenges, take new paths in your faith journey? How are you following the path of Providence? Let us pause to reflect quietly. The song will bring closure to reflection time for now.

Song
"Living Providence"

Living Providence:
deep'ning our relationship with God.

The Vision of Providence
"Grant, O my God, that all who dwell in this house may love you much, may love one another, and may never forget why they came here."
—Mother Théodore Guérin

Mother Théodore held on to her visions of Providence and comforted her sisters even in the midst of severe setbacks: storms at sea, fires that destroyed their barns and harvest, prejudice against Catholics, increasingly ill health, excommunication by the bishop, and deaths of loved ones. Yet, the sisters persisted.

Mother Théodore and the other five Providence foundresses welcomed God's presence in their lives and placed themselves under the protection of the Blessed Virgin Mary the moment they arrived at the Woods and entered the chapel. They were wise women whose gifts of love, mercy, and justice rooted their Providence community for the future.

Today the house of Providence has grown to become a Community of Providence that is home to Sisters of Providence and Providence Associates who embrace the vision of Mother Théodore.

Reflection
Mother Théodore prays, "Grant, O my God, that all who dwell in this house may love you much, may love one another, and may never forget why they came here." What are your visions? What is in your heart that needs healing? How are you love, mercy, and justice in your family, workplace, neighborhood, the world? The song will bring closure to reflection time for now.

Song
"Living Providence"

Living Providence:
deep'ning our relationship with God.

Reflection | Sharing
Think about what you have heard in Mother Théodore's words and story. Let us take a few moments of quiet to reflect further on these questions:

What words of Mother Théodore's speak to you today? When do you put yourself in the hands of Providence? How do you pay attention to living as Providence, deepening your relationship with the God of Providence like Saint Mother Théodore did? Let us pause for quiet reflection.

After a quiet time, I will invite us to share our reflections with one another.

Song
"Place Yourself Gently"

Place yourself gently; place yourself gently in the hands of Providence.
Place yourself gently; place yourself gently in the hands of Providence.

Litany of Saint Mother Théodore

By Sister Jeanne Knoerle, SP, in Praying with the Sisters of Providence of St. Mary-of-the-Woods. *Used with permission.*

A litany is a well-known form of prayer consisting of a series of petitions with a response that is the same for all petitions or for several in succession. Let us pray this Litany of Saint Mother Théodore.

"That we, like you, may abandon ourselves to the will of God,
Pray for us, Saint Mother Théodore.
That we may learn to love as you loved,
Pray for us, Saint Mother Théodore.
That we may truly be children of Providence,
Pray for us, Saint Mother Théodore.
That we may devote ourselves generously to the care of others,
Pray for us, Saint Mother Théodore.
That we may love, forgive, and encourage one another from the bottom of our hearts,
Pray for us, Saint Mother Théodore.
That we may try to bear everything from others without making them bear anything from us,
Pray for us, Saint Mother Théodore.
That we may be gentle with ourselves, acknowledging and correcting our faults but never exaggerating them,
Pray for us, Saint Mother Théodore.
That we may walk in the presence of God, accepting our crosses as you accepted yours,
Pray for us, Saint Mother Théodore.
That we may love and treat Earth as you did, imitating the care of Divine Providence for the birds of the air and the grass of the fields,
Pray for us, Saint Mother Théodore.
That we may strive to develop in our lives that immense charity that sincerely loves persons whose inclinations are most opposed to ours,
Pray for us, Saint Mother Théodore.
That we may share your deep love for God in the Eucharist,
Pray for us, Saint Mother Théodore.
That we may have confidence in that Providence that so far as never failed us,
Pray for us, Saint Mother Théodore."

Saint Mother Théodore Guérin Prayer

"Saint Mother Théodore Guérin, valiant woman of God, intercede for us in our needs. Implore for us through Jesus, the Christ, the gifts of a living faith, abiding hope and steadfast charity, so that through a life of prayer and service with others we may aid in promoting the Providence of God among all peoples. Saint Mother Théodore Guérin, pray for us. Amen."

Song
"Place Yourself Gently"

Place yourself gently; place yourself gently in the hands of Providence.
Place yourself gently; place yourself gently in the hands of Providence.

Loving the Eucharist

Mother Théodore loved the Eucharist. Her times of receiving this sacrament may have been for her the peak of her prayer and the depth of her love for God. In one of her instructions to her sisters she tells them, "How consoling is this mystery of the Eucharist! If we knew how to appreciate it, it would suffice to fortify and sustain us."

Blessing Bread

The blessers hold the bread, wine, and juice toward the community as participants reach toward them.

Come, extend your hands toward this bread and drink.

Blessed are you, Provident God, for giving us "this mystery of the Eucharist," this banquet of love. We take, bless, break, and eat this bread in memory of and in thanksgiving for the love we have known through Saint Mother Théodore Guérin, in thanksgiving for the love we have received, and in thanksgiving for the love we have been inspired to give. May love, mercy, and justice increase.

Blessing Wine and Juice

Blessed are you, Loving Providence, for giving us this fruit of the vine. Young wine reminds us of new love; aged wine, growing richer and fuller, symbolizes long-lasting love. We take, bless, and drink this fruit of the vine in memory of and in thanksgiving for the lasting love you have shared through Saint Mother Théodore Guérin, her sisters, and the Providence Community. May love, mercy, and justice increase.

Let us share the bread and drink, saying to one another: May love, mercy, and justice increase.

Sending Forth to Be a Person of Providence

This guide for contemplation and reflection was created by Sisters of Providence of Saint Mary-of-the-Woods, Indiana. These statements reflect the wisdom and insights of thirteen congregations of women religious who share the title of "Providence" in their names. Printed with permission by the Sisters of Providence of Saint Mary-of-the-Woods, Indiana, SistersofProvidence.org.

Let us send one another forth to walk in Providence with Mother Théodore Guérin. Who is a person of Providence?

"A Person of Providence
is a visible sign of God's Providence
accepting the challenge to make a difference in the world.

respects and reverences the uniqueness of all creation
and respects and manifests deep compassion toward the whole community of life.

is one whose stance and vision
enables each of us to reverence the past, live in the present moment, and embrace the invitation to share in the ongoing creation of the future.

names injustice
when it is recognized, stands against all forms of oppression, and walks in solidarity and hope with oppressed people.

is a risk taker who stands on the edge,
embracing the surrounding tensions and chaos, while continuing to ask the difficult questions.

is aware of the power, movement, and mystery of Providence in all things.

is one whose life and ministry incarnate
God's Providential love, mercy, and justice for the world.

is on fire with the energy of a caring God
and has trust and confidence in an ever-Provident God.

persuades others to find, trust, and live out of an experience of God who never
deserts or belittles or rejects us; who, with us, finds a way when we see no way.

sifts experience
looking for hints of Holy Mystery's plan in every circumstance.

fiercely believes that Providence is
an unstoppable, undefeatable, unending energy toward the good.

lives in—not on—Earth and within all creation.

acts as if all things are possible.

resists all attempts to dominate, control, or subdue creation.

resists the traps of hopelessness and helplessness."

Take Action

Let us put our prayers into action. Here are some possible ways:

- Choose a line from the reflection on "A Person of Providence" that you will put into action this week.
- Say the Saint Mother Théodore Guérin Prayer every day for a week.
- Give service to a neighborhood soup kitchen, food pantry, or prison.
- Pray the Novena to Saint Mother Théodore Guérin for nine days: https://spsmw.org/prayer/novena-saint-mother-theodore-guerin/.
- Order prayer cards, books, gift items from Providence Gift Shop: www.lindenleafgifts.com/category/saint-mother.

Greeting of Peace

Acorns and oak trees are plentiful on the sacred land of St. Mary-of-the-Woods, Indiana, that Mother Théodore walked. Let us exchange acorns with one another, saying, "Walk in Providence," as we greet one another with peace and send one another forth to plant seeds of hope for the next generations.

Song

"This Tough Spun Web" by Carolyn McDade, from This Tough Spun Web *(Surtsey Publishing © 1984; renewed © 1991 Carlyn McDade). Used with permission.*

We are the forest of ten thousand seeds
in shades of green that hold the sun.
With mingled roots our limbs together lean;
we are the many and the one

We are the waters each small drop of rain
Life-spawning ponds and stream-filled sea.
We run the blood that flows in living veins
to live and die that all be free

Chorus:
This circle opening moves with deepened faith
our lives to birth a living dawn.
As love renewed turns in our common way
creating hope we carry on.

We are the wind-filled song that sounds of joy
and cries from dungeons cast away
The deepening dreams of those who labor on
To shape a just and caring way.

We are the sun-fired passionate love
of life,
The burning heart within the soul
We are the love that grows resisting
chains
To free the bound and make us
whole. *Chorus.*

We are the hands proud ache to knead
the bread
From golden seed we raise as corn
We harvest thoughts to feed the
hungering mind,
Translating life into a poem

We are the faith beyond all mystery,
Beneath the deep, yon skies
above
We are the hope in solidarity
Profoundly shaped by human love.
Chorus.

Our healing love, our hands reach out
and touch
the cherished body, the quivering
mind,
Our lives like grass, like bread, like
falling rain
the ordinary, our sublime.

Hold true this tough spun web as hard
times come
and much be lost or taken away.
We struggle not for things that best be
gone,
Integrity rewebs our way. *Chorus.*

Learn More from These Resources

Burton, Katherine. *The Eighth American Saint: The Life of Saint Mother Theodore Guerin, Foundress of the Sisters of Providence of Saint Mary-of-the-Woods, Indiana.* Chicago, IL: ACTA Publications, 2006.

Guérin, Théodore. *Journals and Letters of Mother Theodore Guerin.* Saint Mary-of-the-Woods, IN: Providence Press, 1937.

Mitchell, Penny Blaker. *Mother Theodore Guerin: A Woman for All Time.* 2006. https://www.lindenleafgifts.com/mother-theodore-guerin-woman-all-time.

Neu, Diann L. *Providence Prayers.* Silver Spring, MD: WATERworks Press, 2018.

Sisters of Providence. *Praying with the Sisters of Providence of St. Mary-of-the-Woods.* St. Mary-of-the-Woods, IN: Sisters of Providence, 2017.

———. "Saint Mother Théodore Guérin." SaintMotherTheodore.org.

———. "Saint Mother Théodore Guérin: A Woman for All Time." Video: https://www.youtube.com/watch?v=dELPn595CA4&t=1001s.

———. Website: Sisters of Providence, St. Mary-of-the-Woods, IN. https://spsmw.org/.

11. November

Solidarity with *Comadres* and Martyrs of El Salvador

I hope you come to find that which gives life a deep meaning for you. Something worth living for—maybe even worth dying for.

—Ita Ford, MM, to her niece and godchild

The Comadres *of El Salvador are the mothers in the Americas who fight for human rights by demanding the return of their imprisoned, disappeared, or politically assassinated family members and loved ones. Martyrs of El Salvador include those whose names are unknown as well as Saint Archbishop Óscar Romero, who was killed on March 24, 1980; Ita Ford, Maura Clarke, Jean Donovan, and Dorothy Kazel, who were abducted, raped, and murdered on December 2, 1980; and Jesuits Ignacio Ellacuría, Ignacio Martín Baró, Segundo Montes, Joaquín López y López, Amando López, Juan Ramón Moreno, their housekeeper, Elba Ramos, and her daughter, Celina, who were shot and killed by a Salvadoran military squad on November 16, 1989. They each spoke out against poverty, social injustice, repression, and torture.*

This liturgy invites participants to enter into the story of the Comadres *and to be in solidarity with them and the people of El Salvador. It remembers the martyrs of El Salvador to carry their legacy forward.*

Preparation

Set the table or center space with a white cloth, a lit candle, an unlit candle, a bowl of incense, a bowl of water, and a small bowl with a tablespoon of salt. If you can, add images of the Comadres; *pictures of Ita Ford, Maura Clarke, Jean Donovan, Dorothy Kazel, Óscar Romero, Ignacio Ellacuría, Ignacio Martín Baró, Segundo Montes, Joaquín López y López, Amando López, Juan Ramón Moreno, Elba and Celina Ramos; a map of El Salvador, and artisan crafts from El Salvador around the space.*

Call to Gather

You may wish to tailor this call to your individual or your group's experiences.

We gather to lift up the generations of *Comadres* and martyrs of El Salvador, those unnamed and those known: Ita Ford, Maura Clarke, Jean Donovan, Dorothy Kazel, Archbishop Óscar Romero, Jesuits Ignacio Ellacuría, Ignacio Martín Baró, Segundo Montes, Joaquín López y López, Amando López, Juan Ramón Moreno, their housekeeper, Elba Ramos, and her daughter, Celina.

Comadres (*Comité de Madres Mons. Romero*) was set up in 1977 when disappearances were the order of the day in El Salvador. The group came into existence because relatives of those who were disappeared felt the need to share their grief with partners in misfortune and to unite forces with them. They continue the fight for human rights by demanding the reappearance of their loved ones today.

Maryknoll Sisters Maura Clarke and Ita Ford, Maryknoll Lay Missioner Jean Donovan, and Ursuline Sister Dorothy Kazel, "The Four Roses of December," were abducted, brutally raped, murdered, and buried by the side of the road outside the airport in San Salvador during the US–backed civil war in El Salvador in 1980. Earlier that same year Archbishop Óscar Romero, canonized on October 14, 2018, was assassinated while celebrating Mass with the people during that same conflict. While not yet recognized by the institutional church as saints, today we honor Maura, Ita, Jean, and Dorothy for their work, sacrifice, and miracles.

Jesuits Ignacio Ellacuría, Ignacio Martín Baró, Segundo Montes, Joaquín López y López, Amando López, Juan Ramón Moreno, their housekeeper, Elba Ramos, and her daughter, Celina, were shot and killed by a Salvadoran military squad that entered the University of Central America in San Salvador, El Salvador, on November 16, 1989.

This liturgy is dedicated to the *Comadres* and Mothers of the Disappeared in every country who give hope as they live out their faith in unimaginable circumstances, to the martyrs who gave their lives for justice and solidarity, and to those who are immigrating from El Salvador with their families seeking a better life.

Naming the Circle

To create our circle of solidarity, speak your name and share your connection with or what you know about the *Comadres* and martyrs in El Salvador or Mothers of the Disappeared in Latin America. End with, "I am in solidarity with you."

Quiet Reflection

Let us take a moment in darkness for quiet reflection. One light illuminates a map of El Salvador. We light a bowl of incense so our prayers will reach the heavens and the people of El Salvador.

Song

"Paz, Queremos Paz," Traditional, source unknown.

Paz, queremos paz, y libertad en este mundo.	Peace, we want peace, and liberty in this wide world.

Prayer

"Prayer in a Desperate Advent" by Jean Stokan, in Imagine a World: Poetry of Peacemakers, *compiled by Peggy Rosenthal (Erie, PA: Pax Christi USA, 2005), 125. Used with permission.*

"O May all hearts be broken
with stories of squalor
and horrors of war.

"O May all be haunted
by the screams of the tortured
and the faint whimpering of a hungry
child dying.

"O May Madonna images from Africa,
Iraq, El Salvador,
inner cities everywhere
burn deep
Pieta embraces of unnecessarily
unbroken bodies
pierce our comfort.

"O Dear Compassion
May a path be made ready.

"Through the desperate walls and
gnashing of teeth
O May Justice be birthed.

"O Dear God
Come."

Litany of Solidarity

We Remember . . .

We remember the disappeared throughout Latin America—in Argentina, Chile, El Salvador, Guatemala, Colombia, and Mexico—whose governments used terror against their own people as a means of control.

Response: We hear your cries. *Presente!*

We remember the disappeared of the Salvadoran civil war, those who were tortured, raped, imprisoned, murdered, beheaded, and those who have still not been found.

Response: We hear your cries. *Presente!*

We remember the four churchwomen—Dorothy Kazel, Jean Donovan, Ita Ford, and Maura Clarke—who were raped and killed because of their work for justice and solidarity with the people of El Salvador.

Response: We hear your cries. *Presente!*

We remember those who were massacred at El Mozote—the 809 children, women, and men who were brutally killed on December 11, 1981, and buried in shallow mass graves.

Response: We hear your cries. *Presente!*

We remember the massacre of Jesuits Ignacio Ellacuría, Ignacio Martín Baró, Segundo Montes, Joaquín López y López, Amando López, Juan Ramón Moreno, their housekeeper, Elba Ramos, and her daughter, Celina, who were shot and killed by a Salvadoran military squad that entered the University of Central America in San Salvador, El Salvador, on November 16, 1989.

Response: We hear your cries. *Presente!*

Song

"May My Blood Be" by Linda Bessom, SNDdeN, from Sorrow and Healing *by Carolyn McDade & Friends (Surtesy Publishing © 1993). Used with permission.*

May my blood be a seed of libertion
Que mi sangre sea semilla de liberación

We Lift Up . . .

We lift up the *Comadres* of El Salvador, cofounders Alicia García and María Teresa Tula, and the women who risk their own lives to find their loved ones and the loved ones of others. They persist, even in the midst of threats and imprisonment. They fight for human rights, lead literacy and basic life skills programs for the widows and orphans of the civil war, and give workshops of remembrance so that the people of El Salvador will never forget their history.

Response: We stand in solidarity with you. *Presente!*

We lift up the Mothers of the Plaza de Mayo in Argentina who, every Thursday since 1977, march in the Plaza de Mayo in front of the presidential palace in Buenos Aires. Donning their symbolic white head scarves, they demand the reappearance of their missing children and those forcibly disappeared fighting for democracy during Argentina's dictatorship and dirty war from 1977 to 1983.

Response: We stand in solidarity with you. *Presente!*

We lift up the movements and organizations of mothers that have formed across the world. Wherever sons and daughters go missing, mothers rise up to demand justice: Mothers of the Disappeared in Chile and Mexico, the Saturday Mothers in Turkey, the Mourning Mothers and Mothers of Khavaran in Iran, the Committee of Mothers of Disappeared Migrants in Honduras, and the Tiananmen Mothers in China among others.

Response: We stand in solidarity with you. *Presente!*

We lift up those who are immigrating from El Salvador and other Latin American countries today—the young who fear for their lives because of the increasing violence by gangs and the resurgence of the death squads.

Response: We stand in solidarity with you. *Presente!*

Song

"Paz, Queremos Paz"

Stand, we stand with you, for liberty in this wide world.
Paz, queremos paz, y libertad en este mundo.

We Celebrate . . .

We celebrate the mothers of every country who are rising up and those in solidarity with the mothers, those who do not stay silent, and those who speak out against the status quo.

Response: We honor your courage. *Presente!*

We celebrate Prudencia Ayala, a social activist who led the fight for suffrage and, in 1930, despite public attacks on her gender and indigenous heritage, became the first woman to run for president in El Salvador.

Response: We honor your courage. *Presente!*

We celebrate Óscar Romero, who encouraged the *Comadres* to organize and find their loved ones. He read publicly the names of the disappeared of El Salvador over the radio each week. Romero was martyred in 1980 while presiding at Mass with his parishioners. He was proclaimed a saint in 2018.

Response: We honor your courage. *Presente!*

We celebrate the people of Latin America who today, along with many others, work toward caring for the environment and putting an end to international predatory and harmful mining in their countries.

Response: We honor your courage. *Presente!*

Song

"May My Blood Be"

May my blood be a seed of libertion
Que mi sangre sea semilla de liberación

Quiet Reflection

Let us light a candle of remembrance for the mothers and the martyrs. Let us take a few minutes of quiet to breathe our prayers to the people of El Salvador.

Song

"Cry of Ramah" by Colleen Fulmer, from Cry of Ramah *(© 1985). Used with permission.*

Solo voice sings:

A voice is heard in Ramah, Hiroshima, Salvador;
Women refusing comfort for their children are no more;
no garland of lovely flowers could dispel the ancient grief
or silence the anguished voices that abhor the war machine.

Solo voice speaks:

Ramah was the place of a concentration camp to which the survivors of the destruction of Jerusalem were taken. Poetically, Rachel, mother of the tribes, is imaged crying for her children who have been lost in Jeremiah 31:15.

Crying, grieving, and shedding tears are important. If we deny evil or suppress grief or anger, destructive forces can get stronger.

Solo voice sings:

A voice is heard in Ramah, Hiroshima, Salvador;
Women refusing comfort for their children are no more;
no garland of lovely flowers could dispel the ancient grief
or silence the anguished voices that abhor the war machine.

The Search Goes On

From Circles of Madness: Mothers of the Plaza de Mayo *by Marjorie Agosin (Fredonia, NY: White Pine Press, 1992). Used with permission.*

"Walking, she is soliloquy, an alchemy of life itself, erect, barefoot, majestic in her silence and in the plentitude of her immense open palms. She goes to the river; an embrace of water outlines her crossings, and in the light rippling river, she raises her hands to find him, to discover him and to whisper water sounds in his ear, and she becomes a tree because her arms are two flowery branches while she looks for him, and when he does not appear, she then approaches the sea, the immense territories of the coasts and the dauntless vigor of the surging tide.

"Sometimes she no longer sees the river or she confuses it with the whole sea. Sometimes she returns barefoot in a lonely wet caress and dreams about her sorrows, and she dreams about returning quickly to the river because maybe she will see his brown sun-bleached locks of hair, and if he is not in the river, maybe, yes, surely he will be in the sea. If he isn't in the sea, surely he will be in heaven."

"Ella es un soliloquio entre sus pasos, una alquimia de la vida misma, erguida, descalza, altísima en su silencio y en la plenitud de sus inmensas abiertas palmas. Va hacia el río, un abrazo de agua marca sus travesías y en el río ondulado leve, ella allza sus manos, para encontrarlo, hallarlo, decirle en el oído los sonidos del agua y ella se transforma en árbol, porque sus brazos son dos ramas floridas mientras lo busca en el río, y cuando no aparece entonces, ella se acerca al mar, a los inmensos territorios de las costas y al aliento indomable de la deriva.

"A veces ya no divisa al río o lo confunde con la plena mar. A veces, regresa descalza en una sola caricia mojada y sueña con las penas, y sueña con ir otra vez veloz al río porque a lo mejor verá sus cabellos castaños, soleados, si no está en el río, a lo mejor, sí, seguro que estará en el mar. Si no estará en el mar, seguro en el cielo de la tierra."

Song
"Cry of Ramah"

Solo voice sings:

A voice is heard in Ramah, Hiroshima, Salvador;
Women refusing comfort for their children are no more;
no garland of lovely flowers could dispel the ancient grief
or silence the anguished voices that abhor the war machine.

Reflection | Sharing

We hear the cries of the *Comadres*. We stand in solidarity with them and the people of El Salvador. We honor the dedication of Ita Ford, Maura Clark, Jean Donovan, Dorothy Kazel; Ignacio Ellacuría, Ignacio Martín Baró, Segundo Montes, Joaquín López y López, Amando López, Juan Ramón Moreno, Elba and Celina Ramos, and Óscar Romero.

Why do you cry with the *Comadres*? How do you stand in solidarity with the people of El Salvador? What hope do you get from their story and the legacy of the martyrs?

Let us spend a few minutes in silence. Then, we will share our wisdom.

Blessing with Salt Water

Salt water reminds us of tears. Put salt into the water and mention names of those who cry for justice today.

Let us put salt water on each other's faces to represent the tears of those who are crying. Let us connect with them and pray with all who suffer and all who work for justice.

Song
"May My Blood Be"

May my blood be a seed of libertion
Que mi sangre sea semilla de liberación

A Letter from Ita Ford, MM

Excerpt from a letter written by Ita Ford, MM, martyr of El Salvador, to her niece and godchild, Jennifer Ford, on her sixteenth birthday, August 18, 1980, three months before Ita died. http://www.lovingjustwise.com/ita's_words.htm.

"I hope you come to find
that which gives life a deep meaning for you.
Something worth living for—maybe even dying for—
Something that energizes you, enthuses you,
enables you to keep moving ahead.

"I can't tell you what it might be—
That's for you to find, to choose, to love.
I can just encourage you to start looking,
And support you in that search."

Take Action

Let us put our prayers into action this month. Here are some possible ways:

- Disseminate information about *Comadres* through websites, Facebook, and other social media sites.

- Train immigrants, orphans, and victims of the war in first aid, basic life skills, and human rights; sponsor the formal education and technical training of orphans.
- Advocate to increase the literacy rate of adults and children in your area.

Sending Forth

Let us go forth to carry on the legacy of the *Comadres*, the people of El Salvador, Ita, Maura, Jean, Dorothy, and Óscar Romero.
Let us remain vigilant toward the human rights of El Salvador and Latin America.
Let us remember and tell their stories of dedication and solidarity.

Song

"Our Hearts Cry Out in Longing," words by Jann Aldredge-Clanton (© 2014), music: Appalachian melody I WONDER 12.11.11.12, in Inclusive Songs for Resistance & Social Action *(words © 2014 Jann Aldredge-Clanton). Used with permission.*

Our hearts cry out in longing for justice and peace.
Oh, when will oppression and violence all cease?
Oh, when will the captives all find full release?
Our hearts cry out in longing for justice and peace.

We labor bringing Wisdom Sophia to birth,
To give us the power to make peace on Earth;
With Her all creation reclaims sacred worth;
We labor bringing Wisdom Sophia to birth.

Learn More from These Resources

Agosin, Marjorie. *Circles of Madness: Mothers of the Plaza de Mayo.* Photographs by Alicia D'Amico and Alicia Sanguinetti; translation by Celeste Kostopulos. Fredonia, NY: White Pine Press, 1992.

Carrigan, Ana, and Bernard Stone. *Roses in December.* 56 minutes, documentary, color, English. New Day Films, 1982. https://www.kanopy.com/product/roses-december.

Cerna, Lucía, and Mary Jo Ignoffo. *La Verdad: A Witness to the Salvadoran Martyrs.* Maryknoll, NY: Orbis Books, 2014.

Dennis, Marie, Renny Golden, Scott Wright. *Oscar Romero: Reflections on His Life and Writings.* Maryknoll, NY: Orbis Books, 2000.

Ford, Ita. *Here I Am, Lord: The Letters and Writings of Ita Ford.* Selected with Commentary by Jeanne Evans. Maryknoll, NY: Orbis Books, 2005.

Garcia, J. Malcom. "1980–2015: Memory of El Salvador's Church Martyrs Lives On." *Global Sisters Report.* November 30, 2015. https://www.globalsistersreport.org/news/1980-2015-memory-el-salvadors-church-martyrs-lives-34431.

Markey, Eileen. *A Radical Faith: The Assassination of Sister Maura.* New York: Nation Books, 2016.

Mulligan, Joseph E. *The Jesuit Martyrs of El Salvador: Celebrating the Anniversaries.* Catholic Worker Reprint. Eugene, OR: Wipf and Stock Publishers, 2010.

Proyecto Desaparecidos. www.Desaparecidos.org.

Romero, Óscar. *The Scandal of Redemption: When God Liberates the Poor, Saves Sinners, and Heals Nations.* Walden, NY: Plough Publishing House, 2018.

Sobrino, Jon. *Witnesses to the Kingdom: The Martyrs of El Salvador and the Crucified Peoples.* Maryknoll, NY: Orbis Books, 2003.

Tula, Maria Teresa. *Hear My Testimony: Maria Teresa Tula Human Rights Activist of El Salvador.* Cambridge, MA: South End Press, 1994.

12. December

Reimagine Mary as a Woman Today

And Mary said, "My soul proclaims your greatness, O God."

—Luke 1:46

December and May are months in the Catholic religious calendar that focus on Mary, the first-century BC Galilean Jewish woman of Nazareth and the mother of Jesus. We see her indelible influence in art, culture, and social justice. For many, she has informed the lens through which we experience the world.

This liturgy for December looks at the many faces of Mary and focuses on her as a symbol of those who are oppressed, forgotten, and in search of a home for their children.

Preparation

Put an Advent wreath (if celebrating in December), bread (stollen), napkins, and cup of hot cider for each person on a table or center space.

Naming the Circle

Let us create our circle by speaking our names and sharing in a word or phrase the role Mary has played in our lives or in the lives of others we know.

Call to Gather

The leader gathers up what all have said and uses their reflections to focus the liturgy.

Mary is "the most powerful woman in the world," according to *National Geographic*. Besides having appeared to faithful ones in Fatima, Lourdes, Guadalupe, and Medjugorje, she has made her mark across the ages. From religious iconography to pop culture, socialist revolutions to feminist movements and beyond, she is everywhere and in our everyday lives. Though she is presented in myriad forms and ways today, her presence is as ubiquitous as her name: Mary.

December is filled with feasts of Mary. On the eighth, Immaculate Conception. On the ninth, Conception of the Most Holy Theotokos (Greek title for Mary, the bearer/mother of God). On the twelfth, Our Lady of Guadalupe. On the twenty-fifth, Christmas.

Lighting the Advent Wreath

One person lights the candles marking the week of Advent that the group is celebrating.

Each week of Advent is marked by lighting another one of the candles in the Advent wreath. Tonight we light ___ candle(s) because this is the ___ week of Advent. *Light candles.*

Song

"Spirit of Our Elders" by Kathy Sherman, CSJ, Song of the Universe *(© 2008 Ministry of the Arts), adapted. Used with permission.*

Many faces of Mary, dance, oh dance in me. *(2x)*

Reading

"Searching the Faces of Maria" by Nicola Slee from The Book of Mary *(London: SPCK, 2007), 128–29. Used with permission.*

"We should work to find out if there is a Maria among us, in the faces of our sisters."

—Marcella Althaus-Reid, Argentina

"I'm seeing Maria in this woman of courage
who has left her gender behind
to take on everything new
who battles daily with the sickness in her gut
that is using her body up
who plays electric guitar like an old rock star
and loves the taste of Nigella's food in her mouth
In her face I'm seeing a Maria of tenderness
a Maria of fierce intelligence
a Maria of beautiful fortitude"

Song

"Spirit of Our Elders"

Many faces of Mary, dance, oh dance in me. *(2x)*

"I'm seeing Maria in this woman of fearfulness
who has left her country and children
and lives in a bedsit in Coventry
She came here seeking safety and found only obscurity,
working illegally for the meagre pounds the government won't pay her
I hardly know her but I pray for her daily
In her face that I've never seen
I'm seeing a Maria of desperation
a Maria of tenacity
a Maria desperately missing her people and her children"

Song
"Spirit of Our Elders"

Many faces of Mary, dance, oh dance in me. *(2x)*

"I'm seeing Maria in this solid, straight-talking, uppity woman
who is a tenacious survivor
of a long life of kicks and bruises
She can infuriate
She dominates any group that will allow her into it
She can pierce the crap of church, state or academy in seconds
She speaks truth as well as her own insistent neediness
whether we want to hear it or not
In her face I'm seeing an irksome Maria
a spirited Maria
a Maria who will not take no for an answer"

Song
"Spirit of Our Elders"

Many faces of Mary, dance, oh dance in me. *(2x)*

"I'm seeing Maria in this woman, my friend, who died of cancer
But she would have hated this description,
she who lived passionately to the last day of her life
for her children and husband and her neighbourhood and her beloved Africa
for the work she did to make prison places of justice and humanity
for her God who she hoped, to the end, might yet heal her
In her face I'm seeing a Maria of compassion
a Maria of mercy
a Maria who can't bear the thought of never seeing her two sons grow older"

Song
"Spirit of Our Elders"

Many faces of Mary, dance, oh dance in me. *(2x)*

"Once I start looking I'm seeing Maria everywhere:
in the faces of the sleek, glossy women
in the magazines I'm given to read at the hairdressers
in my mother's face that looks back at me out of the mirror
in the faces of my sisters, which are now, heaven forbid, middle-aged
in the faces of women on the bus into Birmingham
in the distorted faces of Iraqi women on the news whose homes are lying
  in rubble
with nowhere to take their children"

Song
"Spirit of Our Elders"

Many faces of Mary, dance, oh dance in me. *(2x)*

"Too many faces to catalogue or notice or count
I have to work to find their faces of Maria
demanding my attention, my intelligence, my care

"Come closer, Mother, and show me
all the women I've failed to look at closely
who were your presence to me if I'd but realized it
waiting to be recognized, loved, adored"

Song
"Spirit of Our Elders"

Many faces of Mary, dance, oh dance in me. *(2x)*

Litany of Mary of Nazareth

As we reimagine Mary as a woman today, let us pray a litany of Mary of Nazareth.

Reader 1: Praise to you, Divine Providence, Creator of the Universe,
Breathe into us life and creativity.
Praise to you, Guiding Ancestors, Liberator of the Oppressed,
Free us to do the work of justice with peace.
Praise to you, Divine Wisdom, Sophia Spirit,
Enkindle in us a fiery passion for justice.

Reader 2: Mary, Woman of faith . . . guide us.
Woman of vision . . .
Woman of patience . . .
Woman of wisdom . . .
Woman of peace . . .
Woman filled with questions . . .
Woman of truth . . .

Reader 1: Mary, Mother of all cultures . . . be with us.
Mother of those who are immigrants and refugees . . .
Mother of those who have been disappeared . . .
Mother of those living with HIV/AIDS . . .
Mother of those who are sick and dying, especially women with cancer . . .
Mother of those who are abused, violated, and sexually assaulted . . .
Mother of all families . . .

Reader 2: Mary, Model of persistence . . . pray with us.
Model of gracious hospitality . . .
Model of strength . . .
Model of independence . . .
Model of passion . . .
Model of vulnerability . . .
Model of holy rage . . .

Reader 1: Mary, Liberator of the oppressed . . . empower us.
Bringer of justice . . .
Comforter of the afflicted . . .
Provider of sanctuary . . .
Sign of contradiction . . .
Protector of those who are vulnerable . . .
Dreamer of new possibilities . . .

Song

"Blessed is She" by Colleen Fulmer, from Cry of Ramah *(© 1985). Used with permission.*

Blessed is she,
Who believed that the promise made
her by her God
Would be fulfilled, would be fulfilled.

Prayer

Mary of Many Names, empower us with your Wisdom during these days of Advent. Teach us to see clearly that our vision may bring light to the world. Inspire us to act justly, to love tenderly, to set ourselves free, and to heal those who are brokenhearted. Amen. Blessed be. May it be so.

Song

"Blessed Is She"

Blessed is she,
Who believed that the promise made her by her God
Would be fulfilled, would be fulfilled.

Reflection | Sharing

Think about the many faces of Mary raised up here and the other ones you know. Let us take a few moments of quiet to reflect on these questions:

What are your thoughts about Mary? How is she significant in your life or the life of someone you know?

After a quiet time, we will share our thoughts about Mary.

Prayers of the Faithful

Who needs our prayers today? Speak their names so we can pray with and for them.

Our response is: Mary, embrace *Name* with your love and care.

Blessing Bread (Christmas Stollen)

The blesser presents the bread and offers her own blessing, which focuses on Mary's wisdom. She invites the gathered to extend their hands, lifted outwards, as she prays:

Blessed are you, Gracious and Loving Holy Wisdom, for giving us this festive bread. Bless us as we eat and give thanks for the many faces of Mary in the world. *She continues using her own words.* Let us share this bread of life. *Pass the bread around for all to eat.*

Blessing Cider

The blesser focuses her own blessing on the abundance of women's gifts.

Blessed are you, Source of Life and Being, for the warmth of this drink. Bless us as we drink and give thanks for the many faces of Mary in the world and for the abundance of women's gifts. *She continues using her own words.* Let us share this drink of joy. *Pass the cups around for all to drink.*

Prayer

"Magnificat for Today" from Women Church Speaks *(Chicago, 1983).*

The *Magnificat* is a scriptural prayer that speaks of the holiness of women. Let us stand in a circle, put our arms around one another, and pray the *Magnificat* together in three parts.

"*One:* Our souls magnify the holiness that dwells within us.
Two: And our spirits rejoice in the presence of the Holy One.
Three: Because we as women have been touched and called.

"*All:* Yes, from this day forward all generations will call us blessed.

"*One:* For great things have been done through us and those who have gone before us.
Three: Holy is our name and we have shown mercy and strength as women, from age to age.
Two: We have gathered our courage and steadfastness and worked to heal the brokenhearted with tenderness and care.
Three: We have called forth truth and created a new shape for living what we believe to be just.

One: Yes, we have been hungry and have filled each other with good things.
Two: For we have kept our promises and journeyed and struggled in the hope of our dreams . . . touching and healing, laughing and crying . . . questioning and loving . . .

"*All:* Yes, indeed by our living and our faithfulness, by our passion and our courage . . . all generations of women from this day forth will be blessed."

Take Action

Let us put our prayers into action this month. Here are some possible ways:

- Visit a shrine of Mary in your neighborhood and clean it if necessary.
- Sing a Mary song that you remember from your youth or listen to one on YouTube.
- Pray the Litany of Mary of Nazareth in this liturgy and add more to it.
- Engage in Mary-like ministry—feed those who are hungry, donate to those who are poor, visit those who are sick.

Sending Forth

Sing a medley of your favorite, inclusive holiday songs.

Learn More from These Resources

Castañeda-Liles, María Del Socorro. *Our Lady of Everyday Life: La Virgen de Guadalupe and the Catholic Imagination of Mexican Women in America.* Oxford: Oxford University Press, 2018.

Elkins, Kathleen Gallagher. *Mary, Mother of Martyrs.* Feminist Studies in Religion Books, 2018.

Gebara, Ivone, and Maria Clara Bingemer. *Mary: Mother of God, Mother of the Poor.* Maryknoll, NY: Orbis Books, 1987.

Johnson, Elizabeth A. *Truly Our Sister: A Theology of Mary in the Communion of Saints.* New York: Continuum, 2003.

Kateusz, Ally. *Mary and Early Christian Women: Hidden Leadership.* London, UK: Palgrave MacMillan, 2019.

Lee, Courtney Hall. *Black Madonna: A Womanist Look at Mary of Nazareth.* Eugene, OR: Cascade Books, 2017.

National Geographic: Mary: The World's Most Powerful Woman. 2015.

National Geographic: The Story of Mary: From the Biblical World to Today. 2018.

Ruether, Rosemary Radford. *Mary: The Feminine Face of the Church.* Louisville, KY: Westminster Press, 1977.

Slee, Nicola. "Searching the Faces of Maria." In *The Book of Mary.* London: SPCK, 2007.

section two

Step into the Pool

While the water is stirring
I'll step into the pool.

—Sojourner Truth, 1851 Women's Rights Convention in Akron, Ohio

When you pass through the seas, I will be with you;
when you pass over the rivers, you will not drown.

—Isaiah 43:2

I am like a drop of water on a rock. After drip, drip,
dripping in the same place, I begin to leave a mark,
and I leave my mark in many people's hearts.

—Rigoberta Menchú, *Crossing Borders: An Autobiography*

13. January

Recognize Women in Politics

There cannot be true democracy unless women's voices are heard. There cannot be true democracy unless women are given the opportunity to take responsibility for their own lives.

—Hillary Rodham Clinton, July 11, 1997

January is inauguration month in the United States every four years. November is election month. More women than ever are getting involved in politics every year and making historic inroads. Yet, a century after women won the vote in the United States, we still see very few in leadership roles. We need to listen to their voices, tell their stories, and vote! Democracy depends on us and on women in politics.

This liturgy raises up women in politics past, present, and future who make a difference for the well-being of all. It encourages participants to vote.

Preparation

Place on a table a pitcher of water, a large bowl (like a well), and a towel. Invite participants to wear white to honor suffragists who secured women's voting rights a century ago. Place posters, buttons, and pictures of women in politics around the room.

Call to Gather

This is the season of women in politics! As Michelle Bachelet, first woman president of Chile, reminds us, "For me, a better democracy is a democracy where women not only have the right to vote and to elect but to be elected." With an eye towards the US Election Day in November, let us bless the women—past, present, and future—who hold public office. They engage in public service for the good of the nation.

Naming the Circle

Let us create our circle by sharing our names and saying in a word or phrase why we need women in politics.

Song

"Guide My Feet," African American spiritual.

*Guide my feet while I run this race *(3x)*
For I don't want to run this race in vain

*Stand by me . . . *Vote for me . . .

Raising Up Women in Politics

As you call out the name of each woman or group, pour water into a bowl.

Michelle Obama, you passionately advocate for girls' education, for healthy families, for respect for all women. You are a fearless and graceful model as the first African American First Lady and Partner of the United States. Your time is now. *Pour water.*
Response: You make a difference.

Eleanor Roosevelt, you were a pioneer who changed the role of the First Lady through your active participation in American politics. You were a diplomat, journalist, activist, and advocate for a wide range of human rights issues. You served in the first American delegation to the United Nations. Because of your leadership, more women were empowered to enter political life. Your time was then. *Pour water.*
Response: You make a difference.

Hillary Rodham Clinton, you transformed the role of First Lady to one of First Partner. You paved the way as the first female senator from New York, the third female secretary of state, and the first major party nominee for president of the United States. Your time was then. *Pour water.*
Response: You make a difference.

Women in the cabinet and key administrative positions [*name current ones*], you can provide a breath of fresh air combined with professional, activist, philosophical, and technical leadership skills. Your time is now. *Pour water.*
Response: You make a difference.

The [*number*] women in the Senate, [*name current ones*], you bring women's voices, experiences, and insights. Your time is now. *Pour water.*
Response: You make a difference.

The [*number*] women in the House of Representatives, [*name current ones*], you represent the values, needs, and hopes of people in your districts. Your time is now. *Pour water.*
Response: You make a difference.

Women in state and local governments, [*name those from your area*], you attend to the needs and expectations of neighborhoods and communities at the grassroots. Your time is now. *Pour water.*

Response: You make a difference.

Women firsts in political office in the last one hundred years or more—Victoria Woodhull, the first woman to run for President in 1872; Jeannette Rankin, the first white woman elected to Congress in 1916; Hattie Caraway, the first woman to be elected to the Senate and serve a full term in 1932; Shirley Chisholm, the first African American woman elected to Congress in 1968; Geraldine Ferraro, the first woman on a major party's presidential ticket as vice presidential nominee in 1984; Carol Moseley Braun, the first African American woman elected to the Senate in 1992; Janet Reno, the first woman to become attorney general of the United States in 1993; Madeleine K. Albright, the first white woman to serve as secretary of state in 1997; Condoleezza Rice, the first female African American secretary of state in 2005; Nancy Pelosi, the first and only woman speaker of the house in 2007 and again in 2019 and the highest-ranking elected woman in US history, second in the presidential line of succession, immediately after the vice president; Hillary Rodham Clinton, the first female senator from New York in 2001 and the first major party nominee for president of the United States in 2016; [*add others*]—you paved the way for women in politics for the next one hundred years. Your time was vital. *Pour water.*

Response: You make a difference.

Women in training for future political office, you are hope for humankind. Your time is now. *Pour water.*

Response: You make a difference.

For the woman who will one day be president of the United States, we await your leadership and pray that it will come in our lifetime. Your time is now. *Pour water.*

Response: You make a difference.

Girls born today who will be political leaders tomorrow, to you is given the challenge of a world bursting with possibilities. Remember the stories of your foremothers as you make your mark on the global community. Your time is soon. *Pour water.*

Response: You make a difference.

Reflection | Sharing

We have lifted up pioneering women in politics and women who hold public office today. Like these women, we participate in politics by voting, campaigning, writing, and calling our political leaders, attending public hearings, acting on our convictions, and running for public office ourselves.

Let us take a few moments of quiet to reflect on these questions:
What other women in elected public office would you add?
What are your reflections after hearing the names of these women?
How do they make a difference?
After a short time of silence, when you are ready, share your thoughts and feelings with the group. End your sharing by pouring water and saying:
I am *Name*. I am a political woman. I make a difference. I vote!

Take Action

Let us put our prayers into action. Here are some possible ways:

- Vote! And vote for women who make a difference!
- Encourage girls and young women to develop their leadership skills.
- Read more about the women in politics named here.

Sending Forth to Keep the Momentum Going

Let us go forth to vote!
Let us go forth to tell the stories of women in politics.
Let us raise our hands in solidarity, join them together, and close by proclaiming:
We are political women. Our time is now.
We make a difference. We vote.

Song

"We Shall Not Be Moved," African American spiritual.

*We shall not, we shall not be moved. *(2x)*
Just like a tree that's planted by the water
We shall not be moved.

*Fighting for democracy . . . *Young and old together . . .
*Seeking peace and justice . . . *Living lives of witness . . .

Learn More from These Resources

Carmon, Irin, and Shana Knizhnik. *Notorious RBG: The Life and Times of Ruth Bader Ginsburg.* New York: HarperCollins Publishers, 2015.

Clinton, Hillary. *Hard Choices.* New York: Simon & Schuster, 2014.

Day of the Girl. US page. Women's Under-Representation in Politics, for resources for girls and parents. http://www.dayofthegirl.org/women_s_representation_in_politics.

Dolan, Julie, Melissa M. Deckman, Michele I. Swers. *Women and Politics: Paths to Power and Political Influence.* Lanham, MD: Rowman & Littlefield, 2018.

Levy, Debbie. *I Dissent: Ruth Bader Ginsburg Makes Her Mark.* New York: Simon & Schuster Books for Young Readers, 2016.

NETWORK Lobby for Social Justice. https://networklobby.org/.

Newsom, Jennifer Siebel. *Miss Representation.* Documentary available on Netflix. Uncover the glaring realities we live with every day but fail to see.

Obama, Michelle. *Becoming.* New York: Crown Publishing Group, 2018.

———. Speech responding to Donald Trump's treatment of women. https://www.huffpost.com/entry/watch-michelle-obama-donald-trump_n_57ffc2b9e4b05eff5582381a?guccounter=1.

Palmieri, Jennifer. *Dear Madam President: An Open Letter to the Women Who Will Run the World.* New York: Grand Central Publishing, 2018.

The Representation Project. Discover with Marian Wright Edelman's words "You can't be what you can't see." http://therepresentationproject.org.

Zorthian, Julia, Merrill Fabry, and Olivia B. Waxman. "50 Women Who Made American Political History." *Time Magazine.* March 8, 2017. http://time.com/4551817/50-women-political-history/.

14. February

Called to Heal

Nobody can stop the river from flowin'
We are goin' forward and we're flowing like a river.

—Kathy Sherman, CSJ, "Nobody Can Stop the River from Flowin'"

Healing takes many forms—from swallowing grandma's home remedies to having your scalp massaged and shampooed, from receiving a reconciling embrace to sobbing alone, from needing well-being to praying for a miracle. Healing is needed every day. We find healing through a sympathetic listener, a forgiving hug, a belly laugh, an herbal bath, a quiet time with nature, a moving sermon, a special touch, a powerful Eucharist, or a deeply meaningful liturgy.

This liturgy blesses healers, especially health professionals and those in healing ministries, and it sends participants forth to heal.

Preparation

Put a glass bowl filled with water on a table in the center of a circle. Around the bowl, place a stone for each participant.

Call to Gather

From city center and country corner, from business office and home, from different ethnic, class, and religious backgrounds, we are called to heal. We are called to pay attention to health, wholeness, and healing within our communities. We are called to recognize that healing is the process of integrating the body, mind, and spirit to create wholeness, health, and a sense of well-being, even when curing may not occur.

Let us bless one another for the healing ministry to which we have been called. Let us send one another forth to heal.

Naming a Circle of Healers

Let us create a circle of healers. Say your name, add the words "I am a healer," and then give your right hand to the person on your right. For example, "I am Diann. I am a healer." Then I give my right hand to the person on my right, and she speaks.

Song

"Sing of a Blessing." Words and music by Miriam Therese Winter (© Medical Mission Sisters, 1982, 1987). Used with permission.

Leader: Sing, we sing of a blessing.
All: Sing, we sing of a blessing.
Leader: Sing, we sing of a blessing.
All: Sing, we sing of a blessing.
Leader: A blessing of love.
All: A blessing of love.
Leader: A blessing of mercy.
All: A blessing of mercy.
Leader: Love will increase.
All: Love will increase.
Leader: A blessing of peace.
All: A blessing of peace.

Continue echoing the Leader/All format:

Pray now, pray for a blessing. *Echo.* Pray now, pray for a blessing. *Echo.*
A blessing within. *Echo.* A blessing among us. *Echo.*
Love will increase. *Echo.* A blessing of peace. *Echo.*

Live now, live as a blessing. *Echo.* Live now, live as a blessing. *Echo.*
A blessing within. *Echo.* A blessing among us. *Echo.*
Love will increase. *Echo.* A blessing of peace. *Echo.*

Rise up, rise for a blessing. *Echo.* Rise up, rise for a blessing. *Echo.*
A blessing be yours. *Echo.* Now and forever. *Echo.*
Love will increase. *Echo.* A blessing of peace. *Echo.*

A Reading from John 5:4

"An angel of God would come down to the pool from time to time, to stir up the water; the first one to step into the water after it had been stirred up would be completely healed."

Sung Response

"Blessed Is She" by Colleen Fulmer, from Cry of Ramah *(© 1985), https://www.youtube.com/watch?v=P_ZjCQKwYIw. Used with permission.*

Blessed is she who believes
That the promise made her by our God
Would be fulfilled, would be fulfilled.

Blessing the Healers

One: Filled with the sounds, the power, the visions,
the challenges, and the commitments of the work of healing,
let us lay hands on one another and bless one another for healing ministry.

Touch the shoulders of the person on either side of you.
Speak aloud your name. *Naming.*
You are called to the healing ministry for *[name your community].*

Two: Spirit of Health and Healing,
time and again throughout history
you call forth your ministers from the community
and send them to do works of justice:
to heal the sick and broken,
to feed hungry souls,
to give drink to thirsty ones,
to free captives.
Come, Holy Wisdom, Healing Spirit, Regenerative Source,
bless us, your healers, to do your works of healing.
Let us respond with these words:
Pour out your Spirit upon us, Wisdom Sophia.

All: Pour out your Spirit upon us, Wisdom Sophia.

One: We ask you to bless us, your health ministers, who,
in the cry of the people and in the word of the community,
have been called to be healers.
We ask you to pour out your Spirit upon us,
that we may have the gifts of health and healing,
see visions, dream dreams, break bread, do justice.
Let us respond with these words:
Pour out your Spirit upon us, Wisdom Sophia.

All: Pour out your Spirit upon us, Wisdom Sophia.

Two: Pour forth your Spirit, Wisdom Sophia,
on your people with whom we minister.
Pour forth your Spirit on the church,
that the whole People of God may benefit from our work.
Pour forth your Spirit on our families and friends,
that they may offer us loving care, understanding, and support.
Let us respond:

All: Pour out your Spirit upon us, Wisdom Sophia.

Together: When the bread is not enough,
when our hope is dim,
when our energies are frazzled,
refresh us with Your Spirit.
Let us respond:

All: Pour out your Spirit upon us, Wisdom Sophia.

Sung Response
"Blessed Is She"

Blessed is she who believes
That the promise made her by our God
Would be fulfilled, would be fulfilled.

Water Ritual

In the center of our table is a bowl of water representing a sacred well. Holy wells through the ages have been believed to have healing powers. Water is a healing and regenerative force that facilitates life. It is spoken of as the source, the healer, the transformer, the spring of ancient wisdom.

As we pass the water bowl, the sacred well, look into it and visualize the healing powers of the water. Visualize your healing powers.

Reflection | Sharing

Think about what you have experienced in the blessing and water ritual. Let us take a few moments of quiet to reflect on these questions:

What healing powers do you notice in yourself? In others? How do you see them being used for the community?

After a quiet time, we will share a glimpse of our reflections with one another.

A Blessing of Hands

Look at your hands. They tell many stories. Notice their healing power. Who have your hands touched? What do your hands reveal to you about healing? *Pause.* Let us bless these hands together. Imagine the hands of loved ones blessing you.

Blessed be the works of your hands, O Holy One, Sophia Wisdom.
Blessed be these hands that touch life.
Blessed be these hands that nurture creativity.
Blessed be these hands that hold pain.
Blessed be these hands that embrace with passion.
Blessed be these hands that tend gardens.
Blessed be these hands that close in anger.
Blessed be these hands that open in release.
Blessed be these hands that plant new seeds.
Blessed be these hands that harvest ripe fields.
Blessed be these hands that clean, wash, mop, scrub.
Blessed be these hands that become knotty with age.
Blessed be these hands that are wrinkled and scarred from doing justice.
Blessed be these hands that reached out and are received.
Blessed be these hands that hold the hope of the future.
Please add others . . .
Blessed be the works of your hands, O Holy One, Sophia Wisdom.

Take Action

Let us put our prayers into action. Here are some possible ways:

- Meditate on your healing gifts. Give thanks for them, and use one today.
- Share your healing stone with someone in need of healing.
- Bless your hands every morning for a week as you start your day.

Sending Forth

In Celtic mythology, stones have healing qualities. They activate the power of holy wells. Take a stone from around the well to symbolize your healing powers and the healing powers of this community.

Blessed and filled with healing powers, let us exchange these healing stones with one another, remembering that the gift of healing is given by and for the community. Let us send one another forth, exchanging the stones and saying,

"We send you forth to heal."

Song

"Nobody Can Stop the River from Flowin'" by Kathy Sherman, CSJ (© 2008). Used with permission.

Nobody can stop *the river from flowin' (3x)
We are goin' forward and we're flowing like a river.

Nobody can stop *healing from flowin' (3x)
We are goin' forward and we're flowing like a river.

*compassion *hope *peace

Learn More from These Resources

Ehrenreich, Barbara, and Deirdre English. *Witches, Midwives & Nurses: A History of Women Healers.* New York: The Feminist Press, 2010.

"Healing hands images": search online and enjoy the beauty in the variety of hands.

Jung, Patricia Beattie, and L. Shannon Jung, eds. *Moral Issues and Christian Responses.* Minneapolis, MN: Fortress Press, 2013.

Kao, Grace Y., and Ilsup Ahn, eds. *Asian American Christian Ethics: Voices, Methods, Issues.* Waco, TX: Baylor University Press, 2015.

Ruether, Rosemary Radford, with David Ruether. *Many Forms of Madness: A Family's Struggle with Mental Illness and the Mental Health System.* Minneapolis, MN: Fortress Press, 2010.

15. March

Come to Waters of Peace for World Water Day

Drink living water, come to the well.
Tomen agua viva, vengan a mi.

—Colleen Fulmer, *Drink Living Water*

World Water Day, celebrated annually on March 22, focuses attention on the importance of water and the need to preserve it. Water is also a common, sacred source that symbolizes new beginnings, global connections, and personal transformations. Water and peace are both necessary for life.

This liturgy uses the symbol of water on World Water Day to call forth a blessing of peace from the spirits of the universe so that wars over water will cease.

Preparation

Invite seven people to offer a blessing. Encourage them to adapt the script to the experience of the group and to include a variety of languages. Place a bowl, a pitcher of water, and a towel on a central table or, if the celebration is outside, on a rock, tree stump, or the ground.

Call to Gather

This World Water Day, our circle is huge because we invite into it all living things that need water: people, plants, animals, and all life throughout the universe. The world needs oceans, lakes, rivers, waterfalls, water wells, spring protection, rainwater tanks, small dams, sanitation, and hygiene for all. We all need water that is safe, clean, reliable, and free.

Let us gather in peace to bless water, our common, sacred source that symbolizes beginnings, renewal, and new life.

Naming the Circle

Let us say our names and speak a word of why water is so important, saying, "I am *Name*, and I need and bless water because . . . "

Song

"Drink Living Water | Tomen Agua Viva" by Colleen Fulmer and Rufino Zaragosa, from Her Wings Unfurled © *1984. Used with permission.*

Come, you hungry, come, you thirsty;
Drink living water, come to the well.
Come, you weary, bring your burdens;
Drink . . .

Vengen, hambrientos, vengan sedientos;
Tomen agua viva, vengan a mi.
Vengan, cansados, vengan agobiados;
Tomen . . .

Come, you searching, bring your questions; Drink . . .

Vengan, los pobres, vengan los humildes; Tomen . . .

(Add verses that reflect the needs of the group.)

Invoking the Spirits

We gather from the four corners of Earth, from the seven directions of the wind, to remember all people who come to the waters today.

We call on the Spirits of the East, North, West, South, Above, Below, and Center to shower us and Earth with their blessings, especially their gifts of safe, clean, and reliable water.

Each blesser faces her direction and uses her own gestures to invoke the Spirit. If possible, echo the first two lines in a second language. Begin with the direction that is appropriate to the needs of the time, and pray with as many directions as fit your group.

East

Turn to the East with me. Kneel and touch your forehead to the ground in the Muslim prayer posture.

O Great Spirit of the East, Power of Air!
We invoke you and praise your name.
Repeat in Chinese:
偉大的東方精神, 大氣的力量
我們懇求你 讚美你的名!

Breath of Life, Creator of Dawn, Faithful Rising Sun, Come!
By the air that is your breath, send forth your light of peace.

Move your body to greet the Spirit of the East.

O Great Spirit of the East,
be here now as we remember people of the East:
people groping for peace in the Middle East;

people struggling for justice in China;
people migrating to find food in Ethiopia.

The blesser pours water into the bowl.

Spirit of the East, bless us with your power, and restore all waters of the East!

Song
"Give Us Living Water" by the Collegeville Composers Group, Psallite: Sacred Song for Liturgy and Life *(Collegeville, MN: Liturgical Press © 2005). Used with permission.*

Give us living water, welling up within us:
fill us with your Spirit, fill us with your truth.

North
Turn to the North. Let your body and arms reach for the stars.

O Great Spirit of the North, Power of Earth!
We invoke you and praise your name.
Repeat in Swedish:
O stora Ande i norr, jordens kraft.
Vi åberopar Dig och prisar ditt namn.

Mysterious North Star, Fierce Winter Wind, Nourishing Earth Mother, Come!
By the Earth that is your body, send forth your strength for peace.

Move your body to greet the Spirit of the North.

O Great Spirit of the North,
be here now as we remember those of the North:
people protecting the wilderness heritage of Canada;
indigenous people fighting for economic survival in Alaska;
people creating a social and equitable society in Sweden.

The blesser pours water into the bowl.

Spirit of the North, bless us with your power and restore all waters of the North.

Song
"Give Us Living Water"

Give us living water, welling up within us:
fill us with your Spirit, fill us with your truth.

West

Turn to the West. Let your body slowly reach for Earth like the setting sun.

O Great Spirit of the West, Power of Water!
We invoke you and praise your name.
Repeat in Irish:
A Spiorad Mór an Iarthair, Cumhacht an Uisce!
Impímid ort agus molaimid d'ainm.

Cycle of Change, Ever-Colorful Sunset, Peaceful Night Wonder, Come!
By the waters of your womb, send forth your ebb and flow of peace.

Move your body to greet the Spirit of the West.

O Great Spirit of the West,
be here now as we remember the people of the West:
people working for religious, economic, and political justice in Ireland;
people finding new ways trade can go on in a just and equitable manner in common market countries;
migrant farm workers in California.

The blesser pours water into the bowl.

Spirit of the West, bless us with your power and restore all waters of the West.

Song
"Give Us Living Water"

Give us living water, welling up within us:
fill us with your Spirit, fill us with your truth.

South

Turn to the South. Let your body move like a burning flame.

O Great Spirit of the South, Power of Fire!
We invoke you and praise your name.
Repeat in Spanish:
¡Oh, gran espíritu del sur, poder de fuego!
Te invocamos y alabamos tu nombre.

Flame of Justice, Torch in the Night, Liberator of the Oppressed, Come!
By the fire that is your passion, send forth your flame of peace.

Move your body to greet the Spirit of the South.

O Great Spirit of the South,
be here now as we remember women, men, and children of the South:
Mothers of the Disappeared working for human rights in El Salvador, Guatemala, Argentina, and Chile;

the Aboriginal communities protecting Dreamtime stories in Australia;
people crying for freedom in Sierra Leone.

The blesser pours water into the bowl.

Spirit of the South, bless us with your power and restore all waters of the South.

Song
"Give Us Living Water"

Give us living water, welling up within us:
fill us with your Spirit, fill us with your truth.

Above
Rise up. Let your body soar.

O Great Spirit of Above, Power of the Sky!
We invoke you and praise your name.
Repeat in French:
O Grand Esprit d'en haut, Puissance du ciel!
Nous t'invoquons et glorifions ton nom.

Dreamer of Visions, Soaring Mother Eagle, Cloud of Unknowing, Come!
By the sky that is your presence, send forth your vision of peace.

Move your body to greet the Spirit of Above.

Be here now as we remember people of vision:
the elderly living with wisdom in every culture;
feminist leaders with courage and insight in every religion;
people who work to keep outer space free of war in every country.

The blesser pours water into the bowl.

Spirit of Above, bless us with your power and restore all waters.

Song
"Give Us Living Water"

Give us living water, welling up within us:
fill us with your Spirit, fill us with your truth.

Below
Bend over. Let your body reach for the ground.

O Great Spirit of Below, Power of the Sea!
We invoke you and praise your name.
Repeat in Vietnamese:
O Đại thần dưới đây, Sức mạnh của biển!
Chúng tôi gọi bạn và khen ngợi tên của bạn.

Hidden Treasure, Undiscovered Food Source, Connector of Continents, Come!
By the sea that is your depth, send forth your revelation for peace.

Move your body to greet the Spirit of Below.

O Great Spirit of Below,
be here now as we remember those who have endured:
loved ones who have died of every age and in every family;
people dying from and living with HIV/AIDS in every country;
those killed in unjust wars in Afghanistan, Central America, Middle East, Southeast Asia, China, everywhere.

The blesser pours water into the bowl.

Spirit of Below, bless us with your power, and restore the waters.

Song
"Give Us Living Water"

Give us living water, welling up within us:
fill us with your Spirit, fill us with your truth.

Center
Turn to the center and form a circle by putting arms around each other.

O Great Spirit of Everything That Is Center, Power of the Spirit!
We invoke you and praise your name.
Repeat in Swahili:
Ewe Roho Mtakatifu wa Kila kitu ambacho ni Kwako, Nguvu za milima!
Tunakuomba na kusifu jina lako.

Rock of Ages, Untapped Energy, Enduring Strength, Come!
By the mountains that are your integrity, send forth your sacred peace.

Move your body to greet the Spirit of Center.

O Great Spirit of Everything That Is Center,
be here now as we remember women, men, and children who work for integrity:
caregivers to those who are disadvantaged and without a home in every city;
teachers and exemplars to youth in every nation;
those who do the hard and thankless tasks—road builders, street sweepers, mothers and fathers, sisters and brothers in every society.

The blesser pours water into the bowl.

Spirit of Everything Center, bless us with your power, and restore all waters.

Song
"Give Us Living Water"

Give us living water, welling up within us:
fill us with your Spirit, fill us with your truth.

Community Response

Please say after me:

Spirits of the East, North, West, South, *Echo.*
Above, Below, and Center, *Echo.*
we invoke you and praise your names. *Echo.*
Holy Spirits, enkindle countries with your peace, *Echo.*
so safe, clean, reliable, and free water is available to all worldwide. *Echo.*
Amen. Blessed be. May it be so. *Echo.*

Words of Healing to the Waters

Let us send words of restoration to all waters by saying the words "Healing—Cleansing—New Life" together nine times to allow our intention to create this in all waters.

Healing—Cleansing—New Life
Healing—Cleansing—New Life
Healing—Cleansing—New Life
Healing—Cleansing—New Life
Healing—Cleansing—New Life
Healing—Cleansing—New Life
Healing—Cleansing—New Life
Healing—Cleansing—New Life
Healing—Cleansing—New Life

Blessing the Waters

Come! Let us gather around waters of peace.

The leader stands and with a gesture invites everyone to take hands and form a circle around the water.

You who are thirsty, come to the water.
You who are inquisitive, come to the water.
You who are in need of hospitality, come to the water.
What do you need? Tell us and we will invite you to the waters of peace.
For example, "I need patience." To which the group responds, "You who need patience, come to the water."

We have filled our vessels with waters of the East, North, West, South, Above, Below, and Center. Extend your hands outward, and let us bless this water. Send your love and gratitude to the water.

Blessed is this water that quenches our thirst and refreshes our bodies,
gives birth to our children and heals our wounds,
washes our clothes and dishes, wakes us up in the morning, and cooks our food.
Blessed is this water.

Blessing with Water

Come! Let us bless ourselves and one another with this water. Take this blessed water into your hands. With this blessing we bring healing, cleansing, and new life to this water and symbolically to all waters, to ourselves, and to one another.

Bless yourself with water, saying, "Healing—Cleansing—New Life."

Bless others around you with water, saying, "Healing—Cleansing—New Life."

Bless the world outside this room with water, saying, "Healing—Cleansing—New Life."

Take Action

Let us put our prayers into action for water this month. Here are some possible ways:

- Clean up trash around water in your area—a stream, river, pond, lake, well, ocean, creek.
- Keep track of how much water you use each day. Challenge yourself and your family to use less by taking shorter showers and shutting water off when you brush your teeth.
- Think of ways you can reuse water, such as bathwater to water gardens or plants.
- Check for water leaks around your house and fix them.
- Visit an ocean, lake, river, aquarium, and see how many living creatures and plants there are that depend solely on water.

Sending Forth

Filled with the waters of life, let us go forth to love the waters of the world and the waters in our blood and bodies and in one another.
Let us go forth to all corners of the universe where the works of peace and change are desperately needed.
Let us go forth to protect, heal, renew, and give thanks for all water supplies.
Let us go forth to treasure the precious gift of water.
Pour the water onto plants to refresh them.

Song

"Waters of Life" by Jan Novotka, from Lovers of Life *(© 2006 by Jan Novotka's Music LLC [ASCAP]. All rights reserved.) Used with permission.*

Waters of Life, oceans and rivers,
Waters of Life, Womb of all Life.

Hidden within the deep dark waters,
the ocean waters, life came to be.
Wonder and mystr'y fill the ocean.
Waters of Life, inside of me.

Listen anew to roaring rivers, to
flowing river, where life is free.
Beauty and grace abound in river.
Waters of Life, flow through me.

The tears I shed are one with ocean, the
deep dark waters of ancient seas.
Flowing within my blood is river.
Waters of Life, alive in me.

Learn More from These Resources

Emoto, Dr. Masaru. *The Hidden Messages in Water.* Hillsboro, OR: Beyond Words Publishing, Inc., 2004.

———. "Water, Consciousness & Intent." YouTube. https://www.youtube.com/watch?v=tAvzsjcBtx8.

Games and activities for kids: https://kidworldcitizen.org/celebrate-world-water-day-with-games-and-activities-for-all-ages/.

Neu, Diann L. *Return Blessings: Eco-Feminist Liturgies Renewing the Earth.* Cleveland, OH: The Pilgrim Press, 2002.

Water and toilets: https://www.wateraid.org/.

Zenner, Christiana. *Just Water: Theology, Ethics, and Fresh Water Crises*, revised edition. Maryknoll, NY: Orbis Books, 2018.

16. April

Return to Life for Earth Day

I feel you everywhere, inside every cell
there is no place here that you do not dwell
I Feel You Everywhere.

—Jan Phillips, *Ever with You*

Earth Day, celebrated annually on April 22, is a reminder to be grateful for the natural world in which we live and to reflect on how we are caring for it. It provides a unique opportunity to demonstrate support for environmental protection and climate justice. Earth is a collective home to us all who live here, and we must respect it as such.

This liturgy invites participants to reflect on how Earth takes care of us, and it challenges the gathered to take better care of Earth.

Preparation

If you can, gather outside. Set your table with or gather around spring flowers or plants, violets, basil, dill, parsley, cilantro, rosemary, thyme, mint (or any herbs you prefer). You can also make a fruit dessert and herbal tea to be blessed at the end of this liturgy.

Call to Gather

Earth Day calls us to return to life. Look around! Daffodils, tulips, and cherry blossoms are in full bloom or are starting to peek through the soil. The green of Earth is renewed once again. Today we gather to cherish and reflect on Earth's beauty. We gather to remind ourselves that we are stewards of this Earth and that we must protect it. Though we find ourselves in the midst of turmoil, let us not forget to open our eyes to the promise of spring, to find beauty and hope in all Earth has to offer, and to recommit ourselves and our justice movements to care for all creation.

Naming Our Circle

Let us create our circle by sharing our name and speaking one word that comes to mind when we think of Earth Day.

Song

"For the Beauty of the Earth," words: Folliott S. Pierpoint, 1864; alt. music: Chinese folk song, "Mo-li-hua"; adapt. I-to Loh, 1980 (© 1983 I-to Loh) https://www.youtube.com/watch?v=dGt4-KyFwe4.

For the beauty of the Earth,
For the glory of the skies,
For the love which from our birth
Over and around us lies:

Refrain:
Source of all, to you we raise
This our hymn of grateful praise.

Prayer of Directions

The Prayer of Directions has roots in matriarchal cultures and in indigenous traditions. Each direction has a blessing of gratitude to bestow. It is a fitting prayer this Earth Day.

Face East, raise your arms above your head.
Oh Great Spirit of the East, House of Light and the rising sun,
may the new life of spring blossom in us
so we may start each day anew,
and be renewed.

Face North, cross your arms in front of your chest and sway from side to side.
Oh Great Spirit of the North, House of Night and falling rain,
may the cold and uncertain winters in our lives strengthen us
so we may be ready to welcome spring,
and be renewed.

Face West, extend your arms outward in a gesture of receiving.
Oh Great Spirit of the West, House of Transformation and the setting sun,
may sunsets and changes in our lives illuminate us
so we may embrace our journey with gratitude,
and be renewed.

Face South, put your arms around one another.
Oh Great Spirit of the South, House of the Eternal Sun and abundance,
may we harvest an abundance of love, mercy, and justice
so Earth and the universe may blossom, heal,
and be renewed.

Face Up, stretch.
Oh Great Spirit of all that is Above, House of Heaven and home of ancestors,
may our minds and our hearts soar above Earth
so we may know the breadth of the cosmos,
and be renewed.

Face Down, bend over.
Oh Great Spirit of all that is Below, House of Earth and energy,
may we be pulled to deeper places and to the depths of ourselves
so we may have the strength and the courage to face death when it comes,
and be renewed.

Face Center, rest your hands in the palms of the persons on either side of you.
Oh Great Spirit of everything that is Center, Cosmic Source of gratitude,
may we know mutual love
so we may walk a way of beauty and holiness,
and be renewed.

Song
"For the Beauty of the Earth"

For the wonder of each hour
Of the day and of the night,
Hill and vale, and tree and flow'r,
Sun and moon, and stars of light:

Refrain: Source of all, to you we raise
This our hymn of grateful praise.

Litany: Holy Is Your Creation

Climate change is real, and scientists have shown that humans are causing it.
All: Holy is your Creation.
We can make a difference and slow climate change down.
All: We are the stewards of your Creation.
Half of the world's forests no longer exist.
All: Holy is your Creation.
We can use cloth instead of paper products.
All: We are the stewards of your Creation.
In the past forty years, humans have directly or indirectly killed half of all existing wildlife.
All: Holy is your Creation.
We can visit a national or state park to remember the holiness of the natural and wild world.
All: We are the stewards of your Creation.
Sea levels are rising, and by 2100 the White House could have an ocean view.
All: Holy is your Creation.
We can choose public transportation and reduce our carbon footprint.
All: We are the stewards of your Creation.
We can reduce and reuse before recycling.
All: Holy is your Creation.

We can eat less or no meat. Rainforests are being replaced with farms largely used to feed livestock. That same food could feed us instead.

All: We are the stewards of your Creation.

Climate change is real, and scientists have shown that humans are causing it. We also have the power, however, to slow it down.

All: Holy is your Creation; we will be the stewards.

Reflection | Sharing

During this time of celebrating Earth, let us take a few minutes of quiet to reflect on what Earth means to us, and how we have and will steward it.

After a quiet time, plant an herb and share your reflections.

Blessing Herbs

Blessed are you, Holy Creator, for calling forth stewards of creation throughout time, and especially now, when climate change and the future life of Earth is in our hands.

All: Bless us to be stewards of your Creation.

Blessed are you, Holy Healer, for giving us herbs of spring: basil, dill, parsley, cilantro, rosemary, thyme, mint, and so many others. They beautify Earth, flavor foods, have medicinal properties, and nourish the body and soul.

All: Bless us to be healers of your Creation.

Blessed are you, Holy Gardener, for bringing forth fruit from Earth. And for blessing the cooks who made this berry crisp and steeped this mint tea.

All: Bless us as we eat and drink, and remember the delicious parts of life that are gifts of Earth.

Song

"We've Got the Whole Earth in Our Hands," African American spiritual, adapted.

We've got the Whole Earth in our hands—
We've got the trees and the flowers in our hands,
We've got the climate and the oceans in our hands,
We've got the Whole Earth in our hands!

We've got the crops and the water in our hands,
We've got the bees and the butterflies in our hands,
We've got the wind and the rain in our hands,
We've got the Whole Earth in our hands!

We've got the pigs and the pandas in our hands,
We've got adults and children in our hands,
We've got lakes and rivers in our hands,
We've got the Whole Earth in our hands!

Earth Pledge

Let us commit to caring for Earth, our home, by returning Earth to life. Let us join with Earth and with each other as we pledge:

To bring new life to land
To restore waters
To refresh air
To cherish human community
To heal Earth
To remember the children

To protect animals
To treasure trees
To gaze at stars

Take Action for Earth

Let us put our prayers into action. There are thousands of ways that we can help Earth each and every day. Here are a few important ones:

- Reduce waste by choosing reusable options whenever possible. Follow the phrase "Refuse, Reduce, Reuse, Repurpose, and Recycle."
- Quit using plastic straws; they are nonrecyclable and harm animals.
- Vacation locally. Road trips are much more environmentally friendly.
- Support politicians who take scientific evidence seriously.

Sending Forth

You are the beauty of life; go forth to manifest beauty for Earth.
Blessed be the beauty of Earth.
You are the power of life; go forth to manifest power for Earth.
Blessed be the power of Earth.
You are the truth of life; go forth to manifest truth for Earth.
Blessed be the truth of Earth.
You are the gift of life; go forth to manifest gifts for Earth.
Blessed be the gift of Earth.

Song and Video

"Ever with You" by Jan Phillips (© 2012), video and photos by Joni Luna, https://www.youtube.com/watch?v=QuqzU4adEUQ. Used with permission.

I Feel You Everywhere

I feel you in my heart, I feel you in my hands,
I feel you in the stars, I feel you in the sand,
I feel you everywhere, inside every cell
there is no place here that you do not dwell
I Feel You Everywhere.

I feel you in my arms, I feel you in my feet,
I feel you in the eyes of everyone I meet

I feel you everywhere, inside every cell
there is no place here that you do not dwell
I Feel You Everywhere.

Chorus:
I feel you in the clouds, I feel you in the storm,
I feel you in the cold, I feel you in the warm,
There is nowhere I can go and not find you.
I feel you all day long, I feel you late at night,
I feel you in the dark, I feel you in the light,
There is nowhere I can go and not find you.

I feel you when I sing, I feel you when I cry,
I feel you breathing me, I feel you when I sigh,
I feel you everywhere, inside every cell
there is no place here that you do not dwell
I Feel You Everywhere.

I feel you in my words, I feel you in my love,
I feel you all around, I feel you up above,
I feel you everywhere, inside every cell
there is no place here that you do not dwell
I Feel You Everywhere.

Chorus.

I feel you in my womb, I feel you in my breast,
I feel you in the east, I feel you in the west,
I feel you everywhere, inside every cell
there is no place here that you do not dwell
I Feel You Everywhere.

I feel you in the earth, I feel you in the clay,
I feel you when I work, I feel you when I pray,
I feel you everywhere, inside every cell
there is no place here that you do not dwell
I Feel You Everywhere.

Learn More from These Resources

Adams, Carol J., ed. *Ecofeminism and the Sacred.* New York: Continuum, 1993.

Carson, Rachel. *The Sense of Wonder.* New York: Harper & Row, 1956.

Grey, Mary C. *Sacred Longings: The Ecological Spirit and Global Culture.* Minneapolis, MN: Fortress Press, 2004.

Johnson, Elizabeth A. *Ask the Beasts: Darwin and the God of Love.* London: Bloomsbury Publishing, 2014.

Moe-Lobeda, Cynthia D. *Resisting Structural Evil: Love as Ecological-Economic Vocation.* Minneapolis, MN: Fortress Press, 2013.

Neu, Diann L. *Return Blessings: Ecofeminist Liturgies Renewing the Earth.* Cleveland, OH: The Pilgrim Press, 2002.

Rowthorn, Anne, and Jeffery Rowthorn. *God's Good Earth: Praise and Prayers for Creation.* Collegeville, MN: Liturgical Press, 2018.

Ruether, Rosemary Radford, ed. *Women Healing Earth: Third World Women on Ecology, Feminism, and Religion.* Maryknoll, NY: Orbis Books, 1996.

Shiva, Vandana. *The Vandana Shiva Reader.* Lexington: University Press of Kentucky, 2014.

Tucker, Mary Evelyn, ed. *The Sacred Universe: Earth, Spirituality, and Religion in the Twenty-First Century.* New York: Columbia University Press, 2009.

17. May

Reach for the Stars with Sally Ride on National Space Day

All adventures—especially into new territory—are scary.

—Sally Ride, from *To Space and Back*

May 26 is the birthday of Sally Ride (1951–2012), the trailblazing first American woman in space. In 1983, she made a six-day flight aboard the space shuttle Challenger. *She constantly sought ways to make STEM education (Science, Technology, Engineering, Mathematics) more accessible, especially encouraging women and girls to be unceasing in their pursuit of these careers. She reached for the stars, and now she is one.*

This liturgy honors Sally Ride, raises up an American hero and pioneer, and challenges us to dream big and reach for the stars.

Preparation

Gather and place on a table a star (object, picture, or cut from paper), candles, books; a cloth that represents space, stars, or the sky; some popcorn.

Call to Gather

Today we raise up Sally Ride, the trailblazing first American woman in space, because this is her birthday month. Happy birthday, Sally, on May 26.

Sally was interested in science since she was a child. She earned bachelor's degrees in physics and English and a doctorate in physics from Stanford University. In 1983 she became the first American woman to fly in space when she made a six-day flight aboard the space shuttle *Challenger.* She made her second trip to space in 1984.

Dr. Ride was a professor of physics at the University of California, San Diego. She cofounded Sally Ride Science in 2001 along with Dr. Tam O'Shaughnessy and Dr. Karen Flammer to inspire young people in STEM (Science, Technology, Engineering, and Math) and promote STEM literacy. Sally died on July 23, 2012. In 2013, Sally was posthumously awarded the Presidential Medal of Freedom, accepted by her life and business partner, Dr. Tam O'Shaughnessy.

Sally reached for the stars, and now she is one.

Naming the Circle

Let us pass a star around our circle. When you receive it, share your name, and mention a star for which you are reaching.

Song

"Twinkle, Twinkle Little Star," lyrics from the poem "The Star" by Jane Taylor in Rhymes for the Nursery *(London © 1806). Melody from the French nursery rhyme and folk tale Ah! vous dirai-je, maman.*

Twinkle, twinkle, little star,
How I wonder what you are!
Up above the world so high,
Like a diamond in the sky.
Twinkle, twinkle, little star,
How I wonder what you are!

Encountering Sally

Excerpts from Sally Ride: America's First Woman in Space *by Lynn Sherr (New York: Simon and Schuster, 2014).*

Preflight

A Tom Brokaw interview with the Ride sisters before Sally flew, 18

"Brokaw: Are you particularly religious?
Sally: My sister got most of the religion in the family.
Bear, Sally's sister: She's her own person and she certainly has her own belief system and it doesn't have to fit into mine.
Brokaw: Will you see this flight in any spiritual way?
Bear: No [Laughter].
Brokaw: A triumph of man and technology?
Bear: Of woman and technology."

Reporting for duty at NASA, 96

"I had no idea what to expect. I mean, what do you do when you're an astronaut? Who knows? I don't even remember having specific goals other than to fly in space!"

Preflight interview, 1983, 126

"Lynn Sherr: Do you feel under any pressure as America's first female astronaut?
Sally Ride: I do feel that there's some pressure for me not to mess up."

Prime crew press conference, April 29, 1982, 143

"Q: Dr. Ride, apart from the obvious differences, how do you assess the difference in men and women astronauts?
A: Aside from the obvious differences, I don't think there are any."

The Secret, Sally Ride, 1986, 289

"They should let girls be who they want to be, and not pay any attention to the stereotypes."

Excerpt from To Space and Back *by Sally Ride and Susan Okie (New York: William Morrow & Company, 1986), 221*

"All adventures—especially into new territory—are scary."

Excerpt from "A Ride in Space" by Michael Ryan, People, *June 2, 1983*

Joyce Ride, Sally's Mother, tries to explain to the world what she and her husband Dale did right in raising their daughters.

"In a way you could look at it as neglect," she laughs. "Dale and I simply forgot to tell them that there were things they couldn't do. But I think if it had occurred to us to tell them, we would have refrained."

Song

"Star Light, Star Bright," anonymous.

Star light, star bright,
First star I see tonight,
I wish I may, I wish I might,
Have this wish I wish tonight.

In Flight

Excerpts from Sally Ride: A Photobiography of America's Pioneering Woman in Space *by Tam O'Shaughnessy (New York: Roaring Brook Press, 2015).*

Entering Orbit, 104

"It feels like your arms are made of lead. The notebook in your lab seems to weigh a ton. Then suddenly, the shuttle engines stop. The lead in your arms vanishes. Your arms are lighter than air, and your notebook floats up in front of your face. You are in space."

Touching Down, 108–9

"I started to feel heavier and heavier as gravity slowly pulled me into my seat. It was hard to lift my hand or hold my head up. Outside the windows the shuttle was engulfed in a fiery orange glow as we blazed through the air."

Song

"Twinkle, Twinkle Little Star"

Twinkle, twinkle, little star,
How I wonder what you are!
Up above the world so high,
Like a diamond in the sky.
Twinkle, twinkle, little star,
How I wonder what you are!

Legacy

Excerpt from Leadership and America's Future in Space, *nicknamed "The Ride Report" (Washington, DC: NASA, 1986), 226.*

"NASA should embrace Mission to Planet Earth. This initiative is responsive, time-critical, and shows recognition of our responsibility to our home planet. Do we dare apply our capabilities to explore the mysteries of other worlds, and not also apply those capabilities to explore and understand the mysteries of our own world—mysteries which may have important implications for our future on this planet?"

Excerpts from Sally Ride: A Photobiography of America's Pioneering Woman in Space *by Tam O'Shaughnessy*

Sally Ride Science, 133

"Everywhere I go I meet girls and boys who want to be astronauts and explore space. Or they love the ocean and want to be oceanographers, or they love animals and want to be zoologists, or they love designing things and want to be engineers. I want to see those same stars in their eyes in ten years, and know they are on their way!"

Some of Sally's habits, 139

"She . . .
Walked and ran on her toes.
Clicked her tongue to music (instead of humming or singing).
Ate popcorn soaked in milk with a spoon.
Ate watermelon sprinkled in salt.
Never ripped the top off a sugar or tea packet (it might float away!)
Woke up happy almost every day.
Lived in the moment—seldom thought about the past or the future."

Sally left behind a better world because . . ., 144

"She . . .
Thought for herself.
Was true to herself.
Broke gender barriers with her skill, confidence, hard work, and humor.
Inspired girls and boys to be themselves, to be courageous, and to reach for their dreams."

Excerpt from "Sally Ride and the Quest for Social Space," Mary E. Hunt, Feminist Studies in Religion, *March 4, 2016, https://www.fsrinc.org/sally-ride-social-space/.*

"Sally was a hero whose brilliance and focused work helped her to 'reach for the stars' as she advised the rest of us to do. So why was her loving relationship with a fine woman something to cover with a space blanket? . . . What are we doing about the fact that we can visit outer space but we cannot create enough social space to accommodate the range of ways people love? Abolishing heterosexism thus creating space for love is as fitting a way to honor Sally Ride's memory as naming a ship or a lunar impact site after her. Solidarity not outing is the obvious strategy. One doesn't have to be a lesbian or a woman, whatever those words mean now, to participate."

Song

"Star Light, Star Bright"

Star light, star bright,
First star I see tonight,
I wish I may, I wish I might,
Have this wish I wish tonight.

Reflection | Sharing

Think about what you heard Sally Ride saying. Let us take a few moments of quiet to reflect on these questions:

What reflections do you have after listening to Sally? What stars did you wish upon in your life, and what stars are you encouraging in the eyes of those younger than you?

After a quiet time, eat popcorn, Sally's favorite food, and share your reflections.

Thank You, Sally!

For challenging us to reach for the stars
For being America's first woman in space
For opening doors to students in the STEM fields
For loving a woman and reminding us that we must create enough social space to accommodate the range of ways that people love
For showing the world, especially young girls, that women can reach for the stars and fly into space.

Take Action

Let us put our prayers into action. Here are some possible ways:

- Go outside and look at the stars tonight.
- Talk with a young girl about Sally Ride.
- Take time to meditate about the stars for which you are reaching.

Sending Forth

Let us go forth and reach for the stars.
Look up at the stars tonight, and make a wish.
May our dreams come true.

Song

Medley of "Star Light, Star Bright" and "Twinkle, Twinkle, Little Star"

Star light, star bright,
First star I see tonight.
I wish I may, I wish I might
Have this wish I wish tonight.

Twinkle, twinkle, little star
How I wonder what you are
Up above the world so high
Like a diamond in the sky
Twinkle, twinkle, little star
How I wonder what you are

Learn More from These Resources

Edd, Virginia Loh-Hagan. *Sally Ride*. My Itty-Bitty Bio. Ann Arbor, MI: Cherry Lake Publishing, 2018.

Hunt, Mary E. "Sally Ride and the Quest for Social Space." *Feminist Studies in Religion*. March 4, 2016. https://www.fsrinc.org/sally-ride-social-space/.

NASA: search online and discover the stars.

O'Shaughnessy, Tam. *Sally Ride: A Photobiography of America's Pioneering Woman in Space.* New York: Roaring Brook Press, 2015.

Ride, Sally: search online and learn more about this incredible woman.

———. *The Mystery of Mars.* San Diego, CA: Sally Ride Science, 2006.

Ride, Sally, and Susan Okie. *To Space and Back.* New York: William Marrow & Company, 1986.

Sherr, Lynn. *Sally Ride: America's First Woman in Space.* New York: Simon & Schuster, 2014.

18. June

Praise the Sun for Summer Solstice

I am listening to the summer of my soul.
—Macrina Wiederkehr, "Listening to Summer"

The Summer Solstice (June 21 in the Northern Hemisphere, December 21 in the Southern) is the absolute peak of solar power. The sun is at its apex while at its turning point. This is the longest day and shortest night of the year. It signals that changes in light and weather are coming. Nature is at the summit of its sumptuousness, as light and as ripe as it can possibly get. Summer Solstice festivals celebrate the sun and renew the community's ties to Earth.

This liturgy invites participants to feel the rainbow of colors from the sun, to share the fulfillment, passion, and creativity they wish for themselves and for Earth. It is most freeing when celebrated outside but can also be effective inside.

Preparation

Create the space by placing a fire pit (grill) in the center. Light the fire ahead of time. Have a basket of twigs, a candle for each participant, drinks, and ingredients for s'mores: marshmallows, chocolate squares, and graham crackers. Put red and yellow flowers on the table or around the space.

Naming the Circle

Welcome to tonight's celebration of the Summer Solstice, the time of greatest light. The heat of the day is a reminder that summer is around the corner. Give yourself a moment to transition into summer. *Pause.*

To create our circle, speak your name, and say, "I honor the sun and you on this day."

Song

"Lachen," Traditional German round, found in A Circle Is Cast by Libana *(Spinning Records © 1986).*

Lachen, lachen, lachen, lachen,
kommt der Sommer uber das Feld,
uber das Feld kommt der Sommer,
ha ha ha, lachen uber das Feld.

Laughing, laughing, laughing, laughing,
Comes the summer over the field,
Over the field comes the summer,
Ha Ha Ha, Laughing over the field.

Call to Gather

The Summer Solstice, also known as Midsummer's Night, is the longest day and the shortest night of the year. On this night, Earth reaches midpoint on her journey around the sun. In the Northern Hemisphere, we anticipate the coming of summer, as our friends in the Southern Hemisphere prepare for the winter season.

Red, yellow, and orange are the colors for summer solstice: the red of passion, the yellow of the sun, and the orange of the summer bonfire. Red and orange flowers and candles enhance our celebration. This evening may our wishes be fulfilled!

In ancient agricultural rites, fires were lit at summer solstice to renew the sun's energy. Indigenous Europeans built sun shrines: Stonehenge, Woodhenge, and Newgrange. The Aztecs, Mayans, and Incas of Central America, the Chinese, and the Egyptians all built sun shrines. In many of the Native American traditions, this time of year is celebrated as part of a vision cycle, and dances are performed to renew the energy of the sun, the vegetation, and the people. On this day, the Hopi Indians of the Southwest celebrate Niman Kachina when the kachinas, the tribal spirit guides, return to their underground homes until the winter solstice.

In Brazil, people set flower wreaths on fire and float them on the waves to honor the Yoruba sea goddess, Iamanja. In the Christian tradition, summer solstice, or St. John's Eve, marks the birth of John the Baptist, who told of the coming of Christ, the Light. Even today, St. John's fires are lit in the mountains in Europe. The flames of sun and fire remind us of the early Christian community's Pentecost experience of empowerment by the Spirit. In the goddess traditions, summer solstice was known as Litha, the name of a northern European and North African goddess of fertility, power, and abundance.

In feminist circles and Earth-centered communities around the world, the Summer Solstice is being welcomed as a time to renew passions, continue resistance, give thanks for the abundant gifts of Earth, and promise to work for climate justice to protect all things under the sun.

Lighting Summer Solstice Fires

Generation to generation people honor the light and call forth injustices in the world. This evening we spark five fires to welcome compassion, resistance, and justice into spaces that are both dry and barren, bountiful and fertile.

We greet the fire of the North to honor those who bring the enduring spark of the Summer Solstice in a time of historic injustice: immigrants, Muslims, Jews, communities of color, sexual and gender minorities, all of us gathered tonight.

We greet the fire of the South to remember those in South America, Africa, and Australia as they celebrate the Winter Solstice.

We greet the fire of the East in solidarity with those in Asia and the Middle East, especially mothers and children in Syria, Yemen, Afghanistan, and Iraq who are in fear and trembling, dying in the streets.

We greet the fire of the West for the indigenous women who fight for their sacred spaces and the right for their voices to be heard. We light this candle to thank our friends on the front lines of climate change who have shown grace, courage, and resiliency in the face of destructive environmental policies.

We greet the fire of the Center with gratitude for those this season who bring us laughter, lift up our spirits, and warm our souls. We invite you to name them. *Naming.*

Song
"Lachen"

Reading

"Listening to Summer," from The Circle of Life: The Heart's Journey through the Seasons *by Joyce Rupp and Macrina Wiederkehr (Notre Dame: Sorin Books, 2005). Used by permission of Ave Maria Press.*

"Out of her pastel green pitcher
spring is pouring forth summer, and I am listening.
Out of her youthful, energetic body
summer is flowing, and I am listening.

I am listening.

I am listening to Earth leaning closer to the sun.
I am listening to the heat breathing through the gardens,
    drawing life out of seeds,
    calling plants to fruition,
    whispering fulfillment to the flowers.
I am listening to the growing circle of life.

I am listening.

I am listening to the ripening
    in the orchards,
    in the vineyards,
    in the garden,
    in the grain fields.
I am listening to the ripening in my heart.

I am listening.

I am listening to the summer of my soul,
    to the dance of life within me,

to the fruitful struggle of all that yearns for life,
to the perspiration that sweats out toxic poisons.
I am listening to the warmth of summer.

I am listening.

I am listening to the song of the gardener
bringing food to the table.
I am listening to the meadow's promise
of winter hay for hungry cattle.
I am listening to Mother Earth
growing wild with multiple vitamins.

I am listening.

I am listening to summer songs
of leisure and renewal.
I am listening to the sound of happy voices
playing on the beaches,
shouting at the ball games,
sharing stories on the porches.
I am listening to bare feet, laughter, and fishing poles,
to summer picnics and mosquitoes.

I am listening.

I am listening to the spaces in between the green.
I am listening to young birds testing out their wings.
I am listening to morning filling up with sunlight.
I am listening to the music of evening twilight.
I am listening to the night chant of a thousand tiny creatures.

I am listening.

I am listening to fruitfulness
spilling forth from earth's rich womb.
I am listening to happy potatoes
growing round beneath the ground.
I am listening to the green cathedral of the forest,
to the stars that peep through summer branches.

I am listening.

I am listening to spring
handing over summer.
I am listening to the poetry of summer.

I am listening."

Song

"May I Suggest" by Susan Werner, from New Non-Fiction *(Frank Change Music, ASCAP © 2001 Susan Werner), https://youtu.be/eW1DDSQnEYo. Used with permission.*

May I suggest
May I suggest to you
May I suggest this is the best part of your life
May I suggest
This time is blessed for you
This time is blessed and shining almost blinding bright
Just turn your head
And you'll begin to see
The thousand reasons that were just beyond your sight
The reasons why
Why I suggest to you
Why I suggest this is the best part of your life

There is a world
That's been addressed to you
Addressed to you, intended only for your eyes
A secret world
Like a treasure chest to you
Of private scenes and brilliant dreams that mesmerize
A lover's trusting smile
A tiny baby's hands
The million stars that fill the turning sky at night
Oh I suggest
Oh I suggest to you
Oh I suggest this is the best part of your life

There is a hope
That's been expressed in you
The hope of seven generations, maybe more
And this is the faith
That they invest in you
It's that you'll do one better than was done before
Inside you know
Inside you understand
Inside you know what's yours to finally set right
And I suggest
And I suggest to you
And I suggest this is the best part of your life

This is a song
Comes from the west to you
Comes from the west, comes from the slowly setting sun
With a request
With a request of you
To see how very short the endless days will run
And when they're gone
And when the dark descends
Oh we'd give anything for one more hour of light

And I suggest this is the best part of your life

Reflection | Sharing

"This is the best part of your life," sings Susan Werner. And Macrina Wiederkehr challenges, "spring is pouring forth summer, and I am listening." Let us take a few moments of quiet to reflect on these questions:

Where do you get your spark? How are you listening? What fulfillment, passion, and creativity do you wish for yourself and for Earth this Solstice?

After a quiet time, light a candle and share a glimpse of your reflections or, if you prefer, just light a candle.

Remembering Those Who Need Healing

On this Solstice night, we call forth the Summer Solstice fires once again to honor and remember those who need healing.

Let us remember those suffering from violence around the world:

- the victims of war and terror
- the victims of hate, Islamophobia, and racism

Let us lift up those affected by the destructive capabilities of sun and fire:

- the victims of recent fires
- those plagued by drought and famine
- those who lack access to food and clean water

Let us honor those who are most affected by climate change:

- indigenous communities worldwide
- low-income, coastal communities facing the threat of rising sea levels

And for anyone else who is in need of healing . . . *Add your own.*

Together, we respond:

Spark of the Summer Solstice fires,
Give us the courage to act for justice.
Give us the wisdom to work together—East to West, North to South—
in our common struggle for liberation.
Give us compassion to care for all Earth's goodness this Solstice night.

Blessing Summer Solstice Food and Drink

Summer reminds us of lemonade, melons, bonfires, toasting marshmallows, and eating s'mores. Come, toast a marshmallow, put it on a graham cracker with a piece of chocolate, and make a delicious sandwich like Girl Scouts do.

Blessed are you, Holy Ones of the Summer Solstice, for giving us this food and drink to deepen our passions, fulfill our wishes, and sustain our fires. As we eat and drink, may we be nourished to spark energy for justice.

Greeting and Solstice Leap

We came together today to honor the Sun, the Earth, and each other. Let us greet each other again by saying and gesturing with raised open arms, "I honor the Sun and you on this day."

To bring closure to our Solstice celebration let us take the Solstice leap. It is traditional on the Summer Solstice to leap over fire. Those who wish can leap over the candles. Be careful!

For protection in the coming year . . . for the courage to take risks and follow your aspirations . . . for purification from sorrow . . . and for the fun of feeling foolish again . . . jump over the fire . . . *add your own wish . . . leap over the fire.*

Take another leap for the protection of all things under the Sun and on the Earth. *Leap over the fire.*

Take Action

Let us put our prayers into action. Here are some possible ways:

- Watch the sunrise or sunset.
- Take a walk in a park or forest. Kneel in the grass.
- Notice lightning bugs dotting a summer night.
- Read research about climate change. As record high temperatures are being reached all over the world, let us remember that climate change is bringing summer weather unlike any we have experienced. Let the warmth of summer remind us to be considerate of Earth and of our commitments to work for climate justice.
- Share summer crafts with children.
- Read a poem in a hammock.

Sending Forth

Let us go forth mindful of the life-giving power of the Sun,
conscious of the power of our collective spirit,
and aware of the work still to be done on this Earth.

Learn More from These Resources

Oliver, Mary. *Devotions.* New York: Penguin Press, 2017.

Pfeffer, Wendy. *The Longest Day: Celebrating the Summer Solstice.* New York: Puffin Books, 2015.

Stonehenge: read about the monument to celebrate the Summer Solstice.

19. July

Stand with Malala Yousafzai

One child, one teacher, one book, and one pen, can change the world.
—Malala Yousafzai, speech to the United Nations Youth Assembly

July 12 is Malala Day and is the birthday of Malala Yousafzai. At the age of eleven, Malala became a prominent activist for girls' education, which attracted the attention of the Taliban. At fifteen, she was wounded by several gunshots to her head and upper body. At sixteen, she recovered and took her cause to the global stage with an address to the United Nations. At seventeen, she became the youngest recipient of the Nobel Peace Prize. Now, she is a student at the University of Oxford, furthering her fight and proving that triumph over adversity is possible.

This liturgy contemplates what Malala's message of strength, perseverance, and fortitude can teach us.

Preparation

Put a photo and book of Malala, a pen, a candle, a colorful cloth, and books to give to children on the table.

Call to Gather

Malala Yousafzai was born on July 12, 1997, in Mingora, Pakistan. Happy Birthday, Malala! Even from an early age, she never hesitated to speak up about the importance of girls' education and human rights.

When she was traveling home from school on October 9, 2012, at just fifteen years of age, a Taliban gunman shot her in the head, neck, and shoulder because of her views on female education. She narrowly survived the ordeal and received intensive care in England.

In her first public appearance after the attack, which coincided with her sixteenth birthday, Malala addressed the United Nations, calling for more attention to issues affecting the world's most vulnerable girls. The United Nations declares July 12 "Malala Day," which Malala has promised she will dedicate to furthering the cause of underprivileged girls.

At the age of seventeen, in 2014, Malala became the youngest recipient of the Nobel Peace Prize. In her first book, *I Am Malala: The Girl Who Stood Up for Education and Was Shot by the Taliban*, in collaboration with British journalist Christina Lamb, she demands worldwide access to education.

Upon receiving three A's at her A-level examinations, Malala enrolled at Lady Margaret Hall at the University of Oxford. She balanced studying philosophy, politics, and economics with her fight for global girls' education.

Malala survived a horrendous act of violence and continues to advocate for education and peace. Today, let us think about how we can bring her unbroken resilience home to the United States as we struggle to fight for equality in a country made bloody by what seems like daily shootings in schools and houses of prayer.

Let us take a moment of silence together to remember those killed and to contemplate what Malala's message of strength can teach us. *Light the candle in remembrance.*

Naming the Circle

As we create our circle today, let us each speak our names, pass Malala's book around the circle, and say, "I stand with Malala."

Honoring Malala

Let us honor Malala by listening to her words of commitment to international education for women and children. May she inspire us to go out and make a change in the world today.

Listen to Malala

"When the whole world is silent, even one voice becomes powerful."
—Speech at Harvard University in September 2013

Song

"One Voice" by The Wailin' Jennys, written by Ruth Moody, from 40 Days *(Winnipeg: Private Ear Recording © 2004),* https://youtu.be/Bc6HloRYZGc. *Used with permission.*

This is the sound of one voice
One spirit, one voice
The sound of one who makes a choice
This is the sound of one voice
This is the sound of one voice

Listen to Malala

"Honor your daughters, trust them and most importantly, educate them."
—Ziauddin Yousafzai, Malala's father

"Let us make our future now, and let us make our dreams tomorrow's reality."
—Speech at Harvard University in September 2013

Song
"One Voice"

This is the sound of voices two
The sound of me singing with you
Helping each other to make it through
This is the sound of voices two
This is the sound of voices two

Listen to Malala
"Peace in every home, every street, every village, every country—this is my dream. Education for every boy and every girl in the world. To sit down on a chair and read my books with all my friends at school is my right. To see each and every human being with a smile of happiness is my wish."

—I Am Malala: The Girl Who Stood Up for Education and Was Shot by the Taliban *(London: Back Bay Books, 2015), 313.*

"I tell my story not because it is unique, but because it is not. It is the story of many girls."

—Nobel Lecture in Oslo, December 10, 2014

Song
"One Voice"

This is the sound of voices three
Singing together in harmony
Surrendering to the mystery
This is the sound of voices three
This is the sound of voices three

Listen to Malala
"Even if there was a gun in my hand and [the Talib] was standing in front of me, I would not shoot him. This is the compassion I have learned from Mohamed, the prophet of mercy, Jesus Christ and Lord Buddha. This is the legacy of change I have inherited from Martin Luther King, Nelson Mandela and Mohammed Ali Jinnah. This is the philosophy of nonviolence that I have learned from Gandhi, Bacha Khan and Mother Teresa. And this is the forgiveness that I have learned from my father and from my mother. This is what my soul is telling me: be peaceful and love everyone."

—Speech to the United Nations, June 2013

Song
"One Voice"

This is the sound of all of us
Singing with love and the will to trust
Leave the rest behind it will turn to dust
This is the sound of all of us
This is the sound of all of us

This is the sound of one voice
One people, one voice
A song for every one of us
This is the sound of one voice
This is the sound of one voice

Listen to Malala

"Let us pick up our books and our pens, they are the most powerful weapons."
—Speech to the United Nations, July 12, 2013

After the attack on her life, Malala kept working for the rights and equality of children everywhere, even in the face of violence. Let us listen to her call for education through peace in her own words: "Books, not Bullets" at the 2015 Oslo Education Summit: https://youtu.be/bxOfTQYjy9o?t=8m21s.

Reflection | Sharing

Think about what the words you heard Malala speak. Let us take a few moments of quiet to reflect on these questions:

What about Malala's life has touched you? Who encouraged and supported your own education? How do you keep doing justice in the face of discouragement?

After a quiet time, we will share our words of wisdom with this community.

Litany of Solidarity

We pray for the lives lost in Baton Rouge, St. Paul, Dallas, Parkland, *name others*—school shootings averaging one a week. May a quality education help enlighten people to use intellect and compassion to end conflict.

Response: May peace be with us all.

We pray for the end of abuse, of any and all kinds, against women and girls. Like Malala, may they be inspired to rise out of silence, find a voice, and help raise each other out of the darkness of violence.

Response: May peace be with us all.

We pray for all girls worldwide who are denied education or experience a lesser form of education, just because of their gender. May the world realize that in order for humanity to reach its full potential, we must empower both men and women.

Response: May peace be with us all.

We pray for the end of the seemingly universal stream of violence in the United States and abroad, and we reflect on how an upbringing in this world marred by hate affects a child's development.

Response: May peace be with us all.

We pray for the lives and the well-being of peace, education, and human rights activists. May they take care of themselves emotionally and physically and continue to do the important and blessed work that they do. May they keep fighting even when they are tired, keep moving even when they are blocked, keep speaking even when they are silenced. May they inspire us to continue with our own fights for justice.

Response: May peace be with us all.

Listen to Malala

"Education is one of the blessings of life—and one of its necessities."

—*Nobel Peace Prize Lecture, December 10, 2014*

Blessing for Education

Children need books. We have some on our table already. Let us give books to children, especially to newly arrived Americans so they can have their own books, learn to read, and possess the powerful weapon of learning. May we all be committed to contributing to the education of youth.

Take Action

- Read *I Am Malala.*
- Watch *He Named Me Malala* (2015).
- Help empower girls by taking a book to a shelter, reading a book with a child, and supporting educational centers that are important for children such as libraries and community centers.
- Pursue your own education as learning never ends.

Sending Forth

Let us take the courage and strength of Malala into the hearts of young girls.
Let us teach peace to the next generations through our actions.
Let us greet one another with peace and send peace to the world.

Learn More from These Resources

Robins, Sarah J. *Malala: My Story of Standing Up for Girls' Rights.* New York: Little, Brown, 2018.

Yousafzai, Malala: search online and watch a video about her.

———. "Books, not Bullets" at the 2015 Oslo Education Summit. https://youtu.be/bxOfTQYjy9o?t=8m21s.

———. *I Am Malala: The Girl Who Stood Up for Education and Was Shot by the Taliban.* London: Back Bay Books, 2015.

———. *Malala's Magic Pencil.* New York: Little, Brown Books for Young Readers, 2017.

———. *Nobel Lecture.* https://www.nobelprize.org/nobel_prizes/peace/ laureates/2014/yousafzai-lecture_en.html.

20. August

Keep on Moving in Solidarity

Gonna keep on moving forward,
Never turning back, never turning back.

—Pat Humphries, "Keep on Moving Forward"

We move, walk, run, roll, and march to create new roads because some of the ones that we have used in the past do not lead to the places where we need to be. We march to protest injustice. We walk to get inspired. We jog to get involved. We race for the cure. We honor walkers and runners, all who move for a cause, and challenge each to make new roads.

This liturgy invites the gathered to keep on moving in solidarity on the journey for justice, to keep on moving forward so that Earth may survive and all may live joyfully.

Preparation

Choose three places or stations: one for gathering, another for storytelling, and a third for the meal. Gather drums (trash cans, pots and pans, tin boxes). Set the table with bread, wine, juice, and foods. Gather enough luminaries (candles) appropriate for the number of participants: for example, eight luminaries for a group of forty, two for a group of ten.

Call to Gather

Drummers call people to the gathering place. A few use megaphones to call out phrases like: "Walkers needed." "Got shoes for walking?" "Race for the cure." "Ready to Roll?" "March to protest war." "Could you help us find the way?" "Where is the road?" "Does anyone have a flashlight?" When all have gathered, one continues:

Walkers, marchers, protesters, runners, wheelers, crawlers, cyclists, stilt walkers, dancers—travelers on the journey for peace and justice—let us gather to move in solidarity with other movers and causes. Let us challenge each other to make new roads so Earth can survive and people can thrive.

Naming the Circle

Let us take a minute to meet the people with whom we are moving. Introduce yourself to those around you, saying something like: "Hi! I'm Diann. I am a walker."

Litany of Solidarity

Let us begin our journey by sharing a litany of solidarity to remember why we keep on moving forward. Our response to each line is "We move in solidarity." *Update as needed.*

Struggling to make new roads for just causes,
Response: We move in solidarity.
Marching against gun violence after school shootings,
Response: We move in solidarity.
Speaking out against sexual violence with #MeToo,
Response: We move in solidarity.
Questioning social media policy after stolen elections,
Response: We move in solidarity.
Demanding "no nuclear war" in Iran, Syria, North Korea, United States, everywhere,
Response: We move in solidarity.
Shouting "no" to human trafficking and violence against women and girls,
Response: We move in solidarity.
Rallying to support immigrants and protect DREAMers,
Response: We move in solidarity.
Working to prevent climate change and support lower carbon emissions,
Response: We move in solidarity.
Advocating for women's rights, racial equity, health-care reform, and democracy,
Response: We move in solidarity.
Organizing, resisting, persisting for issues that affect every stratum of society,
Response: We move in solidarity.

Procession

Those holding luminaries begin to light a path. The youngest walks along the path carrying a hobo stick (a stick with a bag filled with belongings tied to it) and leads the procession to the place of storytelling. Others follow, singing and moving with purpose, swinging arms, and exaggerating walking.

Song

"Keep on Moving Forward" by Pat Humphries from Same Rain *(Moving Forward Music © 1984), https://www.youtube.com/watch?v=RtiXT5c5jBQ. Used with permission.*

*Gonna keep on moving forward,
Keep on moving forward,
Keep on moving forward,
Never turning back, never turning back.

*Gonna march for peace together . . .
*Gonna race for cures together . . .
*Gonna reach across our borders . . .

Lighting Candles

Those with the luminaries stand at the entrance to the place of storytelling. The participants enter singing "Keep on Moving Forward."

Moving Chant

As I move, the universe moves.
As the universe moves, I move.
Before, behind, on every side.
We move as one.

Reflection | Sharing

How are you moving in solidarity? For which causes do you walk, run, roll, protest? Let us write, pray, or sing a chant that propels us forward.

Take a piece of paper and pencil. Write a personal moving chant. *Pause for writing.*

After a quiet time, I will invite us to share our moving chants with this community. *If the group is ten or fewer, share in the whole. If larger, invite people to share with two or three others.*

Procession

The youngest leads the procession to the place of table sharing.

Song

"Siyahamba / We Are Marching in the Light of God," collected and edited by Anders Nyberg *https://www.youtube.com/watch?v=dwHU3bmGSUo.*

We are *marching in the light of God,
we are *marching in the light of God.
We are *marching in the light of God,
we are *marching in the light of God.
We are *marching, we are *marching,
we are *marching, we are *marching,
We are marching in the light of God.

* Moving . . . *Dancing . . . *Blessing . . . *Praying . . . *Singing

Lighting Candles

Those with the luminaries stand at the entrance to the place of table sharing. The participants enter singing "We Are Moving in the Light of God."

Blessing Bread

The blesser holds the bread, saying:

Praise to you, Companion on the Road, Bread of life,
for you give us this bread to feed our hunger.
We take, bless, break, and eat it in memory of you,
and of all who move for peace, equality, and justice.

Song
"Siyahamba/We Are Marching in the Light of God"

We are *moving in the light of God, we are *moving in the light of God.

Blessing Drink

The blesser holds the wine and juice, saying:

Praise to you, Companion on the Road, Joy of Life,
for you give us this drink to quench our thirst.
We take, bless, and drink it in memory of you,
and of all who race to overcome violence and illness.

Song
"Siyahamba/We Are Marching in the Light of God"

We are *racing in the light of God, we are *racing in the light of God.

Blessing Food

The blesser, or the cooks, hold the food, saying:

Praise to you, Companion on the Road, Manna in the Desert,
for you give us this food.
We take, bless, break, and eat it in memory of you,
and of all children who hunger for food.

Song
"Siyahamba/We Are Marching in the Light of God"

We are *sharing in the light of God, we are *sharing in the light of God.

Eating the Meal and Sharing Stories

Let us eat, drink, and share our stories.

Song
"Keep on Moving Forward"

The singers begin singing at the close of the meal.

*Gonna keep on moving forward,
Keep on moving forward,
Keep on moving forward,
Never turning back, never turning back.

Take Action

Let us put our prayers into action. Here are some possible ways:

- Take action to make change: march, protest, run, roll for a cause.
- Invite a friend to take action with you.

- Go to a march with a high school student.
- Raise money for a charity or movement.

Prayer for Movers

Compassionate and merciful Divinity of many names,
Allah, Yahweh, Holy One, Wisdom Sophia, Goddess, God of All, Providence,
Move with us on this journey for justice.
Hold our hands. Guide our feet.
Protect our bodies. Search our hearts.
Keep us moving forward,
that justice may come,
that Earth survive,
and all may live joyfully.
Amen. Blessed be. May it be so.

Blessing One Another

Walkers, crawlers, runners, strollers, marchers, cyclists, rollers, we are on a journey together. Let us embrace one another and give thanks for companions on the road.

Song and Spiral Dance

"Siyahamba/We Are Marching in the Light of God"

One person begins dancing the gathered into a spiral.

We are *moving in the light of God, we are moving in the light of God.
We are *moving in the light of God, we are moving in the light of God.
We are *moving, we are moving, we are moving, we are moving,
We are *moving in the light of God.

Learn More from These Resources

Artress, Lauren. *Walking a Sacred Path: Rediscovering the Labyrinth as a Spiritual Practice.* New York: Riverhead Books, 1995, 2006.

Dershowitz, Adena Raub. *Women Who March.* Bethesda, MD: Blue Wave Books, 2018.

George, Linda. *Civil Rights Marches.* Cornerstones of Freedom. Danbury, CT: Grolier, 2000.

Otfinoski, Steven. *The Selma Marches for Civil Rights: We Shall Overcome.* Tangled History. North Mankato, MN: Capstone Press, 2018.

The Women's March Organizers and Condé Nast. *Together We Rise: Behind the Scenes at the Protest Heard Around the World.* New York: HarperCollins, 2018.

Walking Prayer resources: search online and be inspired.

21. September

Bless Feminist Ministers

The Spirit of [Divine Wisdom Sophia] is upon me, for [she] has anointed me: God has sent me to bring good news to those who are poor . . .

—Isaiah 61:1

Time and again, throughout history, communities have called forth individuals to bless them to do works of love, mercy, and justice. Feminist ministers work daily to bring about the kindom of God, the Holy One, Divine Wisdom Sophia.

This liturgy celebrates feminist ministries, and blesses feminist ministers for healing ministries, political ministries, community-building ministries, ministries of feminist theologies, gender and racial justice ministries, leadership and organizational ministries.

Preparation

Put a flask of oil, a bowl, and a cloth on a table or in the center space.

Call to Gather

Today we gather to bless feminist ministers. They are inspired by Divine Wisdom and image her. Feel the power of Divine Wisdom with us. We are here to bless *Names of persons,* to praise feminist ministers, and to reclaim feminist ministries for ourselves, our communities, and the church.

Let us begin by speaking our names and describing our ministry in a phrase. An example is: "I am Diann, a feminist minister who creates liturgies and counsels the brokenhearted."

If you are blessing one feminist minister, use: Let us begin by saying our name and offering a word of blessing for *Name*. An example is: "I am Diann. I bless you, *Name*, for comforting me when my mother died."

Song

"God Has Chosen Me" (80405) © 1990, Bernadette Farrell. Published by OCP. 5536 NE Hassalo, Portland OR 97213. All rights reserved. Used with permission.

God has chosen me, God has chosen me
to bring good news to the poor.
God has chosen me, God has chosen me
to bring new sight to those searching
for light:
God has chosen me, chosen me:

Refrain:
And to tell the world that God's
kindom is near,
to remove oppression and break down
fear,
yes, God's time is near, God's time is
near,
God's time is near, God's time is near.

God has chosen me, God has chosen
me
to set alight a new fire.

God has chosen me, God has chosen me
to bring to birth a new kindom on Earth:
God has chosen me, chosen me:

Refrain:
And to tell the world that God's
kingdom is near,
to remove oppression and break down
fear,
yes, God's time is near, God's time is
near,
God's time is near, God's time is near.

Litany of Feminist Ministers

Adapt these names for your tradition.

O Divine Wisdom, Sophia Spirit, Womb of Life, today we remember women ministers, named and unnamed, who throughout time have used their ministry to bring love, mercy, and justice to the world. We call upon these ancestors to help us discover within ourselves your power and ways we can use it for healing. Our response to each name is: "We proclaim your feminist ministry."

Pray the litany in as many languages as possible, or chant it.

Eve and Lilith, you reached for knowledge and found that it was good.

Response in English: We proclaim your feminist ministry.

Sarah, Hagar, Rebecca, Rachel, and Leah, you answered the call of Divine Wisdom and put faith in a covenant with the Holy One.

Response in German: Wir verkünden euer feministisches Amt.

Mary, you were a mother who listened, pondered, and gave birth to Jesus, Sophia's prophet and Miriam's child.

Response in Spanish: Proclamamos tu ministerio feminista.

Mary Magdalene, you were the first to announce Jesus' resurrection, the apostle to the apostles, and the foundation of women-church.

Response in Swahili: Tunatangaza huduma yako kwa wanawake.

Phoebe, you presided at a local church; Prisca, you supported yourself as a minister; Junia, you were imprisoned for your beliefs; Thecla and the other women leaders of the early house-church movement, you were called to a discipleship of equals.

Response in Greek: Εκτιμούμε την φεμινιστική πνευματική ηγεσία σας
Ektimoume tin feministiki pneymatiki igesia sas

Teresa of Ávila, Catherine of Siena, Thérèse of Lisieux, and Hildegard of Bingen, Doctors of our Church, you challenged the corruption of the institutional church.

Response in French: Nous proclamons ton ministère féministe.

Saint Mother Théodore Guérin, Saint Mary MacKillop, Saint Joan of Arc, and all excommunicated women; Sor Juana Ines de la Cruz, Carmel McEnroy, Myra Poole, Ivone Gebara, and all silenced women; and Elizabeth Lang, Theresa Maxis Duchesmin, Louise Lears, Joan Chittister, Margaret Farley, Mary Daly, Theresa Kane, and other dangerous visionaries like us.

Response in Portuguese: Nós proclamamos seu ministerio feminista.

Feminist ministers and theologians, you speak out against oppression in all of its forms.

Response in Chinese: 我们正式宣布你的女權職務

Let us speak aloud the names of other feminist ministers. *Add other names.*

Response: We proclaim your feminist ministry.

Reading

A reading from Isaiah 61:1-6

"The spirit of [Divine Wisdom Sophia] is upon me,
for [she] has anointed me:
God has sent me to bring good news to those who are poor;
to heal broken hearts;
to proclaim release to those held captive
and liberation to those in prison;
to announce a year of favor from [Divine Wisdom],
and the day of God's vindication;
to comfort all who mourn;
to provide for those who grieve in Zion-
to give them a wreath of flowers instead of ashes,
the oil of gladness instead of tears,
a cloak of praise instead of despair.
They will be known as trees of integrity,
planted by [Divine Wisdom] to display God's glory.

They will restore the ancient ruins,
and rebuild sites long devastated;
they will repair the ruined cities,
neglected for generations.
Strangers will tend your flocks;
foreigners will till your fields and dress your vineyards;
but you will be called priests of [Divine Wisdom]
and ministers of our God;
you will enjoy the richness of nations,
and inherit their wealth.
Because your shame was double—
insults and abuses were your lot—
now you will receive a double share in your land,
and everlasting joy will be yours.
For I, [Divine Wisdom], love justice;
I hate robbery and sin.
So I will faithfully compensate you,
And I will make an everlasting covenant with you.
Your descendants will be renowned among the nations;
and your offspring among the people;
all who see you will acknowledge
that you are a people blessed by [Divine Wisdom]."

Reflection | Sharing

We have proclaimed the ministries of our ancestors; we have been challenged by the words of Isaiah; now we ask ourselves, how do I exercise feminist ministry?

After a quiet time, we will share our experiences of feminist ministry *(or, if blessing one person, say:* our experience of *Name's* feminist ministry*).*

Song
"God Has Chosen Me"

God is calling me, God is calling me
in all whose cry is unheard.
God is calling me, God is calling me
to raise up the voice with no power or choice:
God is calling me, calling me:

Refrain: And to tell the world that God's kindom is near,
to remove oppression and break down fear,
yes, God's time is near, God's time is near,
God's time is near, God's time is near.

Affirming Feminist Ministries

Use the following format for a group affirmation. Personalize it if you are blessing one minister. An example is: "I bless you, *Name,* for the feminist ministry that you do, especially . . . "

Let us call forth the many ministries among us. When you hear your ministry called, stand as you are able for an affirmation. You may stand as many times as you wish.

Let us call forth those among us who are in political ministries: peace workers, those who work with immigrants, those who work against trafficking and domestic violence, grassroots organizers, lobbyists, housing advocates, those who hold political office, marchers and protesters, those who vote. Let us extend our hands to those standing and say: "Wisdom's power and compassion to you in your ministry!"

All: Wisdom's power and compassion to you in your ministry!

Let us call forth those among us who are in community-building ministries: those who sustain and nurture religious communities, those who raise future generations of feminists, those who work with women and children in shelters, those who work in partnership with women across religious traditions. Let us extend our hands to those standing and say:

All: Wisdom's power and compassion to you in your ministry!

Let us call forth those among us who are in ministries of feminist theologies: parents, mentors, writers, religious educators and artists, those in media and communication, teachers, and feminist theologians. Let us extend our hands to those standing and say:

All: Wisdom's power and compassion to you in your ministry!

Let us call forth those among us who are in healing ministries: pray-ers, preachers, ecofeminists, liturgy planners, eucharistic celebrants, dancers, musicians, spiritual companions, counselors, those who use massage, reiki, or healing arts. Let us extend our hands to those standing and say:

All: Wisdom's power and compassion to you in your ministry!

Let us call forth those among us who work in gender and racial justice ministries: those who work for racial justice, reproductive justice, LGBTQIA+ justice, healing for those with HIV/AIDS, and eradication of heterosexism, ageism, sexism, and all -isms. Let us extend our hands to those standing and say:

All: Wisdom's power and compassion to you in your ministry!

Let us call forth those among us who are in leadership and organizational ministries: community leaders, fundraisers, pastors, bishops, rabbis, imams, directors of justice organizations, elected officers, team leaders. Let us extend our hands to those standing and say:

All: Wisdom's power and compassion to you in your ministry!

Let us call forth the many feminist ministries of the discipleship of equals. Please stand. Let us extend our hands to those standing and say:

All: Wisdom's power and compassion to you in your ministry!

Blessing Oil

Oil is the sacramental symbol that strengthens us for feminist ministry. Oil represents the Holy Spirit, Divine Wisdom Sophia, who calls us to act justly, love tenderly, and walk humbly. Let us bless this oil by chanting together. OM is the Primordial Sound of the Universe. It is the sound that reverberates in the entire cosmos and in every cell of our body. Let us hum OM together in harmony.

Anointing with Oil

The anointing of those who are called has a long and deep symbolism, going well back into Hebrew Scriptures. Those who are anointed are cleansed, healed, strengthened, and sealed as healers. Let us anoint one another with this holy oil. *The minister pours oil into the bowl, anoints the person next to her, and invites this person to anoint the next person.*

Song

"Blessing Song" by Marsie Silvestro, from Circling Free *(Moon Song Productions © 1983). Used with permission.*

Play, hum, then sing during the anointing.

Bless you my sister, bless you on your way.
You have roads to roam before you're home,
And winds to speak your name.

So go gently my sister, let courage be your song.
You have words to say in your own way
And stars to light your night.

And if ever you grow weary and your heart song has no refrain,
Just remember we'll be waiting to raise you up again.
And we'll bless you our sister, bless you on your way.
And we'll welcome home all the life you've known.
And gently speak your name.

Take Action

Let us put our prayers into action. Here are some possible ways:

- Write a note or send an email to a feminist minister and thank her for her work.
- Get involved in a feminist ministry, perhaps one named here, and share your gifts.

Commissioning Feminist Ministers

Feminist ministers, take your gifts to the city streets and country roads of every neighborhood!

Let us go forth in all directions of the universe to bless and to embrace,
to forgive and to heal,
to welcome and to sanctify.
Let us go forth to the homeless and to the hospitable,
to the hungry and to the full,
to the thirsty and to the justice-seekers.
Let us go forth to the elderly and to those who seek wisdom,
to the exiled and to those who understand freedom,
to the hopeless and to those who see visions.
Let us go forth to church leaders who are unable to perceive the needs of their people,
to government officials who ignore the cries of the poor,
to world leaders who reject the movements for peace.
Let us go forth to people of every race and place,
to the young and to the old of every neighborhood,
to the next generations and to their children of every nation.
Let us go forth in the name of Divine Wisdom, Sophia Spirit,
the God of love and liberation,
the Holy One of power and justice.
Let us go forth to proclaim feminist ministries!
Let us go forth to heal the world!

Song

"Dance-In the New Day" by Kathy Sherman, CSJ, from Dance in the Dawn *(Ministry of the Arts © 1993). Used with permission.*

Prophets go forth to proclaim your stories.
Go with your visions and go with your dreams.
Dreamers go quickly, the night is waiting
For us to dance in the new day.

We gather all into our circle,
Sharing our hopes hand in hand,
And though we are many, we sing with one voice,
A song that all Earth understands.

We go forth to celebrate living,
Our works and our loves and our fears,
The strength of our joy has been nourished in pain,
Our roots watered deeply by tears.

Strengthened around Holy Wisdom,
Trusting her warmth and her flame,
In her we are tender, fierce, loving and strong
As one we go forth in her name.

Learn More from These Resources

Hunt, Mary E. "The Evolution and Revolution of Feminist Ministry: A U.S. Catholic Perspective." *Journal for the Study of Religion* 26, no. 2 (2013): 75–88.

Kim, Grace Ji-Sun, and Jann Aldredge-Clanton, eds. *Intercultural Ministry: Hope for a Changing World.* Valley Forge, PA: Judson Press, 2017.

Lewis, Karoline M. *She: Five Keys to Unlock the Power of Women in Ministry.* Nashville, TN: Abingdon Press, 2016.

Women's Ordination Conference website: https://www.womensordination.org/.

Zagano, Phyllis. *Women in Ministry: Emerging Questions about the Diaconate.* Mahwah, NJ: Paulist Press, 2012.

22. October

The Faces of Breast Cancer

Just when I needed prayer the most, it eluded me.

—Elizabeth Thoman, CHM

October is Breast Cancer Awareness Month, a worldwide annual campaign raising up the faces of breast cancer to highlight the importance of breast awareness, education, and research. About one in eight women born today in the United States will develop invasive breast cancer at some point. The good news is that most women and men can survive breast cancer if it is detected and treated early.

This liturgy invites participants to be in solidarity with those who have or have had breast cancer, their friends, colleagues, and loved ones. It supports women with breast cancer and assures them that they are not alone.

Preparation

Place a table in the center of a circle of chairs and cover it with a cloth. Arrange on it a pink candle, another candle, matches, a basket of pink strips of paper and pens, a bowl for water, a pitcher of water, a basket of shells, a drum, and a Zen bowl. Invite three women to speak the Litany of Remembrance and six women to read quotes from women survivors. If your group is small, invite some to take two parts.

Call to Gather

Light the candle. We gather to be one with all who have or have had breast cancer, their friends, colleagues, and loved ones. We gather during Breast Cancer Awareness month to be in solidarity with survivors and to remember those who have gone before us.

Naming the Circle

Let us create our circle by sharing our names and saying the name of someone who is a survivor of breast cancer or someone who has died of breast cancer. After each naming, we will all respond, "Welcome, *Name*."

Centering Prayer

Let us continue to create our sacred space with a centering prayer. A few people will walk around the circle, drum, or sound a chime. I invite the rest of us to breathe deeply and visualize water flowing over us like a waterfall.

Blessing This Healing Space

Blessed be this sacred, healing space.
When I ponder my past, may I find healing.
When I contemplate my present, may I find healing.
When I face my future, may I find healing.
Blessed be this sacred, healing space.

Song

"Come, Drink Deep" by Carolyn McDade, from Rain Upon Dry Land *(Surtsey Publishing © 1983). Used with permission.*

Come drink deep of living waters
Without cup bend close to the ground
Wade with bare feet into troubled
waters
Where love of life abounds.

I turn my head to sky rains falling
Wash the wounds of numbness from
my soul,
Turn my heart in tides of fierce renewal
Where love and rage run whole.

Come rains of heaven on the dry seed
Rains of love on every tortured land
Roots complacent awaken in
compassion
So hope springs in our hands
Come drink deep.

Litany of Remembrance

As we gather around this well to listen to women's stories, let us remember and name some of the brave and courageous women with breast cancer whose lives have affected ours. Let us respond to each by saying, "We remember you."

Share the following names with three women for each to share one. After each name, sound the Zen bowl and sing the "Call to Prayer Response."

Song

"Call to Prayer Response" by Carolyn McDade, from Songs of Congregational Singing *(Surtsey Publishing © 1991). Used with permission.*

For each part is a part of each other part.
We all are a part of one another.

Barbara Rosenblum, Jewish sociologist, co-author of *Cancer in Two Voices*, died of breast cancer in August 1988.

All: We remember you, Barbara. *Sound the Zen bowl.*
Song: For each part is a part of each other part. We all are a part of one another.

Audre Lorde, poet laureate of New York State in 1991, influential black writer on feminist, racial, lesbian, and sexual issues, died of breast cancer November 17, 1992.

All: We remember you, Audre. *Sound the Zen bowl.*

Song: For each part is a part of each other part. We all are a part of one another.

Sheryl Crow, Jane Fonda, Heidi Heitkamp, Sandra Day O'Connor, Debbie Wasserman Schultz, Gloria Steinem, Ann Romney, Hoda Kotb, Melissa Etheridge, Robin Roberts, Martina Navratilova, Andrea Mitchell, Ruby Dee, Cokie Roberts, Masumi Miyazaki, and so many others surviving breast cancer.

All: We remember you. *Sound the Zen bowl.*

Song: For each part is a part of each other part. We all are a part of one another.

Let us name the women we know who are living with or have died of breast cancer, and we will all respond with "We remember you." *Sound the Zen bowl.*

Share names and respond with "We remember you."

Women who will die today of breast cancer, and women who will survive.

All: We remember you. *Sound the Zen bowl.*

Song: For each part is a part of each other part. We all are a part of one another.

Listen to Women with Cancer

Readers 1–3 read from Chicken Soup for the Soul Healthy Living Series: Breast Cancer *by Jack Canfield, Mark Victor Hansen, and Mary Olsen Kelly (Deerfield Beach, FL: Health Communications, 2005).*

Reader 1: "My world turned upside down at seven o'clock on the morning of March 8 as I stood in the shower. A lump in the breast. A moment of panic. So begins a journey that every woman fears."

—Susanna, health-care provider, ix

Reader 2: "Cancer wakes you up, and you say, 'There must be more out there to life. I wonder what that is.'"

—Jill Eikenberry, actress, 6

Reader 3: "My cancer scare changed my life. I'm grateful for every new, healthy day I have. It has helped me prioritize my life."

—Olivia Newton-John, singer, 1

Reader 4: "What does it mean to say I have survived until you take the mirrors and turn them outward and read your own face in their outraged light?"

—Adrienne Rich, poet, from "Corralitos Under Rolls of Cloud," in *An Atlas of the Difficult World* (New York: W. W. Norton & Co., 1991)

Reader 5: "With one breast or none, I am still me. The sum total of me is infinitely greater than the number of my breasts."

—Alice Walker, author, endorsement for *The Cancer Journals* by Audre Lorde (San Francisco, CA: Aunt Lute Books, 2006)

Reader 6: "Cancer treatment takes all the stuffing out of you. Words jumble together; you have no energy; concentration is impossible. Just when I needed prayer the most, it eluded me."

—Elizabeth Thoman, CHM, photographer, founder of Healing Petals and the Center for Media Literacy, in conversation at WATER, 2015

Song

"Spirit of Life" by Carolyn McDade, in Songs for Congregational Singing *(Surtsey Publishing © 1982; renewed © 1991 Carolyn McDade). Used with permission.*

Spirit of Life, come unto me.
Sing in my heart all the stirrings of compassion.
Blow in the wind. Rise in the sea.
Move in the hand giving life the shape of justice.
Roots hold me close; Wings set me free.
Spirit of Life, come to me, come to me.

Reflection | Sharing

Let us take time now to think about the prayers and spiritual practices that give hope and courage to women with breast cancer, their families, friends, and communities.

Think about the prayers, rituals, liturgies, and spiritual practices that you or someone you know have found helpful as you walk the breast cancer journey so we can empower one another. For example, when examining your breasts, getting a mammogram, feeling a lump, getting chemo, loosing hair, honoring an anniversary, rituals for any part of the breast cancer journey. Let us pause for quiet reflection.

In a minute we will share some of the prayers, rituals, and blessings to give one another hope.

Blessing with Water and Shells

In the center of our table is a bowl of salt water representing the ocean. Salt water has healing and regenerative properties that facilitate life. Born of the ocean, seashells have long been known for their healing qualities.

Look at the well and the seashells and visualize their healing powers. Take a seashell. *Pause.* Put it in the water and share your reflection of a prayer, blessing, or ritual, or just put a seashell in the water. *Each takes a shell and shares.* We will all respond:

All: We are here with you; you are not alone.

Examples of Sharing

This Buddhist prayer helps me to begin each day: "May all be loved. May all be healed. May all be sheltered. May all be free from fear. May I be loved. May I be healed. May I be sheltered. May I be free from fear."

I like visualization and imagery. When I was undergoing radiation treatment, I visualized myself sitting under a waterfall in Hawaii and having the water flow over me and wash away all the cancer cells.

The worry box: I found a box and glued colorful scraps of wrapping paper on the top. Inside it, each morning, I tucked handwritten notes about my worries and fears. Then I closed the lid and went on with the rest of the day, whether it was walking in the woods, listening to music, grocery shopping, paying bills, or cuddling up with my daughter to read a book. The worry box also provided me with a concrete way of saying, Enough!

A friend gave me a "Gratitude Journal" to write down my thoughts. I began to write three things I was grateful for each night.

Song
"Call to Prayer Response"

For each part is a part of each other part. We all are a part of one another.

Take Action

Let us put our healing prayers into action. Here are some possible ways:

- Learn about the signs and symptoms of breast cancer.
- Ask doctors and nurses to speak to women about the importance of getting screened for breast cancer.
- Encourage all women to consult with their doctors about getting mammograms.

Greeting of Peace

Let us close our time together by offering one another a greeting of peace. Take a shell from the basket. Let us send one another forth, exchanging the shells and saying, "We send you forth to heal."

Song
"Spirit of Life"

Spirit of Life, come unto me.
Sing in my heart all the stirrings of compassion.
Blow in the wind. Rise in the sea.
Move in the hand giving life the shape of justice.
Roots hold me close; Wings set me free.
Spirit of Life, come to me, come to me.

Learn More from These Resources

Bolen, Jean Shinoda. *Close to the Bone: Life-Threatening Illness as a Soul Journey.* San Francisco, CA: Conari Press, 2007.

Boucher, Sandy. *Hidden Spring: A Buddhist Woman Confronts Cancer.* Boston, MA: Wisdom Publications, 2000.

Bray, Sharon A. *When Words Heal: Writing through Cancer.* Berkeley, CA: Frog, Ltd. Books, 2006.

Canfield, Jack, Mark Victor Hansen, Mary Olsen Kelly, and Edward Creagan. *Chicken Soup for the Soul Healthy Living Series: Breast Cancer.* Deerfield Beach, FL: Health Communications, 2005.

Dackman, Linda. *Affirmations, Meditations, and Encouragements for Women Living with Breast Cancer.* New York: HarperSanFrancisco, 1991.

Delinsky, Barbara. *Uplift: Secrets from the Sisterhood of Breast Cancer Survivors.* New York: Washington Square Press, 2001.

Dupree, Beth Baughman. *The Healing Consciousness: A Doctor's Journey to Healing.* Boulder, CO: WovenWord Press, 2006.

Faces of Breast Cancer. *The New York Times* website. https://www.nytimes.com/interactive/projects/well/breast-cancer-stories.

Heart, Maria Dancing. *The Last Adventure of Life: Sacred Resources for Living and Dying from a Hospice Counselor.* Findhorn, Forres, Scotland: Findhorn Press, 2008.

Katz, Rebecca, with Marsha Tomassi and Mat Edelson. *One Bit at a Time: Nourishing Recipes for Cancer Survivors and Their Friends.* Berkeley, CA: Celestial Arts, 2004.

Love, Susan M. *Dr. Susan Love's Breast Book.* Boston, MA: Da Capo Press, 2015.

———. Dr. Susan Love's website for women. www.susanlovemd.org.

Mulligan, Gina L. *Dear Friend: Letters of Encouragement, Humor and Love from Women with Breast Cancer.* San Francisco CA: Chronicle Books LLC, 2017.

Muschal-Reinhardt, Rosalie, and The Prism Collective et al. *Rituals for Women Coping with Breast Cancer.* Rochester, NY: Quality Books, 2000.

National Breast Cancer Coalition. www.natlbcc.org.

Neu, Diann L. *Seasons of Survival: Prayers and Rituals for Women with Cancer.* WATERworks Press, 2009.

———. *Seasons of Healing: Journaling and Resources.* WATERworks Press, 2010.

———. *Seasons of Compassion: Resources for Companions of Those Needing Healing.* WATERworks Press, 2011.

Oktay, Julianne S. *Breast Cancer: Daughters Tell Their Stories.* New York: Haworth Press, 2005.

Raz, Hilda, ed. *Living on the Margins: Women Writers on Breast Cancer.* New York: Persea Books, 1999.

Smith Center for Healing and the Arts. Cancer Support Programs. Washington, DC. www.smithcenter.org

Susan G. Komen website. ww5.komen.org/.

Townes, Emilie M. *Breaking the Fine Rain of Death: African American Health Issues and a Womanist Ethic of Care.* Eugene, OR: Wipf & Stock, 2006.

23. November

Give Thanks for Women of Wisdom

I have received much. I am willing to give much in return,
for as I have taught you, there must always be a giving back for what one receives.

—Polingaysi Qoyawayma, *No Turning Back: A Hopi Indian Woman's Struggle to Live in Two Worlds*

November, the season of Thanksgiving in the United States, offers us an opportunity to say thank you. This Thanksgiving, invite your community to express gratitude for the wise women in their lives. Take some time to thank them for their wisdom.

This liturgy honors women of vision—from goddesses to biblical women, notable women in recorded herstory to the women in our personal lives. It connects participants to the wisdom of women, and invites them to dive into their own lived wisdom.

Preparation

On the table place a plate of apples, cider, honey, and bread; three unlit candles that you will light during the liturgy; and a paper heart for each participant. String lights, photos of wise women, and hearts around the room.

Call to Gather

Welcome to our Thanksgiving liturgy. This is the season of gratitude. This is the time to remember ancestors. This is the time to give thanks for all good blessings. Lift your spirit and give thanks today for women of wisdom. Lift your voice and give thanks for life.

Naming the Circle

Let us create our thanksgiving circle by sharing our names and something we are grateful for this season. Example: "I am *Name*, and I am thankful for . . ."

Centering Prayer

Let us center ourselves by breathing together to release the negative energy that manifests in our bodies and minds.

Breathe in hope
Breathe out anxiety

Breathe in gratitude
Breathe out tension

Breathe in rest
Breathe out anger

Breathe in the calm space around you
Breathe out any stress or burdens you may have

Song

"Come to the Circle" by Kathy Sherman, CSJ, from Song of the Universe *(Ministry of the Arts © 2015). Used with permission.*

Come to the circle and tell your story,
Listen and share the world inside you.

Come to the circle, your friends are waiting
to listen and share their stories too.

Prayer

Holy One of Gratitude, Wisdom Sophia, we remember today the women, named and unnamed, who throughout the ages have used their wisdom and gifts to transform the world. We call upon these ancestors to help us discover within ourselves your wisdom and the ways we can use it to bring about justice and peace. Be with us on this journey. Amen. Blessed be. May it be so.

Litany of Goddesses and Biblical Women

Light a candle.

In gratitude, let us remember women who imagined they could make a difference in the world—and did. Our response to each name is: Thanks for your Wisdom.

We remember Kwan Yin, a Buddhist Bodhisattva from China, the Goddess of Compassion, whose name means "She who hears the cries of the world."
Response: Thanks for your Wisdom.
We remember Gaia, the Goddess that embodies Earth itself and all that live and breathe.
Response: Thanks for your Wisdom.
We remember Sarah, Hagar, Rebekah, Rachel, and Leah, for answering the call of Sophia Wisdom and putting faith in a covenant with the Holy One.
Response: Thanks for your Wisdom.
We remember Judith, for fighting for the freedom of her people and for not conforming to any one idea of femaleness.
Response: Thanks for your Wisdom.
We remember Mary, a Galilean Jew and mother, for listening, pondering, and knowing that she had been chosen to give birth to Jesus, a powerful liberator.
Response: Thanks for your Wisdom.

We remember Mary Magdalene, the apostle to the apostles and the foundation of Women-Church, for sharing the first news of Jesus' resurrection.
Response: Thanks for your Wisdom.
We remember Lydia, the businesswoman of purple dye from Thyatira, deaconess, and spiritual leader of the early house-church movement, for being called to a discipleship of equals.
Response: Thanks for your Wisdom.

Song

"We Give Thanks," sung to the tune of "Lilies of the Field Amen."

We give thanks. *Toda* (Hebrew). *Asente* (Swahili). *Merci* (French). *Xiè-Xie* (Chinese).

Litany of Women of Recorded History

Light a candle.

We remember Sor Juana Ines de la Cruz, the Mexican nun, for courageously criticizing misogyny and the hypocrisy of the patriarchy that led to her condemnation by the bishop of Puebla.
Response: Thanks for your Wisdom.
We remember Sojourner Truth, for her defiant declaration of "Ain't I A Woman" as she advocated for freedom by fighting for abolition and women's rights.
Response: Thanks for your Wisdom.
We remember Dorothy Day, for founding the Catholic Worker Movement and believing in radical hospitality with those who are poor.
Response: Thanks for your Wisdom.
We remember Dolores Huerta, for founding the United Farm Workers and continuing to work tirelessly to support immigrants and health-care reform.
Response: Thanks for your Wisdom.
We remember Claudette Colvin, Rosa Parks, and the brave women who sparked the Civil Rights Movement, for refusing segregation.
Response: Thanks for your Wisdom.
We remember Malala Yousafzai, for defying the Taliban in Pakistan and demanding that girls be allowed to receive an education.
Response: Thanks for your Wisdom.
We remember Rachel Carson, for being an ecologist whose book *Silent Spring* advanced the global environmental movement.
Response: Thanks for your Wisdom.
We remember Thea Bowman, FSPA, for being a trailblazing African American sister, the first black sister in her white congregation who encouraged people to stand up for their rights, especially toward racial justice.
Response: Thanks for your Wisdom.

Song
"We Give Thanks"

We give thanks. *Gracias* (Spanish). *Danke* (German). *Arigato* (Japanese).

Litany of Women in Our Lives

Light a candle.

We remember our mothers, grandmothers, ancestors, all women who have been our guides and whose powerful lives have shaped ours.

Response: Thanks for your Wisdom.

We remember women in ministry, feminist theologians, scholars and journalists, women prophets, and all women who speak out against oppression in all of its forms.

Response: Thanks for your Wisdom.

What other women do we wish to remember now? Tell us, and we will respond with "Thanks for your wisdom."

Song
"We Give Thanks"

We give thanks. *Shukran* (Arabic). *Grazie* (Italian). *Obrigato* (Portuguese).

Reflection | Sharing

Let us spend a few minutes in quiet reflection on wise women in our lives.

What women of wisdom came to your mind and heart as you listened? Take a heart, hold it, and write on it a word or phrase about the gratitude you have for these women.

After some quiet time, let us share our reflections.

Blessing Apples, Honey, and Bread

We bless apples, honey, and bread today to taste and see the wisdom of women. Taste the sweetness of this harvest and enjoy community with each other. Extend your hands over these harvest foods and let us bless them together.

Blessed are You, Wisdom of the Harvest, for giving us these apples and this cider that are symbols of women's wisdom. We remember Eve, who reached for knowledge, took a bite of the apple, and found that it was good. She was a wise woman!

Blessed are You, Wisdom of the Harvest, for giving us this honey that adds a touch of sweetness to our wisdom. We remember Sweet Honey in the Rock! Let us pass the apples and honey around our circle, dip the apples into the honey, eat them, and connect with wise women as we enjoy them.

Blessed are You, Wisdom of the Harvest, for giving us this bread that nourishes and strengthens us to be wise women. We take, bless, break, and eat it with gratitude!

Let us eat and drink giving thanks.

Song

"Blessing of Food" by Jan Novotka, from In the Name of All That Is *(© 2002 by Jan Novotka's Music LLC [ASCAP]. All rights reserved.) Used with permission.*

Blessing of food, blessing of drink,
blessing of Earth I receive.
Soil to food: my body at prayer,
uttering thanks for all.

Dust of the stars, dust of the Earth,
Holy Breath breathes in you.
Soil to food: my body at prayer,
uttering thanks for all.

Reading

From Polingaysi Qoyawayma (Elizabeth Q. White), No Turning Back: A Hopi Indian Woman's Struggle to Live in Two Worlds *(Albuquerque: University of New Mexico Press, 1964).*

"I grind with gratitude for the richness of our harvest, not with cross feelings of working too hard. As I kneel at my grinding stone, I bow my head in prayer, thanking the great forces for provision. I have received much. I am willing to give much in return, for as I have taught you, there must always be a giving back for what one receives."

Song

"Love Cannot Be Silenced" by Kathy Sherman, CSJ (Ministry of the Arts © 2012). Used with permission.

Love cannot be silenced. It never has.
It never will.
Let justice roll like a river from the
oceans to the hills.
Rise up, people. Rise up. And stand
with your heads held high.

We are faithful, loving, and wise.
Dancing along side by side.
With a Gospel vision to lead us and
Holy Fire in our eyes.

Take Action

Let us put our prayers into action. Here are some possible ways:

- Place your heart somewhere you can see it every day (examples: keyboard, door, mirror).
- Learn more about one of the holy women named in the litany.
- Express gratitude to wise women in your life by giving them a call or writing them a card.

- Plant a garden as a form of self-care.
- Take a walk outside and enjoy the beauty of Earth.

Sending Forth

Let us go forth in peace with
every breath of gratitude
for the wise and visionary women in our lives, communities, and world.
Let us go forth in joy with
every ounce of knowledge
that wise women are changing the world.
Let us seal our prayer with hugs of gratitude.
Filled with this Wisdom, let us embrace one another as people of wisdom.

Learn More from These Resources

Cohick, Lynn, and Amy Hughes. *Christian Women in the Patristic World: Their Influence, Authority, and Legacy in the Second through Fifth Century.* Grand Rapids, MI: Baker Academic, 2017.

Frankel, Lois. *Ageless Women, Timeless Wisdom: Witty, Wicked, and Wise Reflections on Well-Lived Lives.* New York: Skyhorse, 2017.

Japingo, Lynn. *Preaching the Women of the Old Testament: Who They Were and Why They Matter.* Louisville, KY: Westminster John Knox Press, 2017.

Moore, Rebecca. *Women in Christian Traditions.* New York: New York University Press, 2015.

Yarber, Angela. *Holy Women Icons Project.* www.holywomenicons.com.

24. December

Bringing the Light of Wisdom for Winter Solstice

Light is returning, even though this is the darkest hour.
No one can hold—back the dawn.

—C. Murphy, *Canticles of Light*

December is the month in the Northern Hemisphere when most cultures and religious traditions celebrate rituals that mark the Winter Solstice (December 21 in the Northern Hemisphere, June 21 in the Southern) using the symbol of light. The night is longest and the day is shortest. Winter brings sweet darkness and calls the sun from the womb of night. It invites a long journey inward to draw on natural resources and strengths.

In this liturgy, we enkindle winter festival lights to bring the wisdom of the Hindu Diwali, the Jewish Hanukkah, the Christian Advent and Christmas, the Buddhist Bodhi, the Winter Solstice, the Chinese Dongzhi, and the African American Kwanza into this space. (Add others if you wish). Each festival beseeches the sun to return again, to awaken compassion and justice from generation to generation.

Preparation

Set your ritual space with lights and candles (and matches) appropriate for each December festival of light. Include for Diwali (floral centerpiece and ginger tea), Hanukkah (a menorah and latkes), Advent (Advent wreath and cookies), Bodhi (fig jam to honor the Bodhi fig tree), Winter Solstice (pomegranate), Dongzhi (dumplings), and Kwanza (jollof rice). Place on a table foods that represent these festivals. Have five candles to light for Lighting the Winter Solstice. Have ready the song "Light Is Returning" by C. Murphy on Canticles of Light.

Call to Gather

Welcome to this celebration of Bringing the Light of Wisdom. This is the season of Winter Solstice festivals. Virtually all cultures have their own ways of marking the Winter Solstice by using the symbol of light: lighting candles, placing candles or lights on a tree, burning a Yule log, or decorating houses with extra lights.

Many religious traditions mark the light breaking through the night in autumn and winter: the Hindu Diwali, the Jewish Hanukkah, the Christian Advent and Christmas, the Buddhist Bodhi Day, the Winter Solstice, the Chinese Dongzhi festival, and the African American Kwanzaa. Each beseeches the sun to return again, to awaken in us compassion and justice.

Our celebration focuses on women's gifts of wisdom. Women know how to give birth, *Dar la luce,* or to give the light as they say in Spanish. Women have a special insight into life's mysteries, giving birth to children, ideas, artistic spaces, friendships, and more.

Naming the Circle

Let us create our community tonight by sharing our names and a phrase of what we think of when we hear "bring the light of wisdom." *Sharing.*

We light the festival lights now to bring the wisdom of Diwali, Hanukkah, Advent, Bodhi, Winter Solstice, Dongzhi, and Kwanza into this space.

Song

"Light Is Returning" by C. Murphy, on Canticles of Light *(Out Front Music © 1984), https://www.youtube.com/watch?v=R2vHqAVIiWI. Used with permission.*

Light is returning, even though this is the darkest hour,
No one can hold—back the dawn.

Let's keep it burning, let's keep the light of hope alive,
Make safe our journey—through the storm.

One planet is turning, circling in her path around the sun,
Earth Mother is calling—Her children home.

Lighting Winter Solstice Candles

From generation to generation people honor the darkness and call light from the womb of night. We light five candles to welcome compassion and justice into the world. *Adapt to current events.*

Light the candle of the South:
We light our first candle, the candle of the South, to honor those in the Southern Hemisphere—Australia, Antarctica, New Zealand, Chile, Argentina, Bolivia, Peru, and South Africa—as they celebrate the Summer Solstice. We unite especially with those who have migrated to Mexico and face hostility at the US border.

Light the candle of the East:
We light the candle of the East in solidarity with those in Asia and the Middle East, especially mothers and children in Syria.

Light the candle of the North:
We light the candle of the North for those who are afraid, for immigrants, Muslims, Jews, communities of color, sexual and gender minorities, those who have experienced violence: gun violence, intimate partner violence, and sexual violence.

Light the candle of the West:
We light the candle of the West for those who experience the devastation of wildfires and flooding.

Light the candle of the Center:
We light the Center candle for those who have died this season. We invite you to name them. *Naming.*

Song
"Light Is Returning"

Light is returning, even though this is the darkest hour,
No one can hold—back the dawn.

Let's keep it burning, let's keep the light of hope alive,
Make safe our journey—through the storm.

One planet is turning, circling in her path around the sun,
Earth Mother is calling—Her children home.

Reflection | Sharing

Let us take a few moments of quiet to reflect on these questions:
How is light returning to your life and to life around you?
How will you spread this light?
After a quiet time, let us share our reflections.

Spreading the Light

Let us spread this Winter Solstice light far and wide.

To friends who share joys and sorrows,
the light of friendship to you.

To the people living in war-torn countries,
the light of peace to you.

To women with cancer, and those who are sick,
the light of healing to you.

To families divided by differences,
the light of reconciliation to you.

To children of every race, family, and country,
the light of love to you.

To people in despair,
the light of hope to you.

To those who are without homes,
the light of shelter to you.

To those who are hungry,
the light of food to you.

To those who have no job,
the light of remunerative work to you.

To those who are dying,
the light of a peaceful death to you.

To children being born this day,
the light of life and health to you.

To those who experience discrimination in any form,
the light of justice to you.

To the elected leaders of this administration and the next Congress,
the light of vision and truth for the global community to you.

To women who experience violence from war, rape, and religion,
the light of safety and restitution to you.

To young children growing up today,
the light of equality to you.

Song

"Give Me Oil in My Lamp," Traditional.

Give me oil in my lamp, keep me burning,
Give me oil in my lamp, I pray.

Give me oil in my lamp, keep me burning,
Keep me burning till the break of day.

Blessing Winter Solstice Food and Drink

Come, extend your hands toward this food and remember the work of women, people who are on the margins, and communities of color that spread light through the world.

Blessed be this ginger tea for Diwali, latkes for Hanukkah, biscotti for Advent, fig jam for Bodhi, pomegranate for Winter Solstice, dumplings for Dongzhi, and jollof rice for Kwanzaa.

Blessed be those who bring the light of wisdom daily . . . childcare workers, homemakers, domestic workers, lawyers . . . doctors, healers, secretaries, teachers . . . scientists, engineers, philosophers, social workers . . . writers, artists, musicians, florists . . . farmers, farmworkers, gardeners, theologians, therapists . . .

Blessed be . . . friends who laugh with us and warm us like seasoned drink . . . our children, nieces and nephews, students, colleagues who share their creativity . . . women whose muscle and mind move the world . . . those whose sweat and toil bring liberation and equality . . . teachers and professors, not just those who teach us in the classroom but those who teach us in life, who are so important for our formation . . . *Name others.*

Let us share this food and drink as we give thanks for those who bring the light of wisdom.

Take Action

Let us put our prayers into action:

- Participate in a Festival of Light tradition that is other than your own.
- Read a book to a child about a Winter Solstice tradition.
- Donate to a women's shelter in your area.

Sending Forth

Let us form a circle and bring closure to our time together. Close your eyes and feel the power of the darkness around you and within you. Call forth from within you your light, your creativity, and your healing powers.

Filled with the power of this season,
Let us dedicate ourselves to remaining steadfast under oppression.
Let us enjoy the treasures of being together.
Let us call forth feminist religious voices worldwide.
Let us include those who are left out, nourish those who are afraid, and eradicate the causes of their fears. Let us go forth and spread the good news of equality, dignity, and justice far and wide.

Song

"Give Me Oil in My Lamp"

Give me oil in my lamp, keep me burning,
Give me oil in my lamp, I pray.
Give me oil in my lamp, keep me burning,
Keep me burning till the break of day.

Learn More from These Resources

Conrad, Heather. *Lights of Winter: Winter Celebrations Around the World.* Berkeley, CA: Lightport Books, 2013.

Edwards, Carolyn McVickar. *The Return of the Light: Twelve Tales from Around the World for Winter Solstice.* New York: Marlowe & Company, 2000.

Pfeffer, Wendy. *The Shortest Day: Celebrating the Winter Solstice.* New York: Dalton Children's Books, 2003.

section three

Let Justice Flow like Water

We are not called upon to do all the good that is possible but only that which we can do.

—Mother Théodore Guérin, *Journals and Letters*

Let justice flow like a river, and righteousness flow like an unfailing stream.

—Amos 5:24

Until you dig a hole, you plant a tree,
you water it and make it survive,
you haven't done a thing. You are just talking.

—Wangari Maathai, 2006 speech at the Goldman Awards in San Francisco

25. January

Praying to End Human Trafficking

We shall overcome, someday.
Oh, deep in my heart, I do believe
We shall overcome, someday.

—African American spiritual

January is Human Trafficking Awareness Month and January 11 is National Human Trafficking Awareness Day. Human trafficking is the fastest-growing modern-day manifestation of slavery and second most profitable criminal industry in the world. It must be renounced. It is perpetuated through extensive networks that exist in virtually every corner of the world.

This liturgy focuses on uniting the global community in solidarity with victims and survivors of human trafficking and in praying for a resolute end to this slavery.

Preparation

On a table or center space, place a prayer cloth, photos of victims of human trafficking, blue ribbons, a loaf of multi-grain gluten free bread, a goblet with wine and a goblet with juice, a paper chain, candles, and matches.

Call to Gather

January 11 is National Human Trafficking Awareness Day. Human trafficking is modern-day slavery and is the fastest growing and second most profitable criminal industry in the world. More than 27 million women, men, and children have become victims of human trafficking for labor and sexual exploitation. Trafficking can and does occur in all parts of the world, including around and within the United States. Large sporting events such as the Super Bowl are especially attractive occasions for human trafficking, particularly the sexual exploitation of women.

We gather today to pray and work for an end to human trafficking. Let us begin with a moment of silence in solidarity with the more than 40.3 million people globally who each suffer from this modern form of slavery.

Moment of silence.

Naming the Circle

Let us create our circle of solidarity by speaking our names and saying, "I pray for an end to human trafficking."

Prayer of Solidarity

This human trafficking awareness month, we gather with the global community to be in solidarity with victims and survivors of human trafficking.
All: God of Compassion, be with us.

We seek justice and healing for all people who are affected by human trafficking.
All: Divine Healer, be with us.

We gather to pray, reflect, and renounce this modern-day slavery.
All: Spirit of Justice, be with us.

Song

"Don't Walk Away (Human Trafficking Song)" by Meg Ammons, from Anchors *(cdbaby © 2013), https://www.youtube.com/watch?v=VAhKtNdWisE. Used with permission.*

I was in the news today
A story back on page 16
No photographs
No last names
They save that for the beauty queens

I'm a girl you've never met
A half a world away from you
And though I seem so different
I am someone's daughter too
Aren't we the same?
I bet I'm just as far away
And easy to forget

Don't walk away
Don't walk away
Don't walk away from me
I have a face
I have a name
I have my hopes and dreams
I try and I try to hold on
But it's hard to believe
Anyone notices
Anyone cares
When day after day
They walk away

I'd like to believe
That people are good
And they take to heart
The things they see
That if they thought they should
They would
They'd come for all the girls like me

Aren't we the same?
I bet I'm just far away
And easy to forget
Don't walk away
Don't walk away
Don't walk away from me
I have a face
I have a name
I have my hopes and dreams
I try and I try to hold on
But it's hard to believe
That anyone notices
Anyone cares
When day after day
They walk away

Don't walk away *(5x)*
I'm a girl you've never met
It should be easy to forget me.

Don't walk away *(5x)*

Psalm 34:17-18

"But the just cry out, and YHWH hears, and saves them from all their troubles. YHWH is close to the brokenhearted and rescues those whose spirits are crushed."

Listen to the Stories

We join our tears with those of the victims of human trafficking. Each person forced into slavery has a unique story. Let us listen to some of them and respond with: "We hear your story. We'll work to break your chains."

A's Story, Told at WATER by Heureuse Kaj from the Democratic Republic of the Congo. *Used with permission.*

"Before I joined Wesley Theological Seminary, I worked as a young adult missionary at Help Asian Women's Shelter in Tokyo, Japan, which provides temporary and emergency housing, counseling, and rehabilitation to women and children survivors of domestic violence and human trafficking. Among the many women that I encountered was a seventeen-year-old woman who came to the Help shelter after escaping exploitation by her adoptive mother. The young lady came from a poor family, lost her father at the age of two, and was adopted by a single mother at the age of six. She did not have a chance to go to school because she was used as a babysitter for her adoptive sister and brothers.

"Some years later, her adoptive mother remarried, and the family moved to Japan. Arriving in Japan as a teen, she was hardly allowed to leave the house and was physically abused by her adoptive mother. At the age of seventeen, her adoptive mother started using her for commercial sex without her consent. Defenseless, she had no choice but to abide because when she refused, she was beaten and mistreated. She did this for six months until a friend of the family noticed, helped her escape, and brought her to Help, where I was working. After this experience, my eyes were opened to the reality of human trafficking and I began to reflect on similar situations that were happening in my own community in the Congo that I did not notice."

Response: We hear your story. We'll work to break your chains.

Break paper chains.

Hagar's Story, Adapted from Genesis 16–21

"Hagar was an Egyptian slave-girl working for a rich man, Abraham, and his wife Sarah. After Sarah was unable to bear children, she gave her servant, Hagar, to Abraham. Abraham raped Hagar, and she conceived a child. After becoming pregnant, Sarah grew jealous, abused Hagar, and threw her out of their home. An angel found Hagar wandering alone and blessed her child, who would be called Ishmael, which means 'God hears.'

"Hagar returned to the house of Abraham. Fourteen years later when Sarah bore a son, she forced Hagar and Ishmael to leave their house once again. Returning to exile, God heard their cry and an angel called to Hagar, saying, 'Do not be afraid,' and reminded Hagar of God's blessing and provided a spring of water. They survived, and Ishmael sired a great nation as God promised. The story of Hagar and Ishmael is the story of thousands of women and children today caught in cycles of trafficking, rape, abuse, and exploitation."

Response: We hear your story. We'll work to break your chains.

Break paper chains.

Kolab's Story, Adapted from Equality Now

https://www.equalitynow.org/campaigns/trafficking-survivor-stories

"Kolab's parents sold her for 1,000 dollars as a baby. Later on, her 'foster parents' sent her to work as a servant in the city. She was raped by her employer and after escaping got trapped by two men and forced into drug dealing and brothel work. When she didn't comply with the man in charge of the brothel, she was tortured. Eventually the police shut down the brothel and she found a program to offer her training as a hairdresser."

Response: We hear your story. We'll work to break your chains.

Break paper chains.

Tina's Story, Adapted from Courtney's House

http://www.courtneyshouse.org/

"Courtney's House in Washington, DC, was founded in 2008 by Tina Frundt. A survivor of domestic sex trafficking herself, Tina is relentless in her fight to protect children from sexual exploitation and the devastation that comes from it. Courtney's House helps underage survivors of sex trafficking to recover and reenter society. They work with survivors and train community members and law enforcement to recognize and help trafficked youth."

Response: We hear your story. We'll work to break your chains.

Break paper chains.

Josephine's Story, Adapted from Sisters of St. Joseph of Orange

http://csjorange.org/wp-content/uploads/2017/12/2018-Human-Trafficking-Calendar-and-Flyer.pdf

"Born in South Sudan in 1869, St. Josephine Bakhita was kidnapped as a child and sold into slavery in Sudan and Italy. She was brutally treated by her captors as she was sold and resold more than a dozen times. She spent such a large period of her most formative years in the slave trade that she did not even remember her own name. Bakhita, Arabic for 'fortunate one,' was the name given to her by her kidnappers. When a court case ruled that slavery had been illegal since even before she was born, Josephine was immediately freed and later became a Canossian Religious Sister in Italy, living and working there for the next forty-five years. In the early 1990s, Pope John Paul II publicly honored her during his visit to Sudan. In 2000, she was declared a saint by the Catholic Church."

Response: We hear your story. We'll work to break your chains.

Break paper chains.

Song

"We Shall Overcome," African American spiritual.

Sing this song as those in the Civil Rights Movement do with right arm on top of left arm, then link hands with the person on either side of you.

*We shall overcome, *(3x)* someday.

Refrain: Oh, deep in my heart, I do believe
We shall overcome, someday.

*We shall break these chains . . . *We shall all be free.

Myths and Truths about Human Trafficking

From Out of the Shadows: Exposing the Myths of Human Trafficking, *https://www.acf.hhs.gov/sites/default/files/otip/trafficking_infographic508.pdf. Used with permission.*

"MYTH: Human trafficking is only sex trafficking."
TRUTH: *Light a candle.* Of the 20.9 million victims of human trafficking globally, 68% are trapped in forced labor, 22% are sexually exploited, and 10% are in state-imposed forced labor.

"MYTH: Human trafficking victims will self identify."
TRUTH: *Light a candle.* While 50% of victims had contact with a health care professional, none were identified as a victim.

"MYTH: Human trafficking is not in my community."
TRUTH: *Light a candle.* Cases of potential human trafficking are reported in all 50 states, Washington, DC, and US territories.

"MYTH: Human trafficking only happens to children."
TRUTH: *Light a candle.* Since 2012, National Hotline Cases reported 62% are adults.

"MYTH: Human trafficking only happens to women."
TRUTH: *Light a candle.* Since 2012, National Hotline Cases reported 18% men.

Song

"We Shall Overcome"

*We shall overcome, *(3x)* someday.

Refrain: Oh, deep in my heart, I do believe
We shall overcome, someday.

*We are not afraid . . . *We shall tell the truth . . .

Reflection | Sharing

Let us take a few moments of quiet to reflect on these questions:

What are your reflections after listening to these stories, myths, and truths? What one action can you take to stop the demand for human trafficking?

After a quiet time, break paper chains and light a candle while you share what is stirring in your heart.

Intercessory Prayers

Please respond: We pray.

For the freedom of the millions of victims trapped in commercial sex, forced labor, and forced marriage worldwide.

Response: We pray.

For children around the world who are violently abducted and forced to be child soldiers.

Response: We pray.

For the end of violence against women and new respect for their human dignity.

Response: We pray.

For the success of the awareness campaign to discourage all people from engaging in or soliciting paid sex.

Response: We pray.

For children who are stolen from their parents and used for the harvesting of organs worldwide.

Response: We pray.

For the young girls forced into prostitution at truck stops and at the Super Bowl.

Response: We pray.

For homeless, runaway youth and foster children who are dangerously targeted by traffickers.

Response: We pray.

For justice to come to those who recruit, obtain, move, or purchase humans, especially children, through the use of fraud, coercion, force, manipulation, or any means of exploitation.

Response: We pray.

For strength, hope, and wholeness for those who have been rescued.

Response: We pray.

For the leaders, lawmakers, activists, and all who work day and night to free the enslaved.

Response: We pray.

For those who have died while enslaved, and the children left behind.

Response: We pray.

For those who are trafficked and remain in bondage.

Response: We pray.

Prayer of Solidarity

Holy Compassion, you who hear the cries of those in anguish,
be with us now to bring them to safety and speak out against those who exploit.
Holy Love, you who shout with us no to human trafficking in all its forms,
be with us now to restore freedom to those who are trafficked and their families.
Holy Justice, you who rage with us against the injustices of trafficking,
be with us now to take action to prevent and end this slavery.
Holy Wisdom, you who know the worth of every human being,
be with us to erase this sinful practice from the face of the Earth.

Blessing Bread

Three blessers speak a sentence of blessing. Each holds the bread and prays:

Blessed are you, God of Compassion, for you promise your people food for the journey, nourishment for the struggle.

Blessed are you, Divine Healer, for you sent your people manna as they wandered in the desert.

Blessed are you, Spirit of Justice, for you give us this day our daily bread, and you keep us hungry for a world without human trafficking.

Let us extend our hands, lifted outward, and bless this bread.

Blessing Fruit of the Vine

Three blessers pray a sentence of blessing. Each holds a glass of wine or juice and prays:

Blessed are you, God of Compassion, for you beg us to drink this fruit of the vine in memory of all who have died for justice.

Blessed are you, Divine Healer, for you call us to remember women's lives, women's blood, those who have been wounded, raped, and killed at the time of trafficking.

Blessed are you, Spirit of Justice, for even though we drink, you keep us thirsty for justice.

Let us extend our hands, lifted outward, and bless this fruit of the vine.

The blessers pass the bread and drink around the circle.

Take Action

Let us put our prayers into action. Here are some possible ways:

- Recognize the Signs of Human Trafficking: https://polarisproject.org/human-trafficking/recognize-signs; http://hagarusa.org/about/hagars-story/.
- Demand slave-free products. Buy fair trade when possible.
- Wear a blue heart in solidarity, or donate to the Blue Heart Campaign against Human Trafficking, which works to raise awareness of the plight of victims and to build political support to fight the criminals behind trafficking: http://www.unodc.org/blueheart/en/-get-involved-donate-now.html.
- Ask your local library to have a display in January on the issue of human trafficking.
- Watch the film *I Am Still Here* by director Mischa Marcus: https://www.imdb.com/title/tt4956376/.
- Watch *Lives for Sale*, a documentary on immigration and trafficking produced by Maryknoll and Lightfoot Films in association with Faith & Values Media, with study guide: www.youtube.com/watch?v=qWoalXlkMWc.

Prayer

By Rose Mary Meyer, BVM, https://www.projectirene.org/human-trafficking-ritual/. Used with permission.

"Let us stand and form a heart with our two hands. Take some deep breaths, breathing in gratitude for those working to end human trafficking, and breathing out hope for the future when human trafficking will no longer be a reality.

"Creator of All, for love, peace, and freedom you formed us and all those caught in the web of human trafficking. We pray that justice, peace, compassion, freedom, and mercy may overflow in our hearts and in our actions. May this be so. Amen."

Song

"There Is More Love Somewhere," African American spiritual sung by Bernice Johnson Reagon, from River of Life: Harmony One *(Rounder Records © 1986), https://www.youtube.com/watch?v=2qbqceIK9nc. Permission requested.*

There is *more love somewhere,
There is *more love somewhere,
I'm gonna keep on 'till I find it,
There is more love somewhere.

Repeat using *more hope . . . *more peace . . . *more joy

Sending Forth

The blue ribbon symbolizes human trafficking awareness. As we go forth, let us show our solidarity and commitment by exchanging blue ribbons with one another.

Learn More from These Resources

Courtney's House is a nonprofit that fearlessly searches for children who are being forced into prostitution, embraces the survivors, brings them into a safe environment, and trains community officials. www.courtneyshouse.org.

Fair Girls (formerly FAIR Fund) prevents the exploitation of girls worldwide with prevention education, compassionate care, and survivor-inclusive advocacy, so girls can become confident, happy, healthy young women. http://www.fairgirls.org.

Global Sisters Report. "Sisters Work against Human Trafficking." https://www.globalsistersreport.org/blog/gsr-today/trafficking/sisters-work-against-human-trafficking-55850.

Human Trafficking Enactment Database. http://www.ncsl.org/research/civil-and-criminal-justice/human-trafficking-enactment-database.aspx.

InterCommunity Peace & Justice Center raises awareness by participating in vigils. Use their toolkit to create your own vigil. https://ipjc.org/human-trafficking/.

National Human Trafficking Hotline: (888) 373-7888.

National Runaway Switchboard: (888) RUN-AWAY.

Polaris Project. https://polarisproject.org/.

STOP APP, the first global app available in multiple languages, combines community empowerment, big data management, and antitrafficking expertise to disrupt and prevent human trafficking. All information shared with the STOP APP is fed directly into the Centre for Intelligence-Led Prevention (CfILP), where it is analyzed alongside global data on human trafficking and modern slavery. This data is used to build intelligence on global trends and hotspots of human trafficking, which enables the global organization STOP THE TRAFFIK to disrupt, prevent, and predict this criminal activity. https://www.stopthetraffik.org.

TraffickCam App enables you to help combat sex trafficking by uploading photos of the hotel rooms you stay in when you travel. Traffickers regularly post photographs of their victims posed in hotel rooms for online advertisements. The purpose of TraffickCam is to create a database of hotel room images that an investigator can efficiently search, in order to find other images that were taken in the same location as an image that is part of an investigation. https://traffickcam.com/.

26. February

Witnessing Womanist Wisdom during Black History Month

Our womanist work is to draw on the rugged endurance of black folks in America who outwit, outmaneuver, and outscheme social systems and structures that maim and stifle mental, emotional, and spiritual growth.

—Katie Geneva Cannon, *Katie's Cannon: Womanism and the Soul of the Black Community*

February is Black History Month. Womanist theologians and ministers are on the forefront of the struggles for liberation. They resist racial, gender, and class discrimination and all forms of social oppression. They challenge others to do the same.

This liturgy invites the gathered to learn, to be nourished, and to be inspired by Womanist Wisdom in order to make this world a place of justice, equality, and peace for all.

Preparation

Put books of womanist authors around the room. Many are listed at the end of this liturgy under "Learn More from These Resources." Gather the books named in this liturgy so readers can pick up the book to do the reading. On a table or center space, place African cloths, candles, purple flowers or bulbs, a bowl of soil, a pitcher of water, a basket of African Amerian soul food, sweet corn bread, and goblets of wine and juice.

Call to Gather

During Black History Month and anticipating Women's History Month, we gather to celebrate and support womanist theologians and ministers who are on the forefront of the struggles for liberation. We lift up their memories, life stories, and contributions as we walk the path of justice together. We join our sisters of African descent in the United States to resist racial, gender, and class discrimination and all forms of social oppression. We come to learn, to be nourished, and to be inspired by Womanist Wisdom in order to make this world a place of justice, equality, and peace for all.

Naming the Circle

Let us share our names, and give a glimpse of what we think of when we hear the words "Witnessing Womanist Wisdom."

The Wisdom of Alice Walker, novelist, poet, activist

Alice Walker defines womanist:

"1. From *womanish* (Opp. of 'girlish,' i.e., frivolous, irresponsible, not serious.) A black feminist or feminist of color. From the black folk expression of mothers to female children, 'You acting womanish,' i.e., like a woman. Usually referring to outrageous, audacious, courageous or *willful* behavior. Wanting to know more and in greater depth than is considered 'good' for one. Interested in grown-up doings. Acting grown up. Being grown up. Interchangeable with another black folk expression: 'You trying to be grown.' Responsible. In charge. *Serious.*

"2. *Also*: A woman who loves other women, sexually and/or nonsexually. Appreciates and prefers women's culture, women's emotional flexibility (values tears as natural counterbalance of laughter), and women's strength. Sometimes loves individual men, sexually and/or nonsexually. Committed to survival and wholeness of entire people, male *and* female. Not a separatist, except periodically, for health. Traditionally universalist, as in: 'Mama, why are we brown, pink, and yellow, and our cousins are white, beige, and black?' Ans.: 'Well, you know the colored race is just like a flower garden, with every color flower represented.' Traditionally capable, as in: 'Mama, I'm walking to Canada and I'm taking you and a bunch of other slaves with me.' Reply: 'It wouldn't be the first time.'

"3. Loves music. Loves dance. Loves the moon. *Loves* the Spirit. Loves love and food and roundness. Loves struggle. *Loves* the Folk. Loves herself. *Regardless.*

"4. Womanist is to feminist as purple is to lavender."

Response: Thank you for your Womanist Wisdom, Alice Walker!

Song

"Ella's Song," by Bernice Johnson Reagon of Sweet Honey in the Rock, from Breaths *(Songtalk Publishing Company © 1983). Permission requested.*

Freedom:

We who believe in *freedom cannot
rest,

We who believe in freedom cannot
rest until it comes.

The Wisdom of Mercy Amba Oduyoye, Ghanaian source of inspiration for womanist theology

From Introducing African Women's Theology *(Sheffield, England: Sheffield Academic Press, 2001), 76.*

"Women's struggle for survival in Africa is not only a struggle to stay alive. It seeks a quality of life that can be truly and fully human not only for themselves but also for men. When women refuse to stay on the margins, they are making a statement concerning their understanding of what it means to be human. The spirituality of resistance therefore enables one to hold on to one's humanity. Resisting anonymity is an expression of the belief that our individual humanity is meant to find expression in community."

Response: Thank you for your Womanist Wisdom, Mercy Oduyoye!

Song
"Ella's Song"

Community:
We who believe in *community cannot rest,
We who believe in community cannot rest until it comes.

The Wisdom of Delores S. Williams, womanist theologian, former professor of theology and culture at Union Theological Seminary, first to use the term "womanist theology" in her 1987 *Christianity and Crisis* article, "Womanist Theology: Black Women's Voices"

From Sisters in the Wilderness: The Challenge of Womanist God Talk *(Maryknoll, NY: Orbis Books, 1993), 238–39.*

"The greatest truth of black women's survival and quality of life struggle is that they have worked without hesitation and with all the energy they could muster. Many of them, like Hagar, have demonstrated great courage as they resisted oppression and as they went into the wide, wide world to make a living for themselves and their children. They depended upon their strength and upon each other. But in the final analysis the message is clear: they trusted the end to God. Every important event in the stories of Hagar and black women turns on this trust."

Response: Thank you for your Womanist Wisdom, Delores Williams!

Song
"Ella's Song"

Trust:
We who believe in *trust cannot rest,
We who believe in trust cannot rest until it comes.

The Wisdom of Katie Geneva Cannon, womanist theologian, founder of the Center for Womanist Leadership, professor of Christian ethics at Union Presbyterian Seminary, first woman of African descent ordained by the United Presbyterian Church in the United States, artist

From Katie's Cannon: Womanism and the Soul of the Black Community *(New York: Continuum Publishing, 1995), 135.*

"The womanist writing consciousness does not obscure or deny the existence of tridimensional oppression but rather through full, sharp awareness of race, sex, and class oppression we present the liberating possibilities that exist. Our womanist work is to draw on the rugged endurance of black folks in America who outwit, outmaneuver, and outscheme social systems and structures that maim and stifle mental, emotional, and spiritual growth. Repeatedly, in light of the stated task, womanist thinkers raise the question of reciprocity in this: How do we bring to the forefront the unity of knower and known?"

Response: Thank for your Womanist Wisdom, Katie Geneva Cannon!

Song
"Ella's Song"

Unity:
We who believe in *unity cannot rest,
We who believe in unity cannot rest until it comes.

The Wisdom of Renita J. Weems, writer, scholar of the Hebrew Bible, ordained African Methodist Episcopal Church minister

"Re-Reading for Liberation: African American Women and the Bible," from Womanist Theological Ethics—A Reader, *edited by Katie Geneva Cannon, Emilie M. Townes, and Angela D. Sims (Louisville, KY: Westminster John Knox Press, 2011), 57.*

"A womanist biblical hermeneutic takes as its starting point the fundamental notion that people have power, not texts. . . . Women have to reclaim their right to read and interpret sacred texts for themselves and should not have to defend or apologize for their interpretations to privileged women in the culture who remain ignorant to how class, race, and colonialism shape and divide us as women."

Response: Thank you for your Womanist Wisdom, Renita Weems!

Song
"Ella's Song"

Power:
We who believe in *power cannot rest,
We who believe in power cannot rest until it comes.

The Wisdom of Emilie M. Townes, dean of Vanderbilt University Divinity School, professor of womanist ethics and society

From https://ir.vanderbilt.edu/bitstream/handle/1803/8226/Townes-Womanist Theology.pdf?sequence=1&isAllowed=y.

"A key feature of womanist theology is its evolving character. From its formal beginning in 1985 with the publication of Katie Geneva Cannon's article, 'The Emergence of Black Feminist Consciousness' (*Katie's Canon*, 47–56), it has developed in the following ways: an orientation to Black women's survival in an oppressive social order that is classist, racist, and sexist; a framework for interpreting and critiquing the role of the Black Church; an interrogation of and critique of the Black Churches' appropriation of scripture in oppressive ways; a model for Black women's organizational strength; a critique of Black social stratification; advocacy for justice-based spirituality; the inclusion of ecological concerns; a concern for health care; a consideration of Black sexuality; and the issue of work. Within this evolving character, womanist theology often melds theological and social scientific analysis with cultural studies, literary studies, political economy and often addresses public policy issues affecting African American communities."

Response: Thank for your Womanist Wisdom, Emilie Townes!

Song
"Ella's Song"

Knowledge:
We who believe in *knowledge cannot rest,
We who believe in knowledge cannot rest until it comes.

The Wisdom of Kelly Brown Douglas, dean of Episcopal Divinity School at Union Theological Seminary in New York City

From Faith in Action Series, *https://sojo.net/articles/faith-action/stories-matter-black-mother-her-son.*

"'You are a sacred child of God. God loves you. There is no one greater than you but God.' This was the first story that I told my son, even when he was too young to respond. I told him the story of his divine connection. It was this divine connection that assured his enslaved forbears they were not created to be chattel. For their African faith taught them two very important things: All that is comes from a great High God, and all that comes from this High God is sacred. Clinging to this faith, they knew that though they were enslaved, they were not slaves and that no matter how the world may treat them, God would always regard them as the sacred beings that they were."

Response: Thank for your Womanist Wisdom, Kelly Brown Douglas!

Song
"Ella's Song"

Faith:
We who believe in *faith cannot rest,
We who believe in faith cannot rest until it comes.

The Wisdom of Cheryl A. Kirk-Duggan, professor of theology and ethics at Shaw University Divinity School, ordained elder in the Christian Methodist Episcopal Church, author, musician

From Refiner's Fire: A Religious Engagement with Violence *(Minneapolis, MN: Fortress Press, 2001), 1.*

"She looked in the mirror:
No immediate image did she see;
The vastness of the horizon
Seemed to mock her: she could not see her reflection
Through the skewed lens of dominant culture
She saw nothing
A sister came along,
With dignity and joy,
And a different way of seeing.
She was mesmerized.
A thing she could not fathom
Was about to cross her path,
And that incomprehensible other
Opened her mouth;
And spoke;
And lovingly said: 'You are somebody.'
She looked in her mirror, again.
And this time she saw
Gazing back at her, a beauteous vision:
Nobility and peace.
The empty objectiveness that was but a shadow
Had been replaced
By her mighty image.
And she heard God say:
'That's good!' "

Response: Thank you for your Womanist Wisdom, Cheryl Kirk-Duggan!

Song
"Ella's Song"

Goodness:
We who believe in *goodness cannot rest,
We who believe in goodness cannot rest until it comes.

The Wisdom of Audre Lorde, writer, poet, activist

From Sister Outsider *(Trumansburg, NY: Crossing Press, 1984), 44.*

"We can learn to work and speak when we are afraid in the same way we have learned to work and speak when we are tired. For we have been socialized to respect fear more than our own needs for language and definition, and while we wait in silence for that final luxury of fearlessness, the weight of that silence will choke us. The fact that we are here and I speak these words is an attempt to break that silence and bridge some of those differences between us, for it is not difference which immobilizes us, but silence. And there are so many silences to be broken."

Response: Thank you for your Womanist Wisdom, Audre Lorde!

Song
"Ella's Song"

Speaking:
We who believe in *speaking cannot rest,
We who believe in speaking cannot rest until it comes.

Reflection | Sharing

Think about what you heard from these womanists. Witnessing Womanist Wisdom . . . Struggling, Resisting, Rising Up . . . Womanist is to feminist as purple is to lavender . . . The spirituality of resistance enables one to hold on to one's humanity . . . They trusted the end to God . . . Our womanist work is to draw on the rugged endurance of black folks in America who outwit, outmaneuver, and outscheme social systems and structures that maim and stifle mental, emotional, and spiritual growth . . . Women have to reclaim their right to read and interpret sacred texts for themselves . . . The evolving character of womanist theology . . . You are a sacred child of God . . . And she heard God say: "That's good!" . . . There are so many silences to be broken.

Let us take a few moments of quiet to reflect on these questions:

What have you learned from these womanists? How can you put it into practice?

After a quiet time, as you share your reflection, plant a flower bulb as a symbol of receiving and learning wisdom from womanists.

Song
"Ella's Song"

Freedom:
We who believe in *freedom cannot rest,
We who believe in freedom cannot rest until it comes.

Blessing Bread and Drink

Let us bless this bread and drink together in memory and in honor of the womanists who witness with wisdom.

One person holds the basket of bread. Another holds the goblets of wine and juice.

Blessed are you, God of Goodness, Spirit of Resistance, Holy Trust,
for giving us this bread and drink as gifts and symbols of Womanist Wisdom.

We bless them with gratitude for Womanist Wisdom,
with gratitude for womanist struggles for survival,
with gratitude for a womanist spirituality of resistance,

with gratitude for womanist reclaiming of sacred texts,
with gratitude for womanists breaking silence,
with gratitude for womanists who bring to the forefront the unity of knower and known.

We bless this bread and drink with gratitude for womanists and Womanist Wisdom.

As we eat this bread and drink this fruit of the vine, let us be thankful for the precious gifts of Womanist Wisdom and for the womanists who witness them.

Take Action

Let us put our prayers into action. Here are some possible ways:

- Read womanist theology, especially that written by the women named here and listed in "Learn More from These Resources."
- Learn about and support the Katie Geneva Cannon Center for Womanist Leadership in Richmond, Virginia, www.centerforwomanistleadership.org.
- Learn about Black Lives Matter, http://www.blacklivesmatterdmv.org/.
- Visit the National Museum of African American History and Culture, https://nmaahc.si.edu/.

Sending Forth

Let us go forth to struggle, resist, and rise up, unafraid, to move mountains together because God says, "That's Good."
Let us go forth to resist racial, gender, and class discrimination and all forms of social oppression.
Let us go forth with gratitude for Womanist Wisdom.

Greeting of Peace

Let us greet one another with peace, saying, "Go in peace and rise up."

Song
"Ella's Song"

Freedom:
We who believe in *freedom cannot rest,
We who believe in freedom cannot rest until it comes.

Learn More from These Resources

Baker-Fletcher, Karen. *Sisters of Dust, Sisters of Spirit: Womanist Wordings on God and Creation*. Minneapolis, MN: Fortress Press, 1998.

Brooten, Bernadette J., and Jacqueline L. Hazelton, eds. *Beyond Slavery: Overcoming Its Religious and Sexual Legacies*. New York: Palgrave Macmillan, 2010.

Byron, Gay L., and Vanessa Lovelace. *Womanist Interpretations of the Bible: Expanding the Discourse*. Atlanta, GA: SBL Press, 2016.

Cannon, Katie Geneva. *Katie's Cannon: Womanism and the Soul of the Black Community*. New York: Continuum Publishing, 1995.

———. *Remembering What We Never Knew: The Epistemology of Womanist Theology*. 2nd ed. Richmond, VA: Center for Womanist Leadership Publishing, 2018.

Copeland, M. Shawn. *Knowing Christ Crucified: The Witness of African American Religious Experience*. Maryknoll, NY: Orbis Books, 2018.

Douglas, Kelly Brown. *The Black Christ*. Maryknoll, NY: Orbis Books, 1994.

———. *Stand Your Ground: Black Bodies and the Justice of God*. Maryknoll, NY: Orbis Books, 2015.

Gilkes, Cheryl Townsend. *If It Wasn't for the Women . . . : Black Women's Experience and Womanist Culture in Church and Community*. Maryknoll, NY: Orbis Books, 2001.

Grant, Jacquelyn. *White Women's Christ and Black Women's Jesus: Feminist Christology and Womanist Response*. Atlanta, GA: Scholars Press, 1989.

Hayes, Diana. *Hagar's Daughters: Womanist Ways of Being in the World*. Mahwah, NJ: Paulist Press, 1995.

Kirk-Dougan, Cheryl. *Exorcizing Evil: A Womanist Perspective on the Spirituals*. Maryknoll, NY: Orbis Books, 1997.

———. *Refiner's Fire: A Religious Engagement with Violence*. Minneapolis, MN: Fortress Press, 2001.

Lorde, Audre. *Sister Outsider*. Trumansburg, NY: Crossing Press, 1984.

Martin, Joan M. *More Than Chains and Toil: A Christian Work Ethic of Enslaved Women*. Louisville, KY: Westminster John Knox Press, 2000.

Mitchem, Stephanie Y. *Introducing Womanist Theology*. Maryknoll, NY: Orbis Books, 2002.

Morris, Catherine, and Rujeko Hockley, et al. *We Wanted a Revolution: Black Radical Women 1965–85; New Perspectives*. Durham, NC: Duke University Press, 2018.

Oduyoye, Mercy Amba. *Introducing African Women's Theology*. Sheffield, England: Sheffield Academic Press, 2001.

Sanders, Cheryl. *Living the Intersection: Womanism and Afrocentrism in Theology*. Minneapolis, MN: Fortress Press, 1995.

Townes, Emilie M. *Breaking the Fine Rain of Death: African American Health Issues and a Womanist Ethic of Care*. Eugene, OR: Wipf & Stock, 2006.

———. *Embracing the Spirit: Womanist Perspectives on Hope, Salvation, and Transformation*. Maryknoll, NY: Orbis Books, 1997.

———. *In a Blaze of Glory: Womanist Spirituality as Social Witness*. Nashville, TN: Abingdon Press, 1995.

———. *A Troubling in My Soul: Womanist Perspectives on Evil and Suffering*. Maryknoll, NY: Orbis Books, 1993.

———. *Womanist Justice, Womanist Hope*. Atlanta, GA: Scholars Press, 1993.

Walker, Alice. *In Search of Our Mothers' Gardens: Womanist Prose*. San Diego, CA: Harcourt Brace Jovanovich Publishers, 1983.

Weems, Renita J. *I Asked for Intimacy: Stories of Blessings, Betrayals, and Birthings*. San Diego, CA: Lura Media, 1993.

———. *Just a Sister Away: A Womanist Vision of Woman's Relationships in the Bible*. San Diego, CA: Lura Media, 1988.

Williams, Delores S. *Sisters in the Wilderness: The Challenge of Womanist God Talk*. Maryknoll, NY: Orbis Books, 1993.

27. March

Celebrate International Women's Day

Praise women of the seven continents
for the inspiration and justice they bring to the world.

March is National Women's History Month. Every year on March 8, people around the world celebrate International Women's Day. This is a time to raise up women. It is a month to speak their names, tell their stories, and thank them for sharing their unique gifts with the world. It is a chance to become those women.

This liturgy invites participants to honor and thank women locally, nationally, and internationally for sharing their unique gifts with the world.

Preparation

Gather a globe; candles; a pitcher of water and a bowl; chimes; flowers; injera, tortillas, and rye bread; a glass each of water, wine, and tea; and news articles of women. Use the colors white, purple, and gold for candles, cloths, flowers, and decor. These colors have been used in suffrage and women's liberation movements across history.

Call to Gather

This International Women's Day we come together to honor women and thank them for sharing their unique gifts with the world. Who comes to your mind and heart as you think about International Women's Day and National Women's History Month? Bring specific women from around the world into your consciousness.

Naming the Circle

We will pass a globe around the circle. When you receive it, speak your name, name a woman you bring here today, and tell us a piece of her story as you locate her on the globe. Let us assume that among us we cover this globe, country by country. Begin with "I am part of a world that includes . . . "

Blessing of Solidarity

In solidarity with women around the world, we bless the four elements that correspond to the cardinal points on the compass: Fire to the South, Air to the East, Earth to the North, and Water to the West.

We unite with you, Sisters of the South, and share Fire. *(Light a candle.)*
We unite with you, Sisters of the East, and share Air. *(Play the chimes.)*
We unite with you, Sisters of the North, and share Earth. *(Place flowers on the table.)*
We unite with you, Sisters of the West, and share Water. *(Pour water into the bowl.)*

Song

"We are a Wheel," words by Hildegard of Bingen, musical round by Betty Wendelborn, from Sing Green: Songs of the Mystics, *2nd ed. (Auckland, New Zealand: Pyramid Press © 1999). Used with permission.*

We are a wheel, a circle of life.
We are a wheel, a circle of power.
We are a wheel, a circle of light,
Circling the world this sacred hour.

Litany of Gratitude

Let us thank women for their unique gifts to the world.

Thank you, Michelle Obama, former First Lady of the United States, for promoting education and working to create a healthier country and world.
Response: We are grateful!
Thank you, Malala Yousafzai, Pakistani activist and youngest Nobel Prize laureate, for defying the Taliban in Pakistan and demanding that girls be allowed to receive an education.
Response: We are grateful!
Thank you, Qiu Jin, China's first feminist executed in 1907, for fighting for the emancipation of women at a time when such movements did not exist in China, for refusing to bind your feet, for leaving your loveless marriage to study in Japan, and for starting your own feminist newspaper, *Chinese Women.*
Response: We are grateful!
Thank you, Claudette Colvin, Rosa Parks, and the brave women who sparked the Civil Rights Movement in the United States, for refusing segregation.
Response: We are grateful!
Thank you, Sadako Sasaki, Japanese *hibakusha*, "bomb-affected person," after Hiroshima, for folding one thousand origami cranes before your death, a symbol of the innocent victims of nuclear warfare.
Response: We are grateful!

Thank you, Sally Ride, American engineer, physicist, and astronaut who became the first American woman and the third women overall in space in 1983, for showing the world, especially young girls, that women can reach for the stars and fly into space.

Response: We are grateful!

Thank you, Rigoberta Menchú Tum, K'iche' political and human rights activist from Guatemala and 1992 Nobel Peace Prize laureate, for dedicating your life to publicizing the rights of Guatemala's indigenous women and ethno-cultural reconciliation.

Response: We are grateful!

Thank you, Chimamanda Ngozi Adichie, Nigerian novelist and author, for giving a definition of feminism for the twenty-first century in your book *We Should All Be Feminists.*

Response: We are grateful!

Thank you, Mary Daly, American feminist philosopher and theologian, for challenging us to move *Beyond God the Father.*

Response: We are grateful!

Thank you, Marie Sklodowska Curie, Polish and naturalized-French physicist and chemist, first women to win a Nobel Prize, and first person and only woman to win twice, for your groundbreaking work in the field of radioactivity and for setting a new bar for women in academic and scientific achievement.

Response: We are grateful!

Thank you, Helen Keller, American author, political activist, and lecturer who was deaf and blind, for campaigning tirelessly on behalf of people who are physically challenged and for women's suffrage, labor rights, socialism, and antimilitarism.

Response: We are grateful!

Thank you, Wangari Maathai, Kenyan ecologist who won the 2004 Nobel Peace Prize, for your contribution to sustainable development, democracy, and peace with women to reverse African deforestation.

Response: We are grateful!

Thank you, mothers, grandmothers, ancestors, and all who have nurtured in every family and country, for shaping generations with your inspiration.

Response: We are grateful!

The list is endless. Who else would you add?

Response: We are grateful!

Song

"Moment of Thanks" by Jan Novotka, from Lovers of Life *(©2008 by Jan Novotka's Music LLC. [ASCAP]. All rights reserved.) Used with permission.*

A silent moment of thanks is what I offer, a moment of thanks,
a silent moment of thanks.

Reflection | Sharing

Let us take a few moments of quiet to reflect on these questions:

What did you hear in the women's stories that inspires you? How do you inspire others?

After a quiet time, share your inspiration.

Blessing Bread

One woman holds injera and prays: We bless this injera in solidarity with our sisters in Africa. From the land of the Nile in Egypt to the land of former apartheid in South Africa, women struggle with famines and wars and unite to work against patriarchal domination.

Women of Africa, we are in solidarity with you.

Another holds tortillas and prays: We bless these tortillas in solidarity with our sisters in Central and South America. From the highlands of Guatemala to the rim of Chile, women struggle against US domination of their lands and unite in demanding democracy and justice of their own governments.

Women of Central and South America, we are in solidarity with you.

Another holds rye bread and prays: We bless this rye bread in solidarity with our sisters in Europe. From the land of the former Berlin Wall to the highlands of Russia, women struggle to exercise their rights and unite to make their voices heard.

Women of Europe, we are in solidarity with you.

Blessing Drink

One holds water and prays: We bless this water in solidarity with our sisters in Australia, New Zealand, and the South Pacific. From the outback to the seaside, women struggle to retain their ancient Aboriginal dreamtime beliefs about creation, and they unite in passing on their cultures, arts, and customs.

Women of Australia, New Zealand, and the South Pacific, we are in solidarity with you.

Another woman holds tea and prays: We bless this tea in solidarity with our sisters in Asia. From the Middle East to Beijing, from Japan to the Philippines, women toil in rice fields, sew in sweatshops, and unite in embracing new realities.

Women of Asia, we are in solidarity with you.

Another woman holds wine and prays: We bless this wine in solidarity with our sisters in North America. From the tip of Mexico to the Arctic Ocean, indigenous women struggle against racism and oppression and unite in calling all to care for Earth.

Women of North America, we are in solidarity with you.

Share Bread and Drink

Praising Women of the Seven Continents

Praise women of the seven continents for inspiration and justice they bring to the world.
Praise to you, Sisters of Asia, for your strong resistance to oppression.
Praise to you, Sisters of Africa, for raising your voices in public squares.
Praise to you, Sisters of Europe, for your leadership in peacekeeping.
Praise to you, Sisters of North America, for confronting inequalities of race and class.
Praise to you, Sisters of South America, for struggles that bring about equality.
Praise to you, Sisters in Antarctica, for your scientific research.
Praise to you, Sisters of Australia, for your steadfast demands for justice.

Take Action

Let us put our prayers into action. Here are some possible ways:

- Place pictures of inspirational women around your home.
- Search for a woman online whom you admire, read her biography, and let it inspire you to shape your own story.
- Write a letter or send an email to a woman who has guided you.
- Take a wise woman out to dinner or cook a festive meal for her.
- Make a collage of the names of women who have sparked in you a passion for justice.
- Speak out to end discrimination, violence, and murders of trans women and, in particular, trans women of color.
- Advocate for women's rights to move forward and not regress on issues such as nondiscrimination, comprehensive immigration reform, reproductive justice, and voting rights.

Sending Forth

Let us go forth and continue to raise up women.
Let us speak their names, tell their stories, and thank them for sharing their unique gifts with the world.
Let us be women and men who inspire others.

Greeting of Peace

Breathe deeply. Take in the energy of the candlelight. Play the chimes. Smell the flowers. Bless yourself with the water. Send peace to women in your family, in your community, in your country, and around the world. Blessings to you on International Women's Day and during Women's History Month!

Song

"Dancing Sophia's Circle" by Colleen Fulmer, from Dancing Sophia's Circle *(© 1994). Used with permission.*

Ring us round, O ancient circle,
Great Mother dancing free,
Beauty, strength and Holy Wisdom,
Blessing you and blessing me.

Learn More from These Resources

International Women's Day: visit https://www.internationalwomensday.com/.
Litany of Gratitude: read the women named in this litany to learn more about them.

28. April

Imagine a Church for Our Daughters and Take Them to Work

Today we call on our Church leaders to work with us to build a Church that strikes down every oppressive practice, teaching, and law that assigns women and girls to a subordinate status.

—Declaration for Our Daughters

Take Our Daughters and Sons to Work Day is a fine time to imagine a church for our daughters! How are we creating a church for them now? Women are calling for gender equality. We cannot imagine a church without women.

In this liturgy we celebrate our daughters and commit to bringing about radical inclusion, justice, and equality without qualification for our daughters and sons.

Preparation

Set a table or center space with a flower and an unlit candle for each participant. Place a candle in the center and light it. Gather your choice of bread and wine/juice, and provide a small glass for each participant to be used during the eucharistic prayer.

Welcome and Naming the Circle

Let us share our names, and say in a word or phrase why we need a church for our daughters. "I am *Name.* We need a church for our daughters because . . ."

Call to Gather

Imagine a church without women—our daughters, granddaughters, nieces, goddaughters, neighbors, friends, and their daughters. The shocking headline for the A Church for Our Daughters campaign warns: "Missing: The Next Generation of Catholic Women."

We gather in solidarity with a coalition of thirty Catholic social justice organizations who petitioned the US Catholic bishops for concrete changes to create A Church for Our Daughters.

We gather to listen to Catholic women calling for gender equality. A former codirector of the Women's Ordination Conference, when pregnant with her daughter, asked, "How can I tell her she can be anything she wants to be when she grows up knowing that encouragement falls short when it comes to our religion?"

Kyrie, Have Mercy

Let us pray together the Kyrie. We pause for a moment to consider those times when we did not acknowledge the inequality of women in the church.

Loving Creator, too often we have been unaware of the impact of our liturgy on women and girls. Heighten our awareness with compassion.
Response: Loving Creator, have mercy on us.
Jesus who welcomed all, too often we have ignored your women disciples, the women you taught and healed. Stretch our hearts to challenge the structures in our church that hold women back.
Response: Jesus who welcomed all, have mercy on us.
Sophia Spirit, too often we are silent in the face of church authority and complicit in church discrimination against women and girls. Infuse us with courage that we might speak out more often and more boldly.
Response: Sophia Spirit, have mercy on us.
Inclusive One, draw us into your radical inclusivity. Help us to speak in your name for equal rights and equal rites of women in the church. Call your church to greater integrity and authenticity. Amen. Blessed be. May it be so.

Song

"Yo Soy Mujer (I Am A Woman)" by MaríaElena Del Valle, from The Best of Struggles: Multicultural Women's Project in Music *(Womancenter at Plainville © 1987). Used with permission.*

Yo soy mujer en busca de igualdad
No aguantare ni abuso ni maldad
Yo soy mujer y tengo dignidad
y pronto la justicia sera una realidad.

I am a woman in search of equality
I will not stand for any abuse or malice
I am a woman and I have dignity
and soon justice will become a reality!

Por eso hoy yo vengo hasta aquí
Buscando en mi la fe que tengo en ti
Con esta fe podemos caminar
En lucha de justicia legará la libertad

That's why I've come here today
Looking for faith in me that I have in you
In the struggle for justice
liberty will become a reality

Toda mujer que quiera compartir
Alza los brazos y grita que SI! (QUE SI!)
"Somos la vida, la fuerza, la mujer"
En marcha de justicia empezamos a florecer

All women who wish to take part
Raise your arms and shout, O YES (O YES)
We are the life, the strength, the women
In the march for justice we begin to flourish.

I Confess

We, women of this circle and daughters of the church, want to speak truths about our authenticity, not for penance, but for sharing our realities with the greater Catholic community. We recognize that this confession is a transgressive act as we confess to each other rather than to a male figure of authority. We invite the circle now to confess our doubts, questions, and struggles with our faith.

The circle is open for confessions.

As we confess our insecurities, fears, hopes, and experiences in our faith communities, let us imagine a future church that builds on these confessions to create an environment that serves all its members. Catholic feminist theologians and codirectors of the Women's Alliance for Theology, Ethics, and Ritual (WATER) say, "Inclusive, justice-seeking communities are what our children are growing up to expect. We do well to take our cues from them and settle for nothing less."

Let us imagine this inclusive and affirming space.

Reading

"Declaration for Our Daughters," a petition sponsored by thirty Catholic social justice communities: http://achurchforourdaughters.org/declaration.

"Today, we call on our Church leaders to work with us to build a Church that strikes down every oppressive practice, teaching, and law that assigns women and girls to a subordinate status. We call on our leaders to create a Church that is truly inclusive and alive with the gifts, spirit, and potential of all its members."

Song

"Spirit of Our Daughters," adapted from "Spirit of Our Elders" by Kathy Sherman, CSJ, from Song of the Universe *(Ministry of the Arts © 2015). Used with permission.*

Spirit of our daughters, dance, oh dance in us
Spirit of our daughters, dance, oh dance in us

"A Church for our daughters is a community that . . .

recognizes that all people are created in God's image and equally endowed with the gifts of the Holy Spirit for the common good.

honors the vocations and ministries of all its members, fostering and welcoming all called to priesthood, diaconate, and liturgical leadership.

opens its sacred sacraments to all, as nourishment and ritual without limitations based on gender or sexuality."

Song

"Spirit of Our Daughters"

Spirit of our daughters, dance, oh dance in us
Spirit of our daughters, dance, oh dance in us

"A Church for our daughters is a community that . . .

celebrates the witness and contributions of our foremothers in faith—those in Scripture, those in our tradition, and those who walk with us today.

affirms the spirit of the divine presence in the gifts, needs, and dreams of all God's people.

celebrates and promotes a spirituality that recognizes an inclusive God, beyond gender, and incorporates language that is inclusive and representative of God's feminine, masculine, and non-gendered attributes in liturgy, doctrine, and pastoral practice.

honors women's moral agency to make decisions that impact their health and family life."

Song
"Spirit of Our Daughters"

Spirit of our daughters, dance, oh dance in us
Spirit of our daughters, dance, oh dance in us

"A Church for our daughters is a community that . . .

takes a firm and proactive stand opposing all forms of exploitation and violence perpetrated against women.

advocates for social structures that support and sustain the basic needs of women including access to clean water, clean air, adequate housing, food, security, education, the workforce, political and social engagement, and freedom of movement.

advocates for education for all our children, but especially for our daughters around the world who face daily acts of discrimination and violence in their quest for knowledge."

Song
"Spirit of Our Daughters"

Spirit of our daughters, dance, oh dance in us
Spirit of our daughters, dance, oh dance in us

"A Church for our daughters is a community that . . .

works to dismantle oppressive structures and customs that disproportionately impact women creating inequality in pay, employment opportunities, development of public policy, and property ownership.

works to eradicate destructive forces that triply oppress women of color such as racism, religious intolerance, and unequal access to social goods.

honors and justly compensates the contributions of women working in the Church including equal pay, equal access to job opportunities, healthcare, and paid family leave.

commits to reflect on its own participation in the oppression of women; to repent for unjust acts, systems, and teaching; and to renew structures of leadership to be more inclusive of the People of God at every level."

Song
"Spirit of Our Daughters"

Spirit of our daughters, dance, oh dance in us
Spirit of our daughters, dance, oh dance in us

"We pray together as a family of the faithful with the vision of a Church community that at its core upholds the full equality of all of its members. So that our daughters and yours may know radical inclusion and justice, equality without qualification, and an institution that transforms oppression into love without bounds, let us build a Church for our daughters."

Reflection | Sharing

Think about what you heard in this reading:

What women of faith are important to you? What do you hear them saying about creating a church for our daughters? What do you want to say to church leaders?

After a quiet time, light a candle and share your words of wisdom with this community.

Prayers of the Daughters

Let us pray for the next generation of women and girls.

What do we pray? Our response is: God of love and justice, hear our prayer.

Eucharistic Prayer Honoring Women Who Break Bread and Do Justice

Six people proclaim the eucharistic prayer, each reading a verse:

First blesser: Praise to you, God of our Ancestors, Source of Life,
for you created our daughters, granddaughters, nieces, goddaughters, neighbors, friends, and their daughters in your image and likeness,
the image of love, power, and beauty.

Sung Acclamation
"Come, Come to the Banquet" by the Collegeville Composers Group, Psallite, *(Collegeville, MN: Liturgical Press © 2006).*

Come, come to the banquet: all that I have is yours.
Come, come to the banquet: all that I have is yours.

Second blesser: Praise to you, God of Sarah, Hagar, Rebecca, Rachel, and Leah,
for you promised that all families of Earth would be
blessed through a covenant with our foremothers.

Sung Acclamation
Come, come to the banquet: all that I have is yours.
Come, come to the banquet: all that I have is yours.

Third blesser: Praise to you, God of Mary, Mother of Miriam's Child and Sophia's Prophet,
for you partnered with her in bringing Jesus to birth.

Sung Acclamation
Come, come to the banquet: all that I have is yours.
Come, come to the banquet: all that I have is yours.

Fourth blesser: Praise to you, Divine Wisdom, Sophia Spirit, Companion on the Journey,
for you have built yourself a house, and prepared a rich banquet for us.

Sung Acclamation
Come, come to the banquet: all that I have is yours.
Come, come to the banquet: all that I have is yours.

All pray in unison, extending hands toward the bread, wine, and juice: Praise to you, Divine Wisdom, Sophia Spirit,
for you gave us Jesus, who gathered the community for a meal,
took bread and fruit of the vine, gave you thanks, and gave them to the community, saying:
"Take this, all of you, and eat and drink. This is my body, which is for you.
Do this to remember me."

Sung Acclamation
Come, come to the banquet: all that I have is yours.
Come, come to the banquet: all that I have is yours.

Fifth blesser: Praise to you, God of Thecla, Phoebe, Junia, Prisca,
for you raise up strong women house-church leaders to transform your church.

Sung Acclamation
Come, come to the banquet: all that I have is yours.
Come, come to the banquet: all that I have is yours.

Sixth blesser: Praise to you, Divine Wisdom, Sophia Spirit of Justice and Healing,
for you pour out your Spirit on this bread, wine, juice, and on us gathered here.
You call us to heal a fragmented church and world, to mend broken hearts,
and to feed hungry souls.

Sung Acclamation
Come, come to the banquet: all that I have is yours.
Come, come to the banquet: all that I have is yours.

All: Praise to you Divine Spirit, Justice Seeker, Sophia Wisdom,
for you pour out your Spirit on this Eucharist and on us gathered here.
Bring the new creation: the breaking of bread, the doing of justice, the healing of creation.

Sung Acclamation
Come, come to the banquet: all that I have is yours.
Come, come to the banquet: all that I have is yours.

Blessers pass bread and drink around the group.

Take Action

Let us put our prayers into action. Here are some possible ways:

- Teach your daughter or a young girl a prayer that is important to you, and pray it with her.
- Begin each day by lighting a candle and praying: "Inclusive One, draw us into your radical inclusivity. Help us to speak in your name for equal rights and equal rites of women in the church. Call your church to greater integrity and authenticity. Amen."
- Donate to a woman's group.
- Write a letter to the editor of your religious newspaper.

Sending Forth

In solidarity with our daughters, let us go forth from this circle
to spark courage and hope in those who need healing,
to speak truth to church leaders and government officials,
to tend the bold flames of justice and peace for all.
Let us share the light!

Song

"Sister, Carry On" by Carolyn McDade, from Sister, Carry On *(© 1992 Carolyn McDade). Used with permission.*

Sister, carry on
Sister, carry on
It may be rocky and it may be rough,
But sister, carry on.

Sister, don't lose the dream
Sister, don't lose the dream
Don't sell out for no short time gain
Sister, don't lose the dream

Sister, don't settle too soon
Sister, don't settle too soon
'Til everybody's got their rights
Sister, don't settle too soon

Sister, we share the way
Sister, we share the way
Heart to heart and hand to hand
Sister, we share the way

Stand in solidarity
Stand in solidarity
Together we bring a brand new day
Stand in solidarity

Sister, carry on
Sister, carry on
It may be rocky and it may be rough
But sister, carry on.

Learn More from These Resources

Aquino, María Pilar. *Our Cry for Life: Feminist Theology from Latin America.* Maryknoll, NY: Orbis Books, 1993.

Aquino, María Pilar, and María José Rosado-Nunes, eds. *Feminist Intercultural Theology: Latina Explorations for a Just World.* Maryknoll, NY: Orbis Books, 2007.

Clausen, Janet, and Marilyn Kielbasa, eds. *Listen for a Whisper: Prayers, Poems, and Reflections by Girls.* Winona, MN: Saint Mary's Press, 2001.

Duriga, Joyce. *Helen Prejean: Death Row's Nun.* Collegeville, MN: Liturgical Press, 2017.

Dwyer, Maureen, ed. *New Woman, New Church, New Priestly Ministry: Proceedings of the Second Conference on the Ordination of Roman Catholic Women.* Rochester, NY: Kirkwood Press, 1980.

Farley, Margaret A. *Just Love: A Framework for Christian Sexual Ethics.* New York: Continuum, 2008.

Fiedler, Maureen E., ed. *Breaking Through the Stained Glass Ceiling: Women Religious Leaders in Their Own Words.* New York: Seabury Books, 2010.

Gebara, Ivone. *Out of the Depths: Women's Experience of Evil and Salvation.* Minneapolis, MN: Fortress Press, 2002.

McGuiness, Margaret M. *Called to Serve: A History of Nuns in America.* New York: NYU Press, 2013.

Ms. Foundation for Women and Sondra Forsyth. *Girls Seen and Heard: 52 Life Lessons for Our Daughters.* New York: Tarcher/Putnam Books, 1998.

Pui-lan, Kwok, ed. *Hope Abundant: Third World and Indigenous Women's Theology.* Maryknoll, NY: Orbis Books, 2010.

Pui-lan, Kwok. *Introducing Asian Feminist Theology: Introductions in Feminist Theology.* Cleveland, OH: The Pilgrim Press, 2000.

———. *Postcolonial Imagination and Feminist Theology.* Louisville, KY: Westminster John Knox Press, 2005.

Russaw, Kimberly D. *Daughters in the Hebrew Bible.* Lanham, MD: Fortress Press, 2018.

Steinkuhler, Martina. *Prayers for Young Children.* Grand Rapids, MI: Eerdmans, 2018.

Wexler, Celia Viggo. *Catholic Women Confront Their Church: Stories of Hurt and Hope.* Lanham, MD: Rowman and Littlefield Publishing, 2016.

29. May

Remembering and Letting Go on Mother's Day

In search of my mother's garden, I found my own.

—Alice Walker, *In Search of Our Mothers' Gardens*

The second Sunday of May marks Mother's Day in the United States. Celebrations of mothers can be traced to ancient Greeks and Romans who held festivals to honor mother goddesses Rhea and Cybele. The modern precedent is the early Christian festival of "Mothering Sunday." Having a mother, "other mother," or woman role model is an experience common to people of all classes, races, cultures, and nationalities. We each need to take time to integrate this relationship in our lives.

This liturgy remembers the mothers in our lives—mothers, grandmothers, aunts, godmothers, other mothers, women role models, and mother-friends. It offers an opportunity to reflect on what we have received from our mothers and what we give back in return.

Preparation

Set a table or center space with two candles, matches, a small bowl of salt, a bowl of water, and a quilt, blanket, or shawl.

Call to Gather

Mother's Day, and the season around it, is a time to remember the mothers in our lives—mothers, grandmothers, ancestors, aunts, godmothers, women role models, and mother-friends.

This time can bring a mix of emotions: love, pain, grief after losing a mother, expectation, anticipation about becoming a mom, joy from a shared experience, sadness about unresolved hurts, disappointment, fulfillment, and so much more. It offers an opportunity to connect about joys, hurts, struggles, mislaid dreams, and good times. Our mothers most likely have more influence on us than anyone else, and we are marked by this relationship for better or worse.

Mother's Day is the result of more than one hundred years of women's activism that coincided with women's suffrage and labor movements around the turn of the twentieth century. These efforts of calling women to political resistance and pacifism form the foundation of our commitment to ensure respect and safety for women and girls worldwide. This Mother's Day season we are called to active resistance once again. As Hillary Rodham Clinton said, bringing the audience to their feet at the Gloria Awards in 2018, "Resist, insist, persist, and enlist. That is what we will do."

Candle Lighting

We light two candles: one candle for daughters and the other for mothers.

Naming the Circle

Let us think about what it means to be in relationship to the mothers of our families. Recall the female lineage in your family.

Let us pass a lighted candle. When you receive it, say your name, where you were born, and share the names of your female lineage as you acknowledge yourself as their descendants. *For example, I am Diann Lynn, mother of Catherine Fei Min, daughter of Mary Kathryn, granddaughter of Catherine Anna and Emma Marie, great-granddaughter of Anna, aunt of. . . .*

Continue the naming until the circle is complete.

Mothers in our families, you have named us and have given us life,
be here with us.
Response: Our time is now.

Song

"Womanriver Flowing On" by Carole Etzler Eagelheart, from Womanriver Flowing On *(Atlanta, GA: Sisters Unlimited © 1978). Used with permission.*

Chorus:
Womanriver flowing on
Womanriver flowing on and on *(2x)*
Womanriver flowing on.

Womanriver, how you comfort me,
Flowing on through every century,
Flowing on to what is yet to be,
Womanriver flowing on. *Chorus.*

Listen to a Mother's Day Proclamation

Julia Ward Howe, Boston 1870 from Reminiscences, *1819–1899*

"Arise, then, women of this day! Arise all women who have hearts, whether our baptism be that of water or of tears!

Say firmly: 'We will not have great questions decided by irrelevant agencies. Our husbands shall not come to us, reeking with carnage, for caresses and applause. Our sons shall not be taken from us to unlearn all that we have been able to teach them of charity, mercy and patience. . . .'

From the bosom of a devastated Earth a voice goes up with our own. It says: 'Disarm! Disarm! The sword of murder is not the balance of justice.' Blood does not wipe out dishonor, nor violence indicate possession."

Women of the world, "resist, insist, persist, and enlist," be here with us.
Response: Our time is now.

Listen to Mothers Speak

"I want them to see a mother who loves them dearly, who invests in them, but who also invests in herself. It's just as much about letting them know as young women that it is okay to put yourself a little higher on your priority list."
—Michelle Obama, *Prevention*, January 31, 2012

"Biology is the least of what makes someone a mother."
—Oprah Winfrey, *Woman's Day*, 1988

"Acceptance, tolerance, bravery, compassion. These are the things my mom taught me."
—Lady Gaga, speech at Glamour 2013 Women of the Year Awards

"My mother told me two things constantly. One was to be a lady, and the other was to be independent."
—Ruth Bader Ginsburg, "Tribute: The Legacy of Ruth Bader Ginsburg and WRP Staff," ACLU, https://www.aclu.org/other/tribute-legacy-ruth-bader-ginsburg-and-wrp-staff?redirect=womens-rights/tribute-legacy-ruth-bader-ginsburg-and-wrp-staff

"I cannot forget my mother. Though not as sturdy as others, she is my bridge. When I needed to get across, she steadied herself long enough for me to run across safely."
—Renita Weems, "Hush, Mama's Gotta Go Bye-Bye," in Patricia Bell-Scott et. al., eds., *Double Stitch: Black Women Write about Mothers and Daughters* (Boston, MA: Beacon Press, 1991)

"To describe my mother would be to write about a hurricane in its perfect power."
—Maya Angelou, *I Know Why the Caged Bird Sings* (New York: Random House Publishing Group, 1970)

"In search of my mother's garden, I found my own."
—Alice Walker, *In Search of Our Mothers' Gardens* (New York: Harcourt Brace Jovanovich, 1983)

Mothers who guide us, be here with us.
Response: Our time is now.

Reflection | Sharing

Think about what you heard in these quotes.

What have you learned from the mothers in your life? How will you pass on this learning?

After a quiet time, share your thoughts and feelings with this community.

Renouncing Mother's Legacy

Some aspects of our mothers we need to renounce. We have shed many tears over them. Salt purifies, cleanses, and neutralizes. It is said to repel certain spirits. Put salt into the water as you name aloud something that you want to renounce. This is an opportunity to let go, to give to the water something you don't need anymore.

Let us pour this salt water, which symbolizes our tears shed because of our mothers, onto this aloe plant. Aloe is treasured for its healing properties, and this plant, unlike many others, can drink salt water. *One woman pours the salt water onto the aloe plant.*

Song

"Womanriver Flowing On"

Womanriver flowing on.
Womanriver flowing on and on *(2x)*
Womanriver flowing on.

Reclaiming Mother's Legacy

Some spirits of our mothers we want to reclaim. This quilt *(or blanket, shawl)* represents roots and wings, comfort and healing. I have covered myself with it many times. Come, wrap yourself in this quilt and tell whatever family story you want to share, or just sit silently in the quilt. *Sharing. When the sharing ceases, continue by saying:*

Let us each hold onto the quilt *(blanket, shawl)* as we sing a lullaby.

Song

"Lullaby" by Cris Williamson, from Live Dream *(Bird Ankles Music © 1977), https://www.youtube.com/watch?v=kAxFbzKGSzg. Used with permission.*

Like a ship in the harbor, like a mother and child,
like a light in the darkness, I'll hold you a while.
We'll rock on the water. I'll cradle you deep
and hold you while angels sing you to sleep.

Take Action

Let us put our prayers into action this month. Here are some possible ways:

- Do something special for the mother(s) in your life: make a card, send an email, make breakfast, thank her.
- Put flowers in a room she uses often: bedroom, office, living room, kitchen.
- Take a walk with your mom and connect with the universe together. Look at stars, moon, sun, and give thanks.
- Cook a beautiful, healthy meal together. Use one of your mother's favorite recipes. Set a thoughtful table with tablecloth and candlelight and enjoy the time together.
- Lobby your senator and congressperson to give women equal pay, quality childcare, a living wage, affordable health care including reproductive services, paid sick and family leave, and flexible work schedules.
- Give a gift to a charity in the name of the "mothers" in your life.

Sending Forth

Let us go forth with a blessing for mothers.

Blessed be mothers and caregivers everywhere.

Blessed be women who give birth, women who adopt, women who care for children, women who love with an open heart.

Blessed be women who cannot give birth and women who choose not to be mothers.

Blessed be societies that offer health-care services and economic support to all mothers and children.

Blessed be those who create all kinds of loving families.

Blessed be mothers and caregivers. Now and forever, wherever we are. May it be so.

Song

"Womanriver Flowing On"

Womanriver flowing on
Womanriver flowing on and on *(2x)*
Womanriver flowing on.

Womanriver, how you comfort me,
Flowing on through every century,
Flowing on to what is yet to be,
Womanriver flowing on. *Chorus.*

Greeting of Peace

Let us open our circle by blessing one another with peace.

Learn More from These Resources

Cowen, Lauren, and Jayne Wexler. *Daughters and Mothers.* Philadelphia, PA: Courage Books, 1997.

Davey, Moyra, ed. *Mother Reader: Essential Writings on Motherhood.* New York: Seven Stories Press, 2001.

Hayes, Diana L. *Standing in the Shoes My Mother Made: A Womanist Spirituality.* Minneapolis, MN: Fortress, 2011.

Nugent, Patricia A., ed. *Before They Were Our Mothers: Voices of Women Born Before Rosie Started Riveting.* Saratoga Springs, NY: Journal Arts Press, 2017.

Rupp, Joyce. *Fly While You Still Have Wings: And Other Lessons My Resilient Mother Taught Me.* Norte Dame, IN: Sorin Books, 2015.

Van den Abeele, Véronique. *Still My Grandma.* Grand Rapids, MI: Eerdmans Books for Young Readers, 2006.

Walker, Alice. *In Search of Our Mothers' Gardens.* New York: Harcourt Brace Jovanovich, 1983.

30. June

Grateful, Proud, and Connected for Pride and Equality Day

Gracious and Loving God of Many Names,
we praise you for creating LGBTQIA+ people.

June is Pride and Equality Month, and most major cities in the United States and throughout the world celebrate Pride Day. LGBTQIA+ people have a powerful impact on local, national, and international history.

This liturgy celebrates the rights and achievements of same-sex-loving people. LGBTQIA+ communities are working on and bringing together many struggles for justice—especially for immigrants' rights; against racism, sexism, and classism; in support of Muslims; to protect the environment; and many more.

Preparation

Gather rainbow flags, ribbons or yarns of many colors, rainbow bread, wine and juice, and put them on a table or center space covered with a rainbow cloth.

Call to Gather

Welcome to our Pride and Equality Day Liturgy: Grateful, Proud, and Connected! This day and this month we recognize the impact that lesbian, gay, bisexual, transgender, queer, intersex, asexual people, and allies have on local, national, and international history. Remember the White House, along with many other prominent buildings and monuments, lit up in rainbow colors in 2015 to celebrate marriage equality!

We gather not simply to celebrate the rights and achievements of same-sex-loving people and especially not to capitulate to corporate interests that simply see our rights as a way to expand their markets.

We gather to rejoice that LGBTQIA+ people and allies are working on and bringing together many struggles for justice—especially for immigrants' rights, against racism, in support of Muslims, to protect the environment, and many more. While we will focus tonight on the same-sex-love aspect this day honors, it is also important to be grateful, proud, and connected.

Naming the Circle

Let us share our names and mention in a word or phrase one way we have been changed by an LGBTQIA+ person.

Song

"Singing for Our Lives" by Holly Near, Singer in the Storm *(Oakland, CA: Hereford Music © 1990), https://www.youtube.com/watch?v=johabhyURIw. Used with permission.*

We are justice-seeking people, and we
are singing, singing for our lives.
(2x)

We are a land of many colors . . .
We are queer and straight together . . .
We are a peaceful, loving people . . .

Litany of Pride

Let us name LGBTQIA+ people who have been working for change.
Our response: Proudly, we claim you.

We celebrate Sappho, poet from the Isle of Lesbos, whose words inspire us.
All: Proudly, we claim you.
We celebrate Ruth and Naomi in Scripture whose love models women's commitment to one another.
All: Proudly, we claim you.
We celebrate Gertrude Stein, author and poet, whose writings have influenced generations.
All: Proudly, we claim you.
We celebrate Audre Lorde, womanist poet, who challenges us to expand justice struggles.
All: Proudly, we claim you.
We celebrate Del Martin, Phyllis Lyon, and Edie Windsor, who started the ball rolling for marriage equality.
All: Proudly, we claim you.
We celebrate Janelle Monáe, musical recording artist, who redefines gender roles.
All: Proudly, we claim you.
We celebrate Kimberlé Williams Crenshaw, civil rights advocate, who coined the term "intersectionality."
All: Proudly, we claim you.
What other LGBTQIA+ people do we celebrate? Let us speak their names out loud.
All: Proudly, we claim you.
We celebrate all LGBTQIA+ sisters, brothers, friends, and allies, named and unnamed, known and unknown, who put their lives on the line for justice.
All: Proudly, we claim you.

Song
"Singing for Our Lives"

We are justice-seeking people, and we are singing, singing for our lives. *(2x)*

Calls for Solidarity

Listen to LGBTQIA+ people who call for our solidarity. Think of the ones you know.

Four different people speak.

I am your friend. For a very long time I have been reaching out to you, listening to your dreams, talking with you about my life. I have been your good friend since high school. I pick up your kids at school on Wednesdays. I visit your mother in the nursing home. I run with you through our neighborhood on Thursday evenings. I am right here with you.
Response: You are not alone. We are with you too.

I am your co-worker. I work next to you in so many places. I am the doctor who comforted your dying mother. I teach your children. I am your therapist. I am your waitress and bus driver. I am your pastor, rabbi, cardinal, priest, imam, spiritual guide. I am right here with you.
Response: You are not alone. We are with you too.

I am your colleague. I stand beside you in so many places. I am the campus minister who marched next to you as we advocated for LGBTQIA+ rights and marriage equality. I am the nun by your side at the women's shelter where you volunteer. I am the social worker who supports your sister at the mental health center. I am the immigrant worker who meets you at the food pantry. I am right here with you.
Response: You are not alone. We are with you too.

I am your family member. I am your neighbor. As you support my coming out, you give me courage. As you support LGBTQIA+ people and interconnected issues, you give me strength to say I am right here with you.
Response: You are not alone. We are with you too.

Song

"I Am with You" by Kathy Sherman, CSJ, from Always with You *(Ministry of the Arts © 1992). Used with permission.*

I am with you on the journey, and I will never leave you.

I am with you on the journey, always with you.

The Beatitudes of Dignity

DignityUSA © 2003. Used with permission.

Two people pray alternately.

"Blessed are you, gay, lesbian, bisexual, queer, transgender, straight sister or brother, friend, ally—you are a unique and glorious reflection of God's astounding creativity and love!

"Blessed are you when you dare to bring the truth of who you are into loving relationship with others—you heal and strengthen the body of Christ!

"Blessed are you who challenge stereotypes and caricatures—you bring light to the world!

"Blessed are you who speak out against religious hypocrisy—you help to birth justice and peace!

"Blessed are you when you work for full equality and inclusion—you honor the sacredness of all people!

"Blessed are you when you create new kinds of families, families formed by love rather than by law—you live the truth that all God's people are one family!

"Blessed are you who seek to worship in spirit and in truth, whose prayer arises from humble hearts—the Spirit of Holiness will inspire and guide you!

"Blessed are you who offer comfort to the dying, healing to the sick, food to the hungry, housing to the homeless, presence to the lonely, hope to the hopeless—you are the Gospel, the Good News our aching world so desperately needs to know!

"Blessed are you, reviled and persecuted, yet persistent in faith, hope and love! Rejoice and be proud, for in you God's love is revealed!"

Reflection | Sharing

Think about what you heard in this litany, stories, and Beatitudes:
What are you thinking and feeling this Pride Month?
After a quiet time, let us share our words of wisdom with this community.

Prayer of Gratitude

Gracious and Loving God of Many Names, we thank you for creating LGBTQIA+ people and our friends. Our response is: Gratitude!

For creating all people with dignity and worth,
All: Gratitude!
For honoring the many ways people live and love,
All: Gratitude!

For living with authenticity and integrity,
All: Gratitude!
For working to overcome cruelty and bullying toward LGBTQIA+ children and teens in schools and communities,
All: Gratitude!
For building a world where all people are celebrated and loved,
All: Gratitude!
For celebrating sexual and gender diversity as a blessing that enriches all,
All: Gratitude!
For supporting people as they come out of their closets and into the full life of religious groups, society, families, and the military,
All: Gratitude!
For helping us break through the heterosexism, homophobia, and transphobia in ourselves, our families and friends, our communities and cultures,
All: Gratitude!
For embracing us with your love and care,
All: Gratitude!
For inspiring us with dreams and holy impatience,
All: Gratitude!
For challenging us to believe out loud,
All: Gratitude!

Gracious and Loving God of Many Names, thank you for creating LGBTQIA+ people and our friends. Holy Creator, breathe new energies of kindness and love into the world. Wondrous Wisdom, renew our commitment to work for justice for all.

Eucharistic Prayer

Pick up the bread, wine, and juice. Let us extend our hands toward the bread and drink and bless them together.

Blessed are you, Divine Love, for giving us this bread and drink,
this Pride Eucharist.
As we take, bless, eat, and drink, may we manifest divine love in the world.

Let us eat and drink in solidarity with the LGBTQIA+ community.

Take Action

Let us put our prayers into action and act with pride. Here are some possible ways to act in solidarity.

- Participate in Pride events.
- Wear a rainbow ribbon in solidarity with the LGBTQIA+ community.
- Remember a friend or colleague who has died from a hate crime or HIV/AIDS.

- Advocate to end discrimination against LGBTQIA+ people everywhere, particularly in the workplace, by calling on your legislators to pass the Employment Non-Discrimination Act (ENDA).
- Promote safe places for transgender and gender-nonconforming individuals. Start by working for safe bathrooms, https://ohr.dc.gov/page/safe-bathrooms-dc.
- Donate to a group that works toward LGBTQIA+ equality.
- Give your religious leader a book that will enrich her/his/their understanding of diversity.
- Vote.

Sending Forth

Let us go forth to act with pride.
May we be grateful, proud, and connected.
May we not rest until all stones of injustice have been rolled away.
May we believe out loud!

Song

"Believe Out Loud" by David Lohman, from Fling the Church Doors Open Wide *(David Lohman Music © 2010), https://www.youtube.com/watch?v=VQq0FIOukaA. Used with permission.*

Refrain:
It's time to believe out loud—no more staying silent!
It's time to proclaim aloud the faith that we hold dear.
It's time to reach out to the rejected. It's time to stand up and say, "No more!"
It's time to declare a Word of Welcome, bring everyone through the opened doors.
It's time to believe out loud, it's time to be strong and proud.
It's time to believe, believe out loud.

Our God remains unchanging, yet in so many ways
the Holy One's still speaking, for this we offer praise.
Yet God's all-loving guidance too often goes unheard.
But there is yet more wisdom to break forth from God's Word! *Refrain.*

If thoughts like love and justice are more than hollow words,
we'll listen for the Spirit and let our hearts be stirred.
We'll learn to think in new ways, the doors we'll open wide.
The table's set and ready, bring everyone inside! *Refrain.*

The love of God is boundless, we're never turned away.
And out of this abundance, this gift we must repay.
We've got to stand with millions who've heard the Spirit's call,
and shout it from the mountains: "God's love is meant for ALL!" *Refrain.*

Learn More from These Resources

Berry, Selisse. *Out and Equal at Work: From Closet to Corner Office.* 20th ann. ed. San Francisco, CA: Out & Equal Workplace Advocates, 2016.

Patterson, Gillian, and Callie Long. *Dignity, Freedom, and Grace: Christian Perspectives on HIV, AIDS, and Human Rights.* Geneva, Switzerland: World Council of Churches, 2016.

Rosenberg, Rosalind. *Jane Crow: The Life of Pauli Murray.* New York: Oxford University Press, 2017.

Sanders, Cody J. *A Brief Guide to Ministry with LGBTQIA Youth.* Louisville, KY: Westminster John Knox Press, 2017.

Townsley, Gillian. *The Straight Mind in Corinth: Queer Readings Across 1 Corinthians 11:2-16.* Atlanta, GA: SBL Press, 2017.

Wilson, Nancy. *I Love to Tell the Story: 100+ Stories of Justice, Inclusion, and Hope.* Parker, CO: Books To Believe In, 2016.

31. July

The Saving Grace of Fun

Rejoice in our God always, and again I say Rejoice!
Rejoice! Rejoice! And again I say Rejoice!

Each season gives opportunities for vacation, relaxation, fun, leisure, recreation, and renewal. It is a saving grace. It is an extended Sabbath time. It offers time to slow down, enjoy leisure time, and bask in the saving grace of fun.

This liturgy celebrates fun as an integral part of salvation, a human right that foreshadows the pleasure of eternal life. Celebrate it on vacation, or to remember leisure time.

Preparation

Create a beach scene in the room. Place a cloth that looks like water on a table or center space. Put a large bowl of water on it. Surround the water with sand, seashells, coral, rocks, and driftwood. Put photos of a beach at sunrise and sunset around the space.

Call to Gather

Welcome to this liturgy, "The Saving Grace of Fun." Every season offers a grace-filled time for vacations, play, and fun, even in cities where work never seems to stop. Some of us are used to discussing justice issues, working for social change, even practicing spirituality. But religion also has to do with pleasure, enjoyment, plain fun. These are marks of salvation just as surely as are good works and struggles.

Most of us, understandably, have done so much work, shouldered so many responsibilities just trying to survive that play is usually low on the list of things we do. Today let us invite one another to remember the value and necessity of enjoying life for its own sake, building community and developing ourselves through sports, games, music, dancing, hobbies, recreation, vacation, sabbath time.

In this liturgy we take time to recognize and lift up fun as an integral part of salvation, to see it as a human right. By doing so, we affirm each other in yet another dimension of who we are, and we look forward to the time when the pleasure of eternal life will be ours.

Song

"Come to the Circle" by Kathy Sherman, CSJ, from Song of the Universe *(Ministry of the Arts © 2015). Used with permission.*

Come to the circle and tell your story,
Listen and share the world inside
you.

Come to the circle, your friends are
waiting
to listen and share their stories too.

Naming the Circle

Let us create our circle today by speaking our names, sharing one thing we will do this week that is grace-filled fun, and then stirring the water with our hands.

Prayer

Divine Wisdom of Fun and Grace,
you refresh our whole being with your saving love.
Pour out your blessings this day
and open us to fun-filled wisdom.
Source of Life. Saving Grace. Spirit of Joy.
Amen. Blessed be. May it be so.

Reading

"God Laughing Out Loud" by Mary E. Hunt, from WATERwheel *Vol. 1, No. 2 (Silver Spring, MD: WATERworks Press, 1988). Used with permission.*

"In the beginning God enjoyed herself.
She laughed out loud and laughed some more because it was good.
She sat back and smiled.
She clapped her hands in glee and she imagined her sisters dancing.
She did nothing but enjoy and it was everything.

"God knew that there was work to be done—a world to create,
People to form and a whole cosmos to plan.
She even glimpsed the fact that creation would include meetings
And that there would be injustice to right, and still she laughed,
Knowing that in the end it was all about pleasure.

"She explained to no one in particular that enjoyment is what she intended life to be about.
Pleasure is the first principle.
She knew that other would-be divinities stressed work and obligation.
She reasoned quite astutely that if joy for all were the goal,
Then everyone could rest and relax, at least some of the time.
Just thinking about this made her grin.

"Light years later, when creation came into being
And people began to toil and sweat their way,
She noticed that her first principle had been replaced by work and pain.
So she sent a reminder of her legacy.
She gave it several names: vacation, leisure, relaxation, recreation, fun.
Some thought it was a vestige of days gone by.
But God knew that it was the real thing.
She called it salvation."

Reflection | Sharing

Let us explore together how we have fun and what we enjoy doing for its own sake. Most of us still work; some of us are retired. What we do for fun now tells us something very important about our values.

Think about what you heard in the prayer and reading.

What will you do just for fun? How much time will you dedicate to hobbies? to leisure? How can we encourage each other in the joy of fun as we encourage each other in the pursuit of justice?

Let us share our words of fun-filled grace with one another.

Song

"Rejoice," anonymous.

Rejoice in our God always, and again I say Rejoice!
Rejoice in Sophia Spirit, and again I say Rejoice!
Rejoice! Rejoice! And again I say Rejoice!
Rejoice! Rejoice! And again I say Rejoice!

Blessing Water

Salvation, sabbath time, vacation rest, and water are good friends. We gather around water as a symbol for the saving grace of fun.

Our bodies contain nearly 70 percent water and about 75 percent of Earth's surface is covered by water. Think about this. Each time we play with water, shower, walk in the ocean, jump in a lake, or stomp in a puddle, we bless our bodies, our beings, and the world.

Visualize your favorite body of water. *Pause.* Send love and gratitude to this water. *Pause.* Imagine love flowing from your heart, down your arms, and out of your hands into the water.

Imagine standing under a waterfall, or in a stream, or in the ocean, and imagine water washing away anything you want to release.

Let us bring an offering to the water today. There are seashells, coral, rocks, driftwood, sand, and beach photos around the table. Choose one or several that speak to you about the saving grace of fun in your life now. Put your offering on the table, take some water, bless yourself, and offer a word of gratitude.

Song

"Joyfully You Will Draw Water" by the Collegeville Composers Group, Psallite *(Collegeville, MN: Liturgical Press © 2005). Used with permission.*

Joyfully you will draw water deep from salvation's springs.

Sending Forth

Let us go forth and have fun.
Let go forth to love the waters of the world,
the waters in our blood and bodies, and in one another.
May our vacation be full of joy.
May we be renewed with the waters of leisure.
May we know the saving grace of fun.

Song

"Hip Swinging A Safe Road" by Carolyn McDade, from This Tough Spun Web *(Surtsey Publishing © 1985), words adapted for the occasion. Used with permission.*

Let us stand in a circle, swaying with arms around one another as we sing.

A people are not hurt by fun-filled women;
When women relax their people are not hurt. (2x)

All of us together 'til all of us can go
Hip swinging a safe road, (3x)
Hip swinging a safe, safe road.

A people are not hurt by joyful women;
When women feel joy their people are not hurt. (2x)

All of us together 'til all of us can go
Relaxing toward justice, (3x)
Relaxing toward justice now.

A people are not hurt by playful women;
When women have fun their people are not hurt. (2x)

All of us together 'til all of us can go
At home in our own land, (3x)
At home in our own homeland.

Take Action

- Do something fun every day this week.
- Skip with a child. Laugh just to laugh.
- Learn to be a responsible tourist.

Learn More from These Resources

Check the Travel Section of your local newspaper for vacation options.
Get a map of an area you will be visiting and practice reading it.

32. August

Cherishing Friends on Friendship Day

In each friendship we are brought face to face with ourselves, with one another and with a larger world in which the mysterious forces of attraction work beyond our ultimate control.

—Mary E. Hunt, *Fierce Tenderness*

Friendship Day is celebrated the first Sunday in August. Friendship is a gift that is available to each of us. Friends are more precious than gold. Some are with us for a lifetime; others come in and out of our lives; still others we know for a moment.

This liturgy honors friendships. It was first planned with one woman who gathered her friends for a liturgy and festive meal before she retired to another area of the county.

Preparation

Invite friends to a meal and ask them to bring a special food. Share the meal together as the closure to this liturgy. Place a bowl of water and a vase of flowers in the center of the group. Have a gift for each person, i.e., a shell or rock with a message on it. Make a pot of tea and have a tea cup for each person.

Song

"My Friend You Are a Miracle" by Marsie Silvestro, from Circling Free *(Moonsong Productions © 1983). Used with permission.*

In the early morning time, When the sun begins to shine
I see myself in the mirror of your eyes.
And all the stories shared, exposing what we dare seem to fade into our souls.

Refrain:
My friend, you are a miracle, a song of beauty and of light.
My friend, you are a miracle, the promise of day in my night.

In the early evening time, when the sun begins to die
You see yourself in the tears that I cry.
And all the moments shared, revealing that we care gently fade into our souls. *Refrain.*

Coda: In the early morning time, in the early evening time,
My friend you are a miracle, a miracle, a miracle, my friend.

Naming the Circle

Welcome to this liturgy, "Cherishing Friends." Today we gather to celebrate our friendships, especially our justice-seeking friends.

Who are we here? Who are our friends? Let us introduce ourselves. Speak your name, and the names of one or two justice-seeking friends, and close with the words, "I am a justice-seeking friend." *For example, "I am Diann, friend of Mary and Cheryl, and I am a justice-seeking friend."*

Song

"Make New Friends," Traditional Round.

1. Make new friends,
2. but keep the old.
3. One is silver
4. the other gold.

A circle is round,
it has no end.
That's how long
I will be your friend.

The First Sip of Tea

Let us drink tea, savor the gifts of friendship, and honor our friends. This first sip of tea praises our community of friends. While you sip tea, think of your friends who nourish you. Together let us give thanks for our friends. Please say after me:

Blessed are you, Holy Friend, *Echo.*
for you give us friends who love us fiercely and tenderly, *Echo.*
and you delight us with friends to love. *Echo.*

Call to Gather

As old and new friends our lives cross along many paths: home, work, prayer groups, vacations, children, family, professional organizations, books. We chat, call, write to, listen to, mentor, guide, pray for and with, sing with, laugh with, hug, are present to, chide, and cheer one another. We witness life changes in one another and are steadfast when lives feel chaotic and unsure. We comfort each other in pain, sorrow, and uncertainty. We celebrate new jobs, special events, weddings, births, retirements, funerals.

We are friends as we partner, raise children, go to school, graduate, start businesses, get promoted or not, resign, change jobs, retire, volunteer, donate, pray, work for social justice, age, and die.

Each of us is a treasury of friendship. We cherish in memory our friend's voice, her turns of phrase, his wit or humor, the way she moves, how they dress, how he looks, her insights and wisdom. Just being our friend—being present in person, by letter, by telephone or e-mail—brings comfort, safety, and joy.

The Second Sip of Tea

Let us dedicate this second sip to ourselves. We give thanks for the qualities we have that make it possible for us to be friends with ourselves and others. Take a few minutes while you sip tea to think of qualities you bring to friendship. *Pause.* Name one of them. *Sharing.* Let us give thanks for our friendship qualities, saying:

Blessed are you, Holy Friend, Divine Wisdom Sophia, *Echo.*
for creating us to be friends. *Echo.*

Readings about Friendship

Let us listen to what friends have said about friendship. After each set of three quotes we will sing.

Song
"My Friend You Are a Miracle"

Refrain: My friend, you are a miracle, a song of beauty and of light.
My friend, you are a miracle, the promise of day in my night.

"Each friend represents a world in us, a world possibly not born until they arrive, and it is only by this meeting that a new world is born."
—Anaïs Nin, *The Diary of Anaïs Nin*, vol. 1 (San Diego, CA: Harcourt Brace Jovanovich, 1974)

"Nobody sees a flower—really—it is so small—we haven't time—and to see takes time like to have a friend takes time."
—Georgia O'Keeffe, January 1939, Georgia O'Keeffe Museum, https://www.okeeffemuseum.org/wp-content/uploads/2015/03/taketimetolooksource.pdf

"In each friendship we are brought face to face with ourselves, with one another and with a larger world in which the mysterious forces of attraction work beyond our ultimate control."
—Mary E. Hunt, *Fierce Tenderness: A Feminist Theology of Friendship* (New York: Crossroad, 1991)

Refrain: My friend, you are a miracle, a song of beauty and of light.
My friend, you are a miracle, the promise of day in my night.

"My friends have made the story of my life. In a thousand ways they have turned my limitations into beautiful privileges, and enabled me to walk serene and happy in the shadow cast by my deprivation."
—Helen Keller, *The Story of My Life* (New York: Grosset & Dunlap, 1905)

"She is a friend of my mind. She gather me. The pieces I am, she gather them and give them back to me in all the right order."
—Toni Morrison, *Beloved* (New York: Random House, 1987)

"Walk away from friendships that make you feel small and insecure, and seek out people who inspire you and support you."
—Michelle Obama, *People*, October 20, 2014

Refrain: My friend, you are a miracle, a song of beauty and of light.
My friend, you are a miracle, the promise of day in my night.

"My friends are my estate."
—Emily Dickinson, in Mabel Loomis Todd, ed., *Letters of Emily Dickinson*, vol. 1

"Many people will walk in and out of your life, but only true friends leave footprints in your heart."
—Eleanor Roosevelt

"Hold a true friend with both hands."
—Nigerian Proverb

Refrain: My friend, you are a miracle, a song of beauty and of light.
My friend, you are a miracle, the promise of day in my night.

The Third Sip of Tea

Let us drink this third sip and ask ourselves: What difference have friends made in my life? How have friends invited me to new understandings and commitments in a world so often fraught with injustice? What ways have I helped my friends to see an issue, another person, or a world issue in a new light? How do I signal to children how important friends are to me? *Pause.* Let us share our thoughts with one another. *Sharing.*

Let us celebrate our friends, saying:
Blessed are you, Holy Friend, Wisdom Sophia, *Echo.*
for creating many ways to celebrate friendship. *Echo.*

Prayers for Friends

Let us remember now friends who need our prayers. Speak their names, offer your prayers, float a flower in the water, and we will all respond: "We remember *Name.*"

Refrain: My friend, you are a miracle, a song of beauty and of light.
My friend, you are a miracle, the promise of day in my night.

Take Action

- Take time to tell a friend, "You are a blessing in my life."
- Pray for a friend.
- Share a cup of tea with a friend.
- Have fun with a friend.

Sending Forth

Today we have gathered as friends and celebrated friendships.
Let us go forth remembering justice-seeking friends.
Let us go forth cherishing our friendships.
Let us go forth and make friends in all nations.

Song
"Make New Friends"

1. Make new friends,
2. but keep the old.
3. One is silver
4. the other gold.

A circle is round,
it has no end.
That's how long
I will be your friend.

Learn More from These Resources

Carmichael, Liz. *Friendship: Interpreting Christian Love.* New York: T & T Clark, 2004.

Chittister, Joan. *The Friendship of Women: The Hidden Tradition of the Bible.* Erie, PA: Benetvision, 2006.

Clarkson, Sarah, Sally Clarkson, and Joy Clarkson. *Girls' Club: Cultivating Lasting Friendship in a Lonely World.* Carol Stream, IL: Tyndale Momentum, 2019.

Clausen, Janet. "Voices of Friendship." In *Biblical Women: Exploring Their Stories with Girls.* Winona, MN: Saint Mary's Press, 2002.

Hunt, Mary E. *Fierce Tenderness: A Feminist Theology of Friendship.* New York: Crossroad, 1991.

Moltmann-Wendel, Elisabeth. *Rediscovering Friendship: Awakening to the Power and Promise of Women's Friendships.* Minneapolis, MN: Fortress Press, 2001.

Ringe, Sharon H. *Wisdom's Friends: Community and Christology in the Fourth Gospel.* Louisville, KY: Westminster John Knox Press, 1999.

33. September

Lift Up Peacemakers for International Day of Peace

I will write peace on your wings and you will fly all over the world.

—Sadako Sasaki, *Report from Hiroshima*

Every year on September 21, people around the world come together to advocate for peace in its many forms. They pray and work for peace, especially in the midst of mass shootings in schools and synagogues and threats of nuclear war. During this Hispanic Heritage Month peacemakers focus on the dignity of Central American immigrants at the US and Mexican borders, especially on the safety of the children. What kind of peacemakers do we need today? Where are they? How will we know them? Now, more than ever, we must call and encourage one another to be peacemakers.

This liturgy offers a glimpse into what peacemakers throughout the ages have passed on to the generations that follow after them and challenges participants to become peacemakers.

Preparation

Place on a table or center space covered with a cloth: peace cranes, greenery (olive branches!), thirteen candles and matches, a globe, olives, harvest bread, apples, honey, and water. Place pictures of the peacemakers named here and others around the space.

Naming the Circle

Welcome to a celebration to "Lift Up Peacemakers for International Day of Peace." Today, we remember and reflect on the courage and wisdom of peacemakers past, present, and future who advocate for peace in the face of war, violence, and injustice. We look to their actions, words, and symbols to inspire us to live more peaceful and just lives. They challenge us to take action for peace in our families, communities, neighborhoods, and world.

To create our circle, please speak your name and say, "I strive to be a peacemaker."

Song

"I've Got Peace Like a River," African American spiritual.

I've got peace like a river, *(3x)* in my soul.

Call to Gather

In 1981, the United Nations passed a unanimous resolution calling for the celebration of an International Day of Peace devoted to "commemorating and strengthening the ideals of peace both within and among all nations and peoples." Every year on September 21, people around the world come together to advocate for peace in its many forms.

The theme for this year is [*name it*]. We come together to honor women of peace, many of whom have given their lives to uphold the safety and dignity each person deserves. Our history books often exclude the stories of women peacemakers.

Today, we will hear from women who advocate for peace on global and local levels—women who speak out against suffering and hold communities together in the face of violence. Let us learn by their examples so that we too may become peacemakers and bring peace to our world and communities.

We gather in the spirit of those who have died—may they rest in peace. We gather in the spirit of those who are making decisions, hopeful that our prayers will warm their hearts and open their minds to a moral creativity that will bring peace without bombing and killing. We gather in the spirit of the divine who calls us to live in peace from generation to generation. We gather to call forth peacemakers. *Light a candle.*

We gather because we must. We cannot keep from singing for peace. We cannot keep from praying for an end to violence and the beginning of a new day for our children's children and for us. We gather linked in a special way to the people living in war-torn countries, praying for their safety and hoping with them that this war will end. We gather mourning all who are killed in mass shootings, especially schoolchildren. We gather resisting the separation of families by American policies. *Name others.* We gather to call forth peacemakers. *Light a candle.*

Song
"I've Got Peace Like a River"

I've got peace like a river, *(3x)* in my soul.

Calls for Peace

Let us listen to the wisdom of women peacemakers worldwide.
Light a candle after each quote.

Sadako Sasaki of Japan, symbol of innocent victims of nuclear war: "I will write peace on your wings and you will fly all over the world."

—Report from Hiroshima, *as given in United States Committee for Cooperation with the Japan Council Against A and H Bombs (1961), 48.*

Light a candle.

Anne Frank of Germany and the Netherlands, Holocaust victim: "I see the world being slowly transformed into a wilderness; I hear the approaching thunder that, one day, will destroy us too. I feel the suffering of millions. And yet, when I look up at the sky, I somehow feel that everything will change for the better, that this cruelty too shall end, that peace and tranquility will return once more."

—The Diary of Anne Frank, *July 15, 1944 (New York: Doubleday, 1952).*

Light a candle.

Bree Newsome of the United States, artist and human rights activist: "You come against me with hatred, repression, and violence. I come against you in the name of God. This flag comes down today."

—Antonia Blumberg, "Activist Bree Newsome Reveals Staggering Faith During Confederate Flag Action," Huffington Post, *June 29, 2015.*

Light a candle.

Wangari Maathai of Kenya, recipient of the 2004 Nobel Peace Prize: "Unless we properly manage resources like forests, water, land, minerals and oil, we will not win the fight against poverty. And there will not be peace. Old conflicts will rage on and new resource wars will erupt unless we change the path we are on."

—"Trees for Democracy," The New York Times, *December 10, 2004.*

Light a candle.

Berta Cáceres of Honduras, environmental activist and human rights fighter: "I cannot freely walk on my territory or swim in the sacred river and I am separated from my children because of the threats. I cannot live in peace, I am always thinking about being killed or kidnapped. But I refuse to go into exile. I am a human rights fighter and I will not give up this fight."

—Nina Lakhani, "Remembering Berta Cáceres," Guardian, *March 3, 2016.*

Light a candle.

Mary McLeod Bethune of the United States, educator and Civil Rights activist: "The drums of Africa still beat in my heart. They will not let me rest while there is still a single Negro boy or girl without a chance to prove his [or her] worth."

—Suzanne O'Dea Schenken, From Suffrage to the Senate: An Encyclopedia of American Women in Politics *(Santa Barbara, CA: ABC-CLIO, 1999).*

Light a candle.

Olive Schreiner of South Africa, writer and anti-war campaigner: "No tinsel of trumpets and flags will ultimately seduce women into the insanity of recklessly destroying life, or gild the willful taking of life with any other name than that of murder, whether it be the slaughter of the million or of one by one."

—Woman and Labor *(Mineola, NY: Dover Publications, 1998), 176.*

Light a candle.

Rozina of Iraq, refugee and ISIS attack survivor: "I would like to be an activist and talk about women's rights. I have finished sixth grade and would like to finish my studies but I can't continue in the camp. The camp is my home and my lifeline for now."

—Jane Sloane, Global Fund for Women, https://www.globalfundforwomen.org/refugee-crisis-rozinas-story/#.XIXTAhNKh0t.

Light a candle.

Leymah Gbowee of Liberia, recipient of the 2011 Nobel Peace Prize: "All of our religious teachings have similar rules, such as a commitment to peace and nonviolence, and care for women and widows and orphans. What has destroyed a coming together is man's interpretation of religion. In most societies, today where wars and conflicts are taking place, a lot of those involved in these particular issues have some kind of link."

—Amitabh Pal, The Progressive, *https://progressive.org/dispatches/leymah-gbowee/.*

Light a candle.

Mother Teresa of Calcutta, recipient of the 1979 Nobel Peace Prize: "Today, if we have no peace, it is because we have forgotten that we belong to each other."

—Where There Is Love, There Is God *(New York: Random House, 2010), 330.*

Light a candle.

Rigoberta Menchú Tum of Guatemala, recipient of the 1992 Nobel Peace Prize: "Peace cannot exist without justice, justice cannot exist without fairness, fairness cannot exist without development, development cannot exist without democracy, democracy cannot exist without respect for the identity and dignity of cultures and peoples."

—Irene van Lippe-Biesterfeld with Jessica van Tijn, Science, Soul, and the Spirit of Nature *(Rochester, VT: Bear & Company, 2005).*

Light a candle.

Song

"Dona Nobis Pacem," sixteenth century, anonymous.

Dona nobis pacem, pacem.	Grant us peace, peace.
Dona nobis pacem.	Grant us peace.

Reflection | Sharing

Think about the calls for peace you have heard.

Which peacemakers spoke to your mind and heart as you listened?

After a quiet time, we will pass this globe representing peacemakers around the world. When you receive it, name a woman peacemaker and tell us how she has inspired you.

Litany of Peacemakers

Let us remember other peacemakers who, through the ages, have worked for peace and changed the world. Let us ask them to pray with us for peace at home and in the world. Our response is: Pray for peace.

Buddha, Jesus, and Mohammed, pray for peace.
Sarah, Hagar, and Abraham, pray for peace.
Joan of Arc and Francis of Assisi, pray for peace.
Käthe Kollwitz and Rabbi Heschel, pray for peace.
Harriet Tubman and Martin Luther King Jr., pray for peace.
Sor Juana Ines de la Cruz and Pope John XXIII, pray for peace.
Black Elk and Mahatma Gandhi, pray for peace.
Óscar Romero, Ita Ford, Dorothy Kazel, Maura Clark, and Jean Donovan, pray for peace.
Please share with us the names of other peacemakers, pray for peace.

Song
"Dona Nobis Pacem"

Dona nobis pacem, pacem.	Grant us peace, peace.
Dona nobis pacem.	Grant us peace.

Blessing Food

As the world needs Earth, air, water, and sun, so the world needs peacemakers. In solidarity with peacemakers around the world, let us bless four foods to symbolize our unity.

Hold bread:
We unite with you, Peacemakers of the South. We bless and share bread to nourish our struggles.

Hold olives:
We unite with you, Peacemakers of the East. We bless and share olives to anoint ourselves and others with the oil of peace.

Hold apples:
We unite with you, Peacemakers of the North. We bless and share apples to symbolize our shared harvest.

Hold water:
We unite with you, Peacemakers of the West. We bless and share clean water to refresh us when we are tired.

Blessed are you, Gracious and Loving Peacemaker of the World, for giving us bread, olives, apples, and drink to strengthen us for peacemaking. Grant us peace. Grant each country peace. Grant peace to the world and to the universe. Let us eat and drink together in peace.

Prayer for Peace

Light a candle for peace.

All-merciful God of Many Names,
Yahweh, Allah, Holy One, Great Spirit, Wisdom Sophia,
your power and grace sustain the universe.
Teach us to hallow your names throughout the world.
Response: In your mercy, grant us peace.

You chose Sarah, Hagar, and Abraham to birth many nations.
You continue to speak through prophets and peacemakers.
Forgive us, their offspring, for our wars and misdeeds.
Save us from further terrorism and destruction, that all children and Earth may live in peace.
Response: In your mercy, grant us peace.

Compassionate and merciful God of Many Names,
change the hearts of the United States and all governments and their allies who use violence as a solution to differences.
Help us together find a way to peace that serves every nation.
Response: In your mercy, grant us peace.

Guardian of all life,
guide world leaders toward peace,
guide decision makers to orient their governments toward justice.
Show us how to act responsibly to bring peace and welfare to humankind, Earth, and all creation.
Response: In your mercy, grant us peace.

God of Peace and Justice,
guide all religious communities throughout the world
to work for peace with justice
so that all may have food, housing, prosperity, safety, and peace.
Response: In your mercy, grant us peace.

God of Many Names, fill us with peace.
May our peace radiate to loved ones and all we meet.
May this peace touch communities around the world
so that all may live in peace from generation to generation, forever and ever.
Response: Amen. Blessed be. May it be so.

Take Action for Peace

Let us put our prayers for peace into action. Here are some possible ways:

- Make a peace crane: https://www.youtube.com/watch?v=bd9UlOveEYA.

- Call your Congresspersons and tell them to support immigrants and refugees.
- Learn more about the history of International Day of Peace: https://internationaldayofpeace.org/.
- Make a donation to support victims of natural disasters and wars.

Sending Forth

As we go forth to bring peace to the world, let us promise to speak out against injustice everywhere and witness for peace.
Speak out against hatred toward refugees,
Response: Witness for Peace!
Speak out against war everywhere, especially in [*name a current conflict*],
Response: Witness for Peace!
Speak out against ethnic cleansing,
Response: Witness for Peace!
Speak out against the American government's hostility toward immigrants,
Response: Witness for Peace!
Speak out against human causes of climate change and stand in solidarity with all those affected by recent hurricanes, earthquakes, and other natural disasters,
Response: Witness for Peace!
Speak out against human trafficking,
Response: Witness for Peace!
Speak out against child marriage and sexual assault,
Response: Witness for Peace!
Speak out against white supremacy and racism in all its forms,
Response: Witness for Peace!

Blessing of Peace

May peace be within us. May peace be around us. May peace be beside us. May peace be between us. May we walk peacefully with all Earth's creatures. May peace fill our days and nights. May peace fill the Earth.

Greeting of Peace

Let us empower each other to witness for peace by exchanging peace cranes and greeting one another with the words of Sadako Sasaki:
"I will write peace on your wings and you will fly all over the world."

Song

Let there be peace on earth
And let it begin with me;
Let there be peace on earth,
The peace that was meant to be.
*With God our Creator
* We are family,
* Let us walk with each other
* In perfect harmony.

Let peace begin with me,
Let this be the moment now;
With every step I take,
Let this be my solemn vow:
To take each moment and live each
moment
In peace eternally.
Let there be peace on earth
And let it begin with me.

* *Copyright-protected alternative lyrics.*

Learn More from These Resources

1000 PeaceWomen Across the Globe. Zurich, Switzerland: Scalo, 2005.

Bajaj, Monisha. *Educating for Peace and Human Rights* at TEDxTeachersCollege https://www.youtube.com/watch?v=EOAUPytTPmw.

Ellsberg, Robert, ed. *All the Way to Heaven: The Selected Letters of Dorothy Day.* Milwaukee, WI: Marquette University Press, 2010.

———. *The Duty of Delight: The Diaries of Dorothy Day.* Milwaukee, WI: Marquette University Press, 2008.

Hayward, Susan, and Katherine Marshall, eds. *Women, Religion and Peacebuilding: Illuminating the Unseen.* Washington, DC: Institute of Peace Press, 2015.

The History of Women Strike for Peace. https://womenstrikeforpeace.com/.

Hunt, Swanee. *This Was Not Our War: Bosnian Women Reclaiming the Peace.* Durham, NC: Duke University Press, 2004.

Kroll, Virginia, author, and Nancy L. Clouse, illustrator. *Pink Paper Swans.* Grand Rapids, MI: Eerdmans, 1994.

Neu, Diann L. *Peace Liturgies.* Silver Spring, MD: WATERworks Press, 2011.

Peace treaties: research Treaty of Versailles, Paris Peace Treaty, Jordan-Israeli Peace Treaty, Egypt-Israel Peace Treaty, and others.

Rosenthal, Peggy. *Imagine a World: Poetry for Peacemakers.* Erie, PA: Pax Christi USA, 2005.

Sylvester, Nancy, and Mary Jo Klick, eds. *Crucible for Change: Engaging Impasse through Communal Contemplation and Dialogue.* San Antonio, TX: Sor Juana Press, 2004.

Tisdale, Sallie. *Women of the Way: Discovering 2,500 Years of Buddhist Wisdom.* New York: HarperCollins Publishers, 2006.

Women's International League for Peace & Freedom (WILPF). https://wilpf.org/.

34. October

Breaking Silence to End Domestic Violence

The peace of the Earth be with you, the peace of the heavens too;
The peace of the rivers be with you, the peace of the oceans too.

—Traditional Guatemalan, "The Peace of the Earth Be with You"

National Domestic Violence Awareness Month has been observed every October since 1987. Women and girls of all ages, classes, and cultures are at risk for sexual violence, harassment, and abuse in the streets, at work, at home, and in churches, synagogues, mosques, and other houses of worship. All people are! Such violence has profound and long-term effects on the self-esteem of each person, family, and community.

This liturgy invites the gathered to pray for an end to domestic violence, to be committed to breaking the silence of violence, and to unite in claiming our healing powers.

Preparation

Form a circle of chairs, one for each participant, around a table. Place on this table or center space three candles, four containers (shells or bowls) filled with lavender oil, and a towel. Gather pictures of women and place them around the space.

Call to Gather

Welcome to this liturgy, "Breaking Silence to End Domestic Violence." Thank you for all of your work and for your resilience. Take a deep breath! Most of us are exhausted from the stories of #MeToo, the clergy sex-abuse scandals, and much more. *Name others.* Breathe! We hear stories. We tell stories. The silence of violence continues to be broken. Continue breathing!

How do we heal after silence is broken and horrifying stories are told?

We come together to nourish one another and bring some healing to our minds, bodies, and spirits. We gather with people around the world to mark Domestic Violence Awareness Month. Breathe! We commit ourselves to a lifetime of saying no to violence against women, men, children, animals, Earth. It is a long journey. Keep breathing!

Naming the Circle

Let us share our names and then say, "I support everyone who breaks silence around abusive violence, and I pray for healing."

Prayer

One: Light a candle. Compassionate One, you see us working hard speaking truth to power. Strengthen us.
All: Be with us now and always.

Two: Light a candle. Healing One, you see us growing tired. Refresh us.
All: Be with us now and always.

Three: Light a candle. Loving One, you remind us we are not alone. Surround us with community.
All: Be with us now and always.

Song

"The River Is Flowing," Traditional.

The river is flowing, flowing and growing,
The river is flowing, down to the sea.

Mother Earth carry me, your child I will always be
Mother Earth carry me, down to the sea.

Breaking the Silence

One woman walks to the table, picks up a scarf, ties a knot in it, pulls the scarf over her head and shouts: No! No! No!

Another does the same: No! No! No!

And another: No! No! No!

One: We are angry.
Two: We will not be reasonable any longer.
Three: We are breaking the silence.

One: We are screaming no to domestic violence.
Two: We are shouting no to harassment.
Three: We are crying no to abuse.

One: No! No! No!
Two: In the streets, at work, at home,
Three: No! No! No! in churches, synagogues, mosques, all religious houses.

One: Think of the anger and pain you experience from violence. Take a scarf and tie a knot in it to symbolize your "no" to violence. *Pause.*

Two: We must be angry and shout, "No! No! No!" to the violence women and girls experience. To each violent act you hear, shout out "No! No! No!" and pull your scarf over your head. Let us stand.

One: To the men who harass women walking down the street,
  No! No! No!
Two: To parents, grandparents, and relatives who sexually abuse children,
  No! No! No!
Three: To lovers, spouses, and partners who batter and rape their partners,
  No! No! No!
One: To college men who rape their dates,
  No! No! No!
Two: To women who abuse their female lovers or partners,
  No! No! No!
Three: To the exploitation of women and children by pornography,
  No! No! No!
One: To the forced prostitution and trafficking of youth,
  No! No! No!
Two: To whom else do we say no? Tell us and we will shout,
  No! No! No!

Commitment to Solidarity
One woman begins to tie her scarf to the scarves of the people on either side of her. She motions for all to do the same. When the scarves have all been linked together, she puts her portion of the ring of scarves around her shoulders, motions for others to do the same, and begins singing:

Song

"Singing For Our Lives" by Holly Near, from Singing For Our Lives *(© 1982). Adapted. Used with permission.*

We are a gentle, angry people
And we are singing, singing for our lives. *(2x)*

We are shedding tears together
And we are crying, crying for our lives. *(2x)*

We are women breaking silence
And we are shouting, shouting for our lives. *(2x)*

We are women claiming power
And we are uniting, uniting for our lives. *(2x)*

Reflection | Sharing

Shedding tears, breaking silence, claiming power . . .
How are these affecting your life?
How are you allowing yourself to heal?
After a quiet time, let us share our words of wisdom with this community.

Prayers for Healing

Let us pray. Our response is: "We pray for healing."

For anyone who has been abused physically, emotionally, economically, spiritually, or in any other way,
All: We pray for healing.
For those who help heal the wounds of violence,
All: We pray for healing.
For the children who witness domestic violence,
All: We pray for healing.
For those who are undocumented and most vulnerable to abuse,
All: We pray for healing.
For all survivors, that their strength may only increase,
All: We pray for healing.
For friends and supporters who accompany survivors,
All: We pray for healing.
For the increased will in religions and society to call abusers to accountability,
All: We pray for healing.

For what else shall we pray?

Blessing Oil

The blesser touches the oil and prays:

Pour out your Spirit, Wisdom Sophia, upon this oil.
Enduring Spirit, soothe us with oil when cold winds chill us to the bone.
Comforting Presence, refresh us with oil when we need strength to renew our lives.
Gentle Wisdom, warm us with oil and caress us with cool breezes.
Healing Grace, ease our hurts and bruises with oil when we need to keep open to life's changes.

Anointing with Oil

If you feel called, step up to a bowl of lavender oil, dip in your fingers, and anoint yourself, or invite someone to anoint you, as is appropriate for your healing: face, hands, feet, heart, head. Reclaim your healing powers for yourself and for others.

Song

"The Peace of the Earth Be with You," Traditional Guatemalan, tr. Christine Carson © Christine Carson and WGRG c/o Iona Community, Scotland, GIA Publications, Inc., agent. All rights reserved. Used by permission.

The peace of the Earth be with you,
the peace of the heavens too;
The peace of the rivers be with you,
the peace of the oceans too.
Deep peace falling over you.
God's peace growing in you.

Take Action

Let us put our prayers into action this month. Here are some possible ways:

- Take care of yourself by doing something that gives you joy and comfort.
- Contact your legislators and urge them to support reauthorization of the Violence Against Women Act, one of the country's most effective tools in responding to domestic violence, dating violence, sexual assault, and stalking.
- Wear purple on November 3, All Survivors Day, in solidarity with survivors of abuse.

Sending Forth

Let us go forth from this place
strengthened by this community,
committed to breaking the silence of violence,
and united in claiming our healing powers.

Greeting of Peace

Knowing that our bodies have been hurt in many ways, let us greet one another carefully and lovingly with a healing look, touch, or embrace.

Learn More from These Resources

All Survivors Day, November 3: read about this international day to recognize survivors of sexual abuse.

Alwani, Zainab, and Salma Abugideiri. *What Islam Says about Domestic Violence: A Guide for Helping Muslim Families.* Herndon, VA: FAITH (Foundation for Appropriate and Immediate Temporary Relief), 2003.

Domestic Violence Awareness Month: search for resources. https://nrcdv.org/dvam/DVAM-history.

Fortune, Marie M. *Violence in the Family: A Workshop Curriculum for Clergy and Other Helpers.* Cleveland, OH: The Pilgrim Press, 1991.

Kalmanofsky, Amy, ed. *Sexual Violence and Sacred Texts.* Cambridge, MA: Feminist Studies in Religion Books, 2017.

Magrath, Sue. *Healing the Ravaged Soul: Tending the Spiritual Wounds of Child Sexual Abuse.* Eugene, OR: Cascade Books, 2016.

National Coalition Against Domestic Violence, https://ncadv.org/, is the voice of victims and survivors. They are the catalyst for changing society to have zero tolerance for domestic violence. They do this by affecting public policy, increasing understanding of the impact of domestic violence, and providing programs and education that drive that change.

Spotlight: watch this movie, the true story of how the *Boston Globe* uncovered the massive clergy sexual-abuse scandal in the Catholic Archdiocese of Boston.

35. November

Becoming Saints of Love and Justice on All Saints' Day

We who believe in freedom cannot rest,
We who believe in freedom cannot rest until it comes.

—Bernice Johnson Reagon, "Ella's Song"

November 1 is All Saints' Day. It commemorates all the saints, both known and unknown. Saints of love and justice, women, those who are pushed to the margins, immigrants, trans people, queer people, children of mixed races, people who are differently abled, prophets, those who are brave, protesters, marchers, and others.

This liturgy raises up saints of love and justice, even the unlikely ones, who have passed on their inspiration and legacy from generation to generation. It honors those who have rolled stones away to reveal truth. It challenges participants to be saints.

Preparation

Place a table in the center of a circle of chairs. Put on it flowing cloths to represent currents of water. In the center, place a bowl for water and a pitcher of water. Put many stones of various sizes around the bowl and on the cloth.

Song

"Woke Up This Mornin'," African American spiritual.

Woke up this mornin' with my mind
stayed on *freedom, *(3x)*

Hallelu, hallelu, hallelujah.
*Love . . . . *Justice

Call to Gather

Welcome, Saints of Love and Justice. We gather on All Saints' Day for this liturgy to raise up saints and prophets of generations past and present. During this season we remember the ongoing relationship between the living and the dead. On this day we rejoice that we sit around the table with courageous pioneers and ordinary folk. With them, we take our place in the communion of saints.

Our table is set with stones of many shapes, sizes, and colors. These stones are surrounded by a pitcher of water and an empty basin. Saints are embodied here through photos of people who are special to us, those who have gone before us, our family and friends.

Why stones? Stones represent those things that need to be removed in order to reveal a larger truth. *Put a few stones into the bowl.* Stones also represent local and national events and milestones. *Put stones into the bowl.* Some stones need an outside force to move them, even another stone to push up against them giving a ripple effect. *Rub two stones together and put them into the bowl.*

Why saints? Saints are those people who use prophetic imagination to roll stones away. They are recognized as being holy, in a close relationship to God, the Divine Holy One. They are exemplary models, extraordinary teachers, wonder workers, and sources of benevolent power.

Why water? Water, the source of life, represents the currents of love and justice that splash on the stones of injustice to wear them away. Water symbolizes the flow of people, especially women, people of color, and all who are marginalized and made poor. Together, we roll stones away and reveal truth. *Pour a little water into the bowl.*

Naming Our Circle

Look around. Notice the faces among us. Turn to those around you and introduce yourself saying, "Hi! I'm Saint *Name*. I am an image of God."

Song

"Ella's Song," Bernice Johnson Reagon, from We All . . . Everyone of Us *(Flying Fish Records © 1983). Permission requested.*

We who believe in *freedom cannot rest,
We who believe in *freedom cannot rest until it comes.
*Love . . . *Justice

Reading from Matthew 28:1-2

"After the Sabbath, as the first day of the week was dawning, Mary of Magdala came with Mary to inspect the tomb. Suddenly, there was a severe earthquake, and an angel of God descended from heaven, rolled back the stone, and sat on it."

Naming Stones of Injustice

There are many stones that saints of love and justice have rolled away and sat on. Some have died, literally and figuratively, in the process. What are stones of injustice that have been and still need to be rolled away in our communities? We invite you to come forward, name one, and place a stone into the water.

Song
"Ella's Song"

We who believe in *justice cannot rest,
We who believe in *justice cannot rest until it comes.

Litany of Saints

Many saints among us and before us have rolled away stones of injustice. Let us name these saints, thank them, and ask them to guide us, strengthen us, and embolden us.

All you saints, prophets, elders, and ancestors of our tribe and families of choice who have a profound impact on our religious communities and social institutions.
Response: Guide us. Strengthen us. Embolden us. *Pour water.*
All you saints who fight against racism, sexism, classism, transphobia, biphobia, and all other -isms and phobia.
Response: Guide us. Strengthen us. Embolden us. *Pour water.*
All you communities of saints who defy white supremacy and work to decenter whiteness.
Response: Guide us. Strengthen us. Embolden us. *Pour water.*
All you saints who challenge the status quo through experiencing arrest, persecution, and trials.
Response: Guide us. Strengthen us. Embolden us. *Pour water.*
All you saints living with chronic illnesses, HIV/AIDS, or cancer and your loved ones who care for you.
Response: Guide us. Strengthen us. Embolden us. *Pour water.*
All you saints who are brave and speak truth to power.
Response: Guide us. Strengthen us. Embolden us. *Pour water.*
All you saints who . . . Who else shall we name? Tell us.
Response: Guide us. Strengthen us. Embolden us. *Pour water.*

Reflection | Sharing

Think about sainthood. Yours or someone else's.

Who is someone you consider a saint? What is a saintly quality that this person has? How will you be a saint?

After a quiet time, let us share our reflections with one another. *Share in whole group or one to one.*

Song
"Ella's Song"

We who believe in *truth cannot rest,
We who believe in *truth cannot rest until it comes.

Blessing with Water

Touch the water. Water, the source of life, represents the currents of love and justice that splash on the stones of injustice to wear them away. We are the water, the currents. Let us bless our bodies.

Touch your eyes, saying: Bless my eyes, that I may see stones of injustice and have the courage to roll them away.
Touch your ears: Bless my ears, that I may hear the stones of bigotry and have the courage to roll them away.
Touch your mouth: Bless my mouth, that I may taste the stones of bitterness and have the courage to roll them away.
Touch your hands: Bless my hands, that I may embrace those who have been stoned by their persecutors.
Touch your whole body: Bless my body, that I may love passionately.

Song

"Joyfully You Will Draw Water" by the Collegeville Composers Group, Psallite *(Collegeville, MN: Liturgical Press © 2005). Used with permission.*

Joyfully you will draw water deep from salvation's springs.

Commitment to Roll Away Injustice

Take a stone and carry it with you as your commitment to roll away a stone of injustice. *Sing "Joyfully You Will Draw Water" during stone taking.*

Blessing All Saints

Look into the face of the person next to you and see a saint. Look around at the communion of saints in which you are gathered this moment. You are a saint of love and justice. We are saints of love and justice together. Raise your hands in blessing over the heads of those saints around you. *Pause.*

Divine Creator of All, we come from your sacred womb and image you. Bless us yet again, and continue to surprise us with the sacred in our own lives, in the lives of our ancestors, and in the lives of those we meet. May we bless others as we struggle, laugh, dance, and stumble toward the new creation. Amen. Blessed be. May it be so.

Take Action

Let us put our prayers into action. Here are some possible ways:

- Tell a teenager a story of a "saint" who lives in your community: someone who works against racism, sexism, classism, transphobia, biphobia, and the intersection of all -isms.
- Take an elder out to dinner and thank them for their justice work.

Sending Forth

Let us go forth to act as saints.
May the currents of love and justice flow through us.
May we not rest until all stones of injustice have been rolled away.
As we go forth, let us proclaim boldly,
Together: We are saints of love and justice.

Song

"When the Saints Go Marching In," African American spiritual.

Oh when the saints go marching in,
When the saints go marching in;
Oh how I want to be in that number
When the saints go marching in.

When love and justice flow this way
. . .
Oh when the stones are rolled away
. . .

Learn More from These Resources

Chervin, Ronda. *Treasury of Women Saints.* Cincinnati, OH: Franciscan Media, 2015.

Lee, Michael E. *Revolutionary Saint: The Theological Legacy of Oscar Romero.* Maryknoll, NY: Orbis Books, 2018.

Pierpont, Julia. *5 Writers Who Should Be Feminist Saints.* https://lithub.com/5-writers-who-should-be-feminist-saints/.

———. *The Little Book of Feminist Saints.* New York: Random House, 2018.

36. December

Telling Love's Story on World AIDS Day

I see the face of AIDS everywhere
now on the streets of my world
because I see it in myself
one of the worried well.

—Fran Peavey, "Face of AIDS"

World AIDS Day, held each year on December 1, is an opportunity for people worldwide to unite in the fight against HIV/AIDS, to show their support for people living with the disease, and to remember those who have died. It originated at the 1988 World Summit of Ministers of Health on Programs for AIDS Prevention. Since then, every year United Nations agencies, governments, and civil society join together to campaign around specific themes related to AIDS. The AIDS Memorial Quilt Project mirrors the reality that we walk amid life and death daily.

This liturgy reminds us that we are people living with the reality of HIV/AIDS—those who are infected with this virus, those who have lost loved ones, those who care for them, and every one of us struggling to eradicate this disease. It calls us to respond with love, compassion, and support.

Preparation

Along with a candle, a red ribbon, and a pin for each participant, place a larger candle, a loaf of bread, and a glass of water on a cloth that is significant for the occasion. Use a quilt panel or blanket of a loved one, if possible.

Naming the Circle

Welcome to this place of remembrance. In our time together this World AIDS Day, we will focus on "Telling Love's Story." Think of yourself or those you know who are living with HIV/AIDS, those who have died of AIDS-related causes, those who have been affected by HIV/AIDS. Let us create our sacred circle by sharing our names and the names of those we remember, and then honoring them by pinning ourselves with these red ribbons.

Call to Gather

Continue by lighting the larger candle and saying:

These beloved ones are with us in this circle now. Remembering them reminds us that we are all people living with HIV/AIDS—those we have just named and those who have lost loved ones from this disease. AIDS has changed our lives individually and collectively, country to country.

Our beloved friends carry or have carried in their bodies this debilitating disease. Some have been discriminated against, most have been loved deeply, but all of their lives have been changed by this disease. Each has surely felt anger and pain, hope and fear, support and loneliness. They are here with us now, reminding us that we must respond to AIDS with love, tears, rage, compassion, and hope.

How are we responding to AIDS? Our gathering tonight is one response. Let us quiet ourselves, reflect, and remember.

Song

"They Are Falling All Around Me" by Bernice Johnson Reagon, from B'lieve I'll Run On . . . See What the End's Gonna Be *(Redwood Records, reissued Calico Tracks Records © 1975). Permission requested.*

They are falling all around me. *(3x)*
The strongest leaves of my tree.

Every paper brings the news that *(3x)*
The teachers of my sound are moving
on.

Death comes and rests so heavy. *(3x)*
Your face I'll never see no more.

But you're not really going to leave
me. *(3x)*

It is your path I walk
It is your song I sing
It is your load I take on
It is your air I breathe
It's the record you set that makes me
go on
It's your strength that helps me stand
You're not really going to leave me.

I will try to sing my song right. *(3x)*
Be sure to let me hear from you.

Reading

"Face of AIDS" by Fran Peavey, from A Shallow Pool of Time: One Woman Grapples with the AIDS Epidemic *(© 1988). Used with permission.*

"I see the face of AIDS
in my world on every continent
in my country in every state
in my city in each neighborhood

"I see the face of AIDS
It is a face contorted in fear
a deep fear
of blood, of sex, of death, of homosexuals
fear of Africans and Haitians
fear of people different from the self.

"Plague in our times, In our family
Can you believe it?

"Terror in newspaper headlines
national and municipal budgets stretched
insurance companies unable to cope with the bills
johns unwilling to use condoms for their illicit pleasure
parents unable to control their children's sexual explorations
Ignorance and fear mixed as thick as peanut butter.

"I see the face of AIDS,
it is a face thin, old, worn before its time
eyes receding in their sockets
staring beyond the thin veil of present reality
seeing a life beyond and unsure of the route.

"I see the face of AIDS
a baby born of a virus-infested woman,
a baby needing love
yet abandoned by a mother too ill to care.
But of course mothers are never too ill to really care
about losing life
their babies'
or their own.

"I see the face of AIDS in the quiet saint of our times
who steps forward to care for this babe,
for the mother,
for all infected
for as long as they shall live.

"I see the face of AIDS
in my neighbor who comes home from the hospital
in an ambulance
to the arms of his lover who carries him into the house
like a bride

"They live out their lives in quiet retreat together
sleeping in the same bed
each terrified of going on alone.

"I see the face of AIDS
in the outraged crowd gathering to protest
too high a price
being charged for an elixir which offers hope to the
hopeless.

"I see the face of AIDS everywhere
now on the streets of my world
because I see it in myself
one of the worried well."

Litany of Solidarity

To each petition, we respond: We know the face of HIV/AIDS. We are here, right here in your midst.

Left side: We are friends, partners, lovers, family, and neighbors.
All: We know the face of HIV/AIDS. We are here, right here in your midst.
Right side: We are care sharers, justice workers, health-care professionals, social workers, and ministers.
All: We know the face of HIV/AIDS. We are here, right here in your midst.
Left: We are students, teachers, friends, parents, sisters, and brothers.
All: We know the face of HIV/AIDS. We are here, right here in your midst.
Right: Some of us are wise elders; some are caring adults; some are searching youth; some are wonder-filled children.
All: We know the face of HIV/AIDS. We are here, right here in your midst.
Left: Some of us are lesbian; some of us are gay; some straight; some bi; some trans; some allies and friends.
All: We know the face of HIV/AIDS. We are here, right here in your midst.
Right: Some of us have or might get HIV/AIDS.
All: We know the face of HIV/AIDS. We are here, right here in your midst.
Left: Some of us feel angry and sad, fearful and fragile, vulnerable and alone.
All: We know the face of HIV/AIDS. We are here, right here in your midst.
Right: We are multicolored and many cultured; we are one world.
All: We know the face of HIV/AIDS. We are here, right here in your midst.

Left: All of us are people of faith who long for the day when HIV/AIDS is a distant memory.

All: We know the face of HIV/AIDS. We are here, right here in your midst.

The person who began this litany says: What else shall we add to this litany? Tell us and we will respond . . .

All: We know the face of HIV/AIDS. We are here, right here in your midst.

Song

"They Are Falling All Around Me"

They are falling all around me, *(3x)*
The strongest leaves on my tree.

Poem

"The Concert" by Ken Cierpial, who died with AIDS on October 23, 1992, from the private collection of Bob Canavello.

"For my soulmate, Bob Canavello

"I have learned how to learn,
How to read,
How to practice.

"But today, I am getting ready for my life's performance
By forgetting everything I know
And letting everything go.

"Look! How I am now dancing between the notes
Of the music that my soul plays!"

Reflection | Sharing

HIV/AIDS affects all of us and takes us to places where we would not dare to go. Think about what you heard in the songs, readings, and responses.

How is HIV/AIDS affecting you? What is the love story you tell? What would you want on your quilt panel or headstone when you die?

After a quiet time, let us share our thoughts and feelings with this community.

Prayers of the Faithful

Compassionate Holy One, open our hearts, minds, and hands so that we may connect ourselves to the global community of others responding to HIV/AIDS as we pray:

We remember all those people in this country and around the world who are living with HIV/AIDS.

Response: Justice demands that we remember and respond with compassion.

We remember all who care for people living and dying with HIV/AIDS in their homes, in hospices, and in support centers.

Response: Justice demands that we remember and respond with compassion.

We remember all who are involved in research and hospital care, that they may respect the dignity of each person.

Response: Justice demands that we remember and respond with compassion.

We remember all partners who are left mourning for their loved ones.

Response: Justice demands that we remember and respond with compassion.

We remember all parents and partners who learn the truth of their loved ones' lives through the process of facing their death.

Response: Justice demands that we remember and respond with compassion.

We remember . . . Please finish the sentence and we will respond.

Blessing Bread and Water

We remember by blessing bread and water, symbols of nourishment and thirst. Let us extend our hands toward this bread and water.

Blessed are you, Nourishing One, for giving us bread to strengthen us for the long journey. May its healing power rise within us.

Blessed are you, Thirst Quencher, for giving us water to keep us alive in the desert. May its life-giving power flow through us.

As we eat and drink, let us remember.

Lighting Candles

One person takes a small candle, lights it from the large one, encircles it around the large one and says:

I light a candle of _______ . *For example, hope.*
Come, take a candle, light it, and say, "I light a candle of _____." *For example, forgiveness, thanks, sorrow.*

Prayer of Hope

When all candles are lighted, continue:

We bring together many candles, many lights.
As those who keep the night watch await the dawn,
we remain vigilant,
until a cure for HIV/AIDS is found,
until those dying with HIV/AIDS are comforted,

until truth sets us free,
until love drives out injustice,
until compassion reigns.
We shall not give up the fight.

Song

"We Shall Not Give up the Fight," collected and edited by Anders Nyberg © 1984, Peace of Music Publishing AB, admin. Walton Music Corp., a division of GIA Publications, Inc.

We shall not give up the fight.
We have only started. *(3x)*
We shall not give up the fight.
We have only started. *(3x)*

Together we'll have victory,
Hand holding hand. *(3x)*
Together we'll have victory,
Hand holding hand. *(3x)*

Never, ever put to flight,
We are bound to win. *(3x)*
Never, ever put to flight,
We are bound to win. *(3x)*

Take Action

Let us put our prayer into action this month. Here are some possible ways:

- Learn how HIV is transmitted, how it can be forestalled, and how people in this country and around the world are living with it.
- Treat those living with HIV with kindness, respect, and compassion.
- Wear a red ribbon, the universal symbol of HIV mindfulness and support.
- Participate in a candlelight vigil in your community, or organize one with singers, musicians, dancers, poets, storytellers, and religious leaders.
- Demand research funding for HIV/AIDS and government support for people living with it.

Sending Forth

Let us open our circle of support and compassion now.
Let us take our candles with us and use them in marches against HIV/AIDS.
Let us go forth to respond to HIV/AIDS with love, tears, rage, compassion, hope, and action.

Greeting of Peace

Responding is hard and exhausting work. We need all the hugs we can get. Receive an embrace for all that may be required of you in remembering and responding to HIV/AIDS. Let us embrace one another with peace.

Learn More from These Resources

The AIDS Memorial Quilt Project: http://www.aidsquilt.org/about/the-aids-memorial-quilt. How to Make a Panel for the Quilt for someone you love: http://www.aidsquilt.org/make-a-panel/step-by-step-instructions.

Bennett, Marilyn, director. *From Selma to Stonewall: Are We There Yet?* Watch on Amazon Prime or Vimeo, 2016.

Cherry, Kittredge, and Zalmon O. Sherwood, eds. *Equal Rites: Lesbian and Gay Worship, Ceremonies, and Celebrations.* Louisville, KY: Westminster John Knox Press, 1995.

DIGNITY USA is organized to unite gay, lesbian, bisexual, transgender, queer, and intersex Catholics, as well as our families, friends, and loved ones in order to develop leadership and be an instrument through which we may be heard by and promote reform in the church: https://www.dignityusa.org/.

Kugle, Scott Siral al-Hagg. *Living Out Islam: Voices of Gay, Lesbian and Transgender Muslims.* New York: New York University Press, 2014.

Metropolitan Community Churches (MCC) has been at the vanguard of civil and human rights movements by addressing issues of race, gender, sexual orientation, economics, climate change, aging, and global human rights: https://www.mccchurch.org/.

Wilson, Nancy. *I Love to Tell the Story: 100+ Stories of Justice, Inclusion, and Hope.* Parker, Co: Books to Believe In, 2016.

section four

Be Well!

The tree that is beside the running water
is fresher and gives more fruit.

—Teresa of Ávila, *The Interior Castle*

When you do things from your soul,
you feel a river moving in you, a joy.

—Rumi, "Moving Water"

When you learn, teach.
When you get, give.

—Maya Angelou, "Our Grandmothers"

37. January

A Cup of Blessings for the New Year

This is the season of endings and beginnings.
Let the Spirit of Blessings surround me as I give thanks.

The New Year offers time to reflect on endings and beginnings, an opportunity to recognize blessings and await more. Your life can be viewed as three cups. At times you are empty, waiting to receive. Other days you are filling with possibilities. Another time you are overflowing.

This liturgy invites you to look at your cup of blessings to reflect on what you need, to give thanks for what you have been given, and to think about what you will give to others.

Preparation

Be ready to fill your favorite cup with a drink you enjoy: water, tea, cappuccino, wine, juice, coffee, hot chocolate, or another beverage.

Centering Prayer

This is the season of endings and beginnings.
Let the Spirit of Blessings surround me as I give thanks.

A Story of Three Cups

Once upon a time there were three cups. The first was empty, waiting, ready to receive and hold whatever was poured into it. The second was filling with possibilities, pleasing the senses with anticipation. The third brimmed to overflowing, inviting the thirsty to receive its powers.

Look at Your Empty Cup

My cup, empty now, will soon be filled with drink.
Blessed are You, Holy One, for the potential you offer me.

Fill Your Cup with a Drink of Choice

In filling this cup, I see possibilities of the universe pouring forth through me.
Blessed are you, Source of Life, for filling my cup again and again.

Hold Your Brimming Cup

This brimming cup is full of refreshment and renewal.
Blessed are you, Holy Wisdom, for giving me your gifts of empowerment.

Begin to Drink

With this first sip, I give thanks for liberating streams in my life. *Pause.*
With this second sip, I respect the diverse blessing cups given by and to others. *Pause.*
With this third sip, I offer the waters of life to a thirsty world. *Pause.*

Reflect | Meditate | Journal

Think of this cup of blessings for the New Year. Notice the beauty emanating from it—an empty space, a place for mystery, a possibility waiting to be filled, a hunger yearning to be satisfied, a brimming cup ready to share.

What do I need in this cup? What do I accept from this cup? What will I give with this cup?

Take time now to meditate, write in a journal, draw, paint, dance, talk with a friend, or do something else that gives you a pleasurable way to embody your own wisdom.

Closing Prayer

This is the season of endings and beginnings.
Let the Spirit of Blessings surround me as I give thanks.

Take Action for a Blessing

- Fill the empty cup of another by calling, sending a card or an email, having a conversation, or reaching out just because.
- Thank someone for some kind action they have done for you or for the good of the world.
- Feel your power and use one of your gifts to help someone else.

Learn More from These Resources

Emoto, Masaru. *Water Crystal Healing: Music and Images to Restore Your Well-Being.* Hillsboro, OR: Beyond Words Publishing, Inc., 2006.

Polacco, Patricia. *The Blessing Cup.* New York: Simon & Schuster, 2013.

38. February

Goodbye Winter, Hello Spring!

May all be well again.

This winter has been a hard and long one for many: more ice and wind, less warmth; more grey skies and snow, less sun; a time for more hibernation and less community. A thaw and a green world must be around the bend!

This liturgy invites you to pay attention to spring renewal: days growing longer, crocuses peeking out from Earth, and birds returning to sing. Say goodbye to winter and hello to spring renewal.

Preparation

Put your favorite spring plant or herb in front of you: crocus, daffodil, tulip, mint, rosemary, basil, and others.

Centering Prayer

Breathe out winter. Breathe in spring. (3x)

Go, Winter, Go!

Depart from my life, deadening Spirit of Winter.
Response: Go, winter, go.
Be gone, all slippery ice, slushy sleet, dangerous snow, and piercing winds.
Response: Go, winter, go.
Be gone, all ice, sleet, and cold in my personal life: snide remarks, judgmental statements, cruel jokes, nasty gossip, untruthful comments, anger, and jealousy.
Response: Go, winter, go.
Be gone, times of loneliness and harshness.
Response: Go, winter, go.
Be gone . . . . What do you wish to let go of?
Response: Go, winter, go.

Hear my prayer and go, Spirit of Winter. Depart from my neighborhood, from my community, and from my life for another year. Be gone. Be gone. Be gone.

Reflect | Meditate | Journal

Winter and spring represent seasons of our lives. This year, what of this winter do I want to maintain? What do I need to let go of this season? What is the springtime for which I hope? What changes do I need to make to live into spring? Take time for reflection and journaling.

Hello Spring

Source of Life, Provident God,
you who bring forth crocuses and daffodils,
praise to you for blessing Earth with beauty.
Renew all life with flowing water, blooming flowers,
singing birds, and spring light.

May I notice the renewal of Earth.
May my eyes open to the bulbs peeking out of the soil.
May my ears hear the song of the birds.
May my feet touch Earth gently.
May I return blessings to sea and sky.

May Earth be renewed.
May waters be clean.
May air be pure.
May the sun shine brightly with energy.
May all be well again.
Amen. Blessed be. May it be so.

Take Action to Renew Earth

- Let go of fear, anger, jealousy, judgment, and negativity. Welcome friendship.
- Plant something green—an herb, vegetable, flower, kindness. Put your hands in soil.
- Notice spring alive in your neighborhood—flowers blooming, birds nesting, and children playing.
- Clean up a creek. Skip stones across the water.
- Invite friends to have a picnic at the park. Look for four-leaf clovers.
- Get caught in a spring shower. Dance in the rain.
- Pack up winter clothes; take out spring clothes. Donate some to a shelter.
- Do spring-cleaning. Decorate your home with fresh tulips and daffodils.
- Make an impact in an instant: donate to a favorite charity.

Learn More from These Resources

Climate change: read about the effects of climate change on the seasons and share what you learn with a friend.

Greene, Rhonda Gowler, author, and Anne Wilson, illustrator. *The Beautiful World That God Made.* Grand Rapids, MI: Eerdmans Books for Young Readers, 2002.

Rosenberg, Madelyn, author, and Jana Christy, illustrator. *Happy Birthday, Tree! A Tu B'Shevat Story.* Park Ridge, IL: Albert Whitman and Company, 2012.

39. March

Thank ReSisters Worldwide

True resistance begins with people confronting pain . . .
and wanting to do something to change it.

—bell hooks, *Yearning: Race, Gender, and Cultural Politics*

International Women's Day, March 8, and every day is a day to thank ReSisters: women who are resisting, insisting, persisting, and organizing for justice. They are giving people voice and hope worldwide. The world needs ReSisters always, but especially today.

This liturgy invites you to honor silence breakers, thank feminists and womanists of the #MeToo and Time's Up movements, and celebrate Women's Marches.

Preparation

Place pictures of ReSisters around your table and space. Put a pussy hat on the table. Have a candle, with matches, for each ReSister you name.

Listen to ReSisters

ReSisters are speaking out around the world. They are resisting, insisting, persisting, and organizing for justice. Take time now to honor ReSisters and silence breakers, to thank feminists and womanists of the #MeToo and Time's Up movements.

Light a candle of gratitude as you name each woman.

"I don't want to be remembered as the girl who was shot. I want to be remembered as the girl who stood up."

—Malala Yousafzai: An Inspiration for Everyone *by J. D. Rockefeller (J. D. Rockefeller, 2016)*

"The likelihood that your acts of resistance cannot stop the injustice does not exempt you from acting in what you sincerely and reflectively hold to be the best interests of your community."

—*Susan Sontag,* At the Same Time: Essays and Speeches *(New York: Farrar, Straus and Giroux, 2007)*

"True resistance begins with people confronting pain . . . and wanting to do something to change it."

—bell hooks, Yearning: Race, Gender, and Cultural Politics *(New York: Routledge, 2015)*

"As women, we must stand up for each other."

—Michelle Obama, 2009 State Department Women of Courage Awards

"There is no gate, no lock, no bolt that you can set upon the freedom of my mind."

—Virginia Woolf, A Room of One's Own *(Orlando, FL: Harcourt, 1929)*

"It's the fire in my eyes,
And the flash of my teeth,
The swing in my waist,
And the joy in my feet.
I'm a woman
Phenomenally."

—Maya Angelou, Phenomenal Woman: Four Poems Celebrating Women *(New York: Random House, 1978)*

Reflect | Meditate | Journal

What did you hear in the words of these ReSisters that challenges you? What did you hear that comforts you? Who are ReSisters you know? How are you a ReSister?

Solidarity with ReSisters on the Seven Continents

The world needs ReSisters always, and especially at this time in history. In solidarity with those who speak out and act up, unite with women ReSisters on the seven continents.

I march with you, Women ReSisters of North America, and advocate for women's rights, racial equality, immigrant protection, health-care reform, and democracy.

I protest with you, Women ReSisters of Asia, and declare "no more nuclear war."

I revolt with you, Women ReSisters of Africa, and shout no to human trafficking, no to violence against women, and no to civil war.

I organize with you, Women ReSisters of Europe, and confront climate change by protecting nature and working for clean water.

I demonstrate with you, Women ReSisters of Latin and Central America, and work for human rights by demanding the reappearance of your imprisoned, disappeared, or politically assassinated family members and loved ones.

I unite with you, Women ReSisters of Antarctica, and applaud your scientific research.

I rally with you, Women ReSisters of Australia and New Zealand, and call for a deep respect for indigenous people and the reform of sexual assault laws.

Send Blessings of Peace

Breathe deeply. Send blessings of peace to ReSisters in your family, in your community, in your country, and around the world. Bless yourself with peace.

Take Action

Put your prayers into action this month. Here are some possible ways:

- Send an email of thanks to a woman ReSister who has inspired you.
- Support and vote for women who are running for office.
- Put pictures of ReSisters around your home or office. Tell the stories of ReSisters.
- Engage on issues from sexual assault and racial equality to immigrant protections and gun violence.
- Stand with women of color, underpaid workers, disenfranchised voters, young women, and mothers who need help.
- Organize. Resist. Persist.

Learn More from These Resources

Burke, Tarana: read about this activist who founded the #MeToo campaign in 2006.

Dáil, Paula vW., and Betty L. Wells. *We Rise to Resist: Voices from a New Era in Women's Political Action.* Jefferson, NC: McFarland Company, Inc., 2018.

Gaines-Cirelli, Ginger. *Sacred Resistance: A Practical Guide to Christian Witness and Dissent.* Nashville, TN: Abingdon Press, 2018.

Mohanty, Chandra Talpade, and Linda Carty. *Feminist Freedom Warriors: Genealogies, Justice, Politics, and Hope.* Chicago, IL: Haymarket Books, 2018.

40. April

Earth Day Prayer

With all creation, I praise you, Divine Providence:
Breathe your life through me!

Earth Day, April 22, invites us to give thanks for our planet home, and it challenges us to pay attention to climate change and global warming that threaten Earth and the Cosmos. This Earth Day act green, that Earth may live!

This liturgy invites you to praise Divine Providence with all creation.

Preparation

Go outside to be with nature for this Earth Day prayer.

Centering Prayer

Spirit of the Cosmos, breathe your life through me.

Praise Divine Providence

Call upon Earth, our planet home, with its beautiful depths and soaring heights, its vitality and abundance of life.
With all creation, I praise you, Divine Providence:
Thank you, Earth! Breathe your life through me!

Call upon the mountains, the high green peaks and meadows filled with flowers, the knobs and the foothills.
With all creation, I praise you, Divine Providence:
Thank you, Mountains! Breathe your life through me!

Call upon the waters that rim Earth, horizon to horizon, that flow in our rivers and streams, that fall upon our gardens and fields.
With all creation, I praise you, Divine Providence:
Thank you, Waters! Breathe your life through me!

Call upon the land that grows our food, the nurturing soil, the fertile fields, the abundant gardens and orchards.
With all creation, I praise you, Divine Providence:
Thank you, Land! Breathe your life through me!

Call upon the forests, the great trees reaching strongly to the sky with Earth in their roots and the heavens in their branches.

With all creation, I praise you, Divine Providence:
Thank you, Forests! Breathe your life through me!

Call upon creatures of the fields, forests, and seas, our siblings, the wolf and deer, the eagle and dove, the great whale and the dolphin, the beautiful orca and salmon.

With all creation, I praise you, Divine Providence:
Thank you, Creatures! Breathe your life through me!

Call upon all those who have lived on Earth, our ancestors and our friends who dreamed the best for future generations and on whose lives our lives are built.

With all creation, I praise you, Divine Providence:
Thank you, Ancestors! Breathe your life through me!

Reflect | Meditate | Journal

When do I praise Divine Providence? How does Providence breathe life through me?

Take Action

- Go for a walk in the woods to reconnect with Earth.
- Pick up litter in your neighborhood.
- Stop using disposable plastic, especially straws.
- Eat less meat. Try a vegan diet. Buy local produce. Compost.
- Recycle—food, electronics, plants, clothes, paper, containers, and more.
- Reduce your carbon footprint—fly and drive less; walk, bike, bus, train.

Learn More from These Resources

Earth Day: search online for current resources.

Neu, Diann L. *Return Blessings: Ecofeminist Liturgies Renewing the Earth.* Cleveland, OH: The Pilgrim Press, 2002.

Roberts, Elizabeth, and Elias Amidon. *Earth Prayers: 365 Prayers, Poems, and Invocations.* New York: HarperSanFrancisco, 1991.

Sayre, April Pulley. *Thank You, Earth: A Love Letter to Our Planet.* New York: HarperCollins, 2018.

41. May

You Are the Salt of the Earth

Blessed are you when you use your healing powers.

"You are the salt of the Earth" (Matt 5:13), the Scriptures remind us. How are you salt? What salty characteristics do you want to take on?

This liturgy invites you to explore the story of salt and bless yourself with salt water. It is a healing ceremony. If you can celebrate it at the ocean, the ultimate body of salt water, go there.

Preparation

Sprinkle salt into one bowl. Have another bowl with water in it. Invite a friend or several to join you, if you wish. Gather in silence, sing, or play music.

Story of Salt

From the dawn of time salt has been used as a seasoning, a preservative, and a link to the spirit world. Ancient people knew its amazing healing powers and traded it ounce for ounce with gold. Salt is a symbol of hospitality. It has been used to protect against enemies, catastrophes, and evil spirits. Houses, altars, bells, and religious articles have traditionally been blessed with salt.

Salt is a symbol of rebirth, resurrection, reincarnation. Not surprisingly, the alchemical symbol for salt is the same as that for the water element: a line through a circle marking above and below sea level.

A "covenant of salt" is an indissoluble alliance between friends. Bread and salt create a binding commitment. "Salt of the Earth" suggests trustworthiness, wisdom, stability, and strength. Salt purifies; water washes clean. Salt and water combine in a miracle solution that electrifies cells and sustains human growth. Salt and water are both important elements for the body to function properly. The ocean and our tears are salt water.

Centering Prayer

Sit calmly and quiet your mind.
Holy Wisdom *(or a name you use for the Divine)*, surround me with healing.

Pause and ponder: "You are the Salt of the Earth."

Blessing Salt Water

Hold the bowl of salt in your left hand, saying:
Blessed are you, Healing Source, Flavorful One, Great Purifier,
for you bring forth salt from the Earth.

Hold the bowl of water in your right hand, saying:
Blessed are you, Womb of Life, Ocean Wave, Holy Water,
for you hold and maintain everything by your powers.

Add the salt to the water, saying:
Blessed are you, Salt-Water, Spirit-Body, Purifier-Cleanser,
for you renew the whole of my being and all of creation.

Pause and ponder: "You are the Salt of the Earth."

Reflect | Meditate | Journal

Sit near the bowl of salt water. Imagine that salt water is cleansing every part of your body, every part of your being. *Pause.*

Ask yourself: What negative energy do I need to wash away? What harmful spirits do I need to purify? Let hurts, fears, disappointments, worries surface. *Pause.* Let them flow out of you and dissipate in the salt water. Take time to feel deeply cleansed. *Pause.*

Hold the bowl of salt water. Imagine that salt water is rejuvenating you and Earth. *Pause.* Touch the salt water.

Ask yourself: What good works will I do to bring about love, mercy, and justice? *Pause.* Take time to make a commitment.

Pause and ponder: "You are the Salt of the Earth."

Blessing with Salt Water

Dip your hands into the salt water and bless yourself.
Blessed are you when you use your healing powers.
 You are the Salt of the Earth.
Blessed are you when you free yourself of negative energy.
 You are the Salt of the Earth.
Blessed are you when you are full of life, vigor, and zest.
 You are the Salt of the Earth.
Blessed are you when you do good works.
 You are the Salt of the Earth.
Blessed are you when you share love, mercy, and justice with those who are pushed to the margins, especially women.
 You are the Salt of the Earth.
Blessed are you when you offer hospitality.
 You are the Salt of the Earth.

Blessed are you when you believe in miracles.
  You are the Salt of the Earth.
Blessed are you when you share your resources and your wisdom.
  You are the Salt of the Earth.

Closing Prayer

Holy Wisdom *(or the name you use for the Divine)*, thank you for surrounding me with healing. Send me forth to live as the Salt of the Earth.

Take Action for a Blessing

- Soak your body in salt water at the ocean or in a bathtub with sea salts added.
- Bake a loaf of salt-rising bread. See recipe book listed below.

Learn More from These Resources

Bardwell, Genevieve, and Susan Ray Brown. *Salt Rising Bread: Recipes and Heartfelt Stories of a Nearly Lost Appalachian Tradition.* Pittsburgh, PA: St. Lynn's Press, 2016.

Kurlansky, Mark, author, and S. D. Schindler, illustrator. *The Story of Salt.* London: Puffin Books, 2014.

42. June

Drawing from Wisdom's Well

May Wisdom be in my heart and in my perceiving.

Divine Wisdom calls, and those who hear her gather around her well. At birth and baptism Divine Wisdom calls girls and women to feminist ministry. She challenges them to proclaim their gifts and to act with wisdom.

This liturgy invites you to praise Divine Wisdom with seven women, representing the seven pillars of the house of Divine Wisdom and the seven continents, to call upon Divine Wisdom to bless all waters, and to bless the gathered with her power.

Preparation

Place a bowl of water, a towel, sprigs of rosemary and lavender on a table.

Call to Gather

Welcome to Wisdom's Well! In the center is a bowl filled with water to represent Divine Wisdom's Well. Gather here to remind you of your birth and baptism when she first called you to feminist ministry.

Wells throughout the ages were places where the community gathered, welcomed one another, remembered together, blessed one another, and sent each other forth with water for their homes and their communities. Many women of the Bible make their entrances by a well, and many commentators have noted the well as a feminine, womb-like symbol, a hidden source of life.

In Celtic spirituality a custom called "well dressing" involved placing plants, flowers, or herbs near a source of water as a way of honoring the precious gift of water from Divine Wisdom. Today put rosemary and lavender, symbols of remembrance, around the well to help you remember and be remembered. You are an image of Divine Wisdom.

Praise Divine Wisdom

Praise to you, Divine Wisdom, for raising up Miriam to dance your people to promised lands.

Response: Bless me with wisdom.

Praise to you, Divine Wisdom, for empowering Mary Magdalene, the apostle to the apostles, the first to proclaim Jesus' resurrection, and the foundation of women-church.

Response: Bless me with wisdom.

Praise to you, Divine Wisdom, for raising up Teresa of Ávila, Catherine of Siena, Thérèse of Lisieux, and Hildegard of Bingen, Doctors of the Church, who challenged the corruption of the institutional church.

Response: Bless me with wisdom.

Praise to you, Divine Wisdom, for empowering feminist ministers and theologians, all who speak out against oppression in all its forms, and women who break bread and do justice.

Response: Bless me with wisdom.

Reflect | Meditate | Journal

Think about the women whose names you have just heard.

Which woman do you feel especially connected to and why? How would you like your litany verse to be written? Start with "Praise to you, Divine Wisdom, for . . ." *Pause for quiet reflection.*

Prayer for Wisdom

Take some water from Wisdom's Well to connect with your birth and baptism and to your call to feminist ministry. If you wish, touch each part of your body as you pray for wisdom.

Touch your heart and say: May Wisdom be in my heart and in my perceiving.
Touch your head and say: May Wisdom be in my mind and in my thinking.
Touch your mouth: May Wisdom be in my mouth and in my speaking.
Touch your hands: May Wisdom be in my hands and in my working.
Touch your feet: May Wisdom be in my feet and in my walking.
Touch your body, especially any other part you want blessed: May Wisdom be in my body and in my loving.
May Wisdom be with me all the days of my life.
Amen. Blessed be. May it be so.

Take Action

Put your prayers into action this month. Here are some possible ways:

- Pray the Prayer for Wisdom every day for a week and connect with your own wisdom.
- Bless yourself with water each day for a week and ask Divine Wisdom to bless you with her wisdom.
- Share your wisdom by writing a letter to the editor of your local newspaper.

Learn More from These Resources

Aquino, María Pilar, and Elisabeth Schüssler Fiorenza, eds. *In the Power of Wisdom: Feminist Spiritualities of Struggle.* London: SCM Press, 2000.

Healy, Elizabeth. *In Search of Ireland's Holy Wells.* Dublin, Ireland: Wolfhound Press, 2002.

The women named in this liturgy: read about them to learn more about those who have gone before us.

43. July

Hand in Hand—Imagine!

Blessed are these hands when they . . .

Imagine the many ways you are connected to family, friends, and colleagues around the world. Hands reach out and link you to others.

This liturgy invites you to imagine yourself hand in hand with loved ones wherever they live.

Preparation

Choose your favorite handmade object, and put it in a special place near you. Pick a treasured gift, a pottery vessel, a weaving, a quilt, jewelry, an article of clothing. Or gather photos of you and loved ones. Invite a friend or several to join you if you like. Play music of your choice if you wish. Rest your body in a comfortable place, relax, and imagine.

Centering Prayer

Center yourself through your five senses, mindful that your hands especially provide a unique way to experience your sense of touch.

Notice five things you see. Name each item in your mind. Maybe you look at your hands. Take in the sights around you.

Pay attention to four things you feel. Maybe you clasp your hands together and notice the feeling of your skin. Maybe you feel the texture of your clothing or the seat you are sitting on.

Listen to three things you hear. Maybe it's the sound of your breathing. Maybe it's something off in the distance.

Observe two things you smell. Maybe your hands or your clothing carry a scent.

Take note of one thing you taste. Maybe you take a sip of a drink nearby. If nothing is nearby, imagine the taste of something you love.

Now that you are centered, imagine that you are hand in hand with dear friends, near and far away. Through the centuries, the creative and healing power of the Divine has been represented through the gestures of the human hand.

Bless Your Hands

Think of the lives your hands have touched and the incredible work you do.

Blessed are my hands when they nurture creativity and cradle new life.
Blessed are my hands when they care for Earth, recycle, and grow gardens.
Blessed are my hands when they protect loved ones.

Response: Look at your hands. Rub them together. Feel the warmth. Place them on any part of your body that needs energy or healing.

Bless the Hands of Friendship

Remember the many ways you and your friends join hands together.

Blessed are my hands when they embrace with love, respect, and dignity.
Blessed are my hands when they comfort a loved one living with illness, disabilities, cancer, HIV/AIDS, or pain-filled uncertainties.
Blessed are my hands when they reach out in understanding to sustain friendships.

Response: Look at your hands. Rub them together. Feel the warmth. Place them on any part of your body that needs energy or healing.

Bless the Hands of Justice

Think of those whose hands bring about love, mercy, and justice.

Blessed are my hands when they care for those who are aged, infirm, lonely, desperate.
Blessed are my hands when they stop violence, vote for equality, and bring about social change.
Blessed are my hands when they hold banners, create signs of solidarity, or embrace circles of community.

Response: Look at your hands. Rub them together. Feel the warmth. Place them on any part of your body that needs energy or healing.

Bless a New Season

Think of all the emotions that you experience: wonder, alienation, doubt, excitement, dread, ecstasy, hope, and more. Acknowledge these feelings as part of yourself.

Blessed are my hands when they open tightly clenched fists to let go of fears and reach out with trust.
Blessed are my hands when they feel the warmth of sunshine, the coolness of water, and the wonder of new places.

Blessed are my hands when they *(add your own).*

Reflect | Meditate | Journal

What invitations and challenges did you hear in this blessing of your hands? When will you reach out to a family member or friend, visit someone in a nursing home or an elderly person who lives at home, comfort a friend who is living with cancer or who is seriously ill?

Take Action with Your Hands

- Pick flowers and give a bouquet to a friend.
- Pull weeds, compost, and beautify your yard.
- Hug a child and say, "I love you."
- Go swimming and feel the refreshing water on your hands and whole body.
- Massage your hands. According to the ancient healing technique of hand reflexology, you can heal your whole body when you massage your hands because you target key zones of your body to relieve stress, tension, and imbalances.

Learn More from These Resources

Hand massage: watch a video online to learn how to give one.

Hand reflexology chart: search this online to learn more about healing.

Kullman, Susan, and Marvelle Thompson. *Blessed Are These Hands: An Exploration and Celebration of Women's Values.* Claremont, CA: blurb.com, 2010.

44. August

Bless Me with Creative Hope

Hope is a song in a weary throat.

—Pauli Murray, *Dark Testament*

Many people are weary from war, illness, inequality, abuse, lies, and injustices of all forms. They yearn for signs of creative hope.

This liturgy invites you to think hopefully about the future and make your visions concrete. You can share it with your family, community, or other group of friends at the beginning of a holiday meal or special time of sharing.

Centering Prayer

Light a candle.

God of Many Names,
Yahweh, Allah, Holy One, Divine Wisdom,
bless me with creative hope for my weary journey.
Bless people in every nation with mercy, love, and justice.

Listen to Hope

"Hope is a song in a weary throat."

—*Pauli Murray,* Dark Testament and Other Poems *(New York: Liveright Publishing, 1970)*

"Hope is a very unruly emotion."

—*Gloria Steinem,* Outrageous Acts and Everyday Rebellions *(New York: Henry Holt and Company, 2019)*

"'Hope' is the thing with feathers -
That perches in the soul -
And sings the tune without the words -
And never stops - at all -"

—*Emily Dickinson, in T. W. Higginson and Mabel Loomis Todd, eds.,* Poems by Emily Dickinson *(1861)*

Reflect | Meditate | Journal

What are my sources of hope? What are my hopes and dreams for the future? What creative action will I do to bring creative hope to my weary journey and a weary world?

Prayer of Hope

God of Many Names,
Yahweh, Allah, Holy One, Divine Wisdom,
thank you for your promise of hope.
Empower me to be hopeful as I act justly, love tenderly, and walk with you.

Take Action

- Be kind. Have empathy.
- Listen to the story of someone who is different from you.
- Find your hope, hold on to it, and share it.

Learn More from These Resources

Campbell, Joan Brown. *Living into Hope: A Call to Spiritual Action for Such a Time as This.* Woodstock, VT: SkyLights Paths Publishing, 2010.

Chavez, Matthew "Levee." *Signs of Hope: Messages from Subway Therapy.* New York: Bloomsbury, 2017.

Chittister, Joan. *Radical Spirit: Twelve Ways to Live a Free and Authentic Life.* New York: Convergent Books, 2017.

Chittister, Joan, and Rowan Williams. *Uncommon Gratitude: Alleluia for All That Is.* Collegeville, MN: Liturgical Press, 2010.

Murray, Pauli. *Dark Testament and Other Poems.* New York: Liveright Publishing, 1970.

———. *Song in a Weary Throat: Memoir of an American Pilgrimage.* New York: W.W. Norton & Company, 1987.

Steinem, Gloria. *Outrageous Acts and Everyday Rebellions.* New York: Henry Holt and Company, 2019.

Tobin, Mary Luke. *Hope Is an Open Door.* Nashville, TN: Abingdon Press, 1981.

45. September

Pray for Peace on Earth

Teach us to hallow your names throughout the world
and to make friends with people of all cultures.
Then, together, we will bring peace on Earth.

Peace on Earth, or world peace, is the absence of war and violence. While there are many theories for how peace could be achieved, respecting and valuing differences in people and cultures tops the list.

This liturgy invites you to imagine living in different parts of the world and praying for peace on Earth. After your individual prayer, use this liturgy for the beginning of a holiday meal or a special time of sharing with your family, community, or group of friends.

Preparation

Put a cloth on the dining table and place a candle on it for each person.

Centering Prayer

Breathe in peace. Breathe out peace. *(3x)*

Praying for Peace on Earth

Imagine living in the mountains of Afghanistan.
You wear a veil and search for food to eat.
Five times a day you pray to Allah for peace on Earth.

Imagine living in a crowded city in China.
You shop at street stalls and ride your bike to work.
Every day you pray to the Buddha for peace on Earth.

Imagine living in the Hopi Nation.
You make beautiful pottery and live in the pueblo.
Every day you pray to the Great Spirit for peace on Earth.

Imagine living on the west coast of Africa.
You grow yams and walk five miles to school.
Every day you pray to Oshun for peace on Earth.

Imagine living on the other side of town or in another state.
You have different neighbors, a different job, a different lifestyle.
Every day you pray to your God for peace on Earth.

Lighting Candles

Imagine people around the world praying for peace every day.
Light a candle and say, "I pray with you for peace on Earth."

Reflect | Meditate | Journal

What does peace on Earth mean to you? How can you bring it about in your life and the lives of others?

Prayer for Peace

Merciful and peace-loving God of Many Names and Many Peoples, your compassion and grace sustain the universe. Teach us to hallow your names throughout the world and to make friends with people of all cultures. Then, together, we will bring peace on Earth.
Amen. Blessed be. May it be so.

Take Action

- Look up "peace on Earth" and gaze at the beautiful images you find.
- Write to friends in another country and wish them peace.
- Think "Peace on Earth" the next time you are in the midst of a conflict with someone and let it make a difference in your reactions and the outcome.

Learn More from These Resources

Diamond, Louise. *The Peace Book: 108 Simple Ways to Create a More Peaceful World.* Berkeley, CA: Conari Press, 2001.

McKenna, Megan. *She Who Brings Peace.* Erie, PA: Pax Christi, 2003.

Parr, Todd. *The Peace Book.* New York: Little, Brown Books for Young Readers, 2017.

"The Peace Pilgrimage": search online (Lugo to Santiago de Compostela, Spain).

46. October

Grant Me Healing

Healing in front of me, healing behind me;
Healing above me, healing below me;
Healing in my body, healing in my soul.
Companion on the Journey! Grant me healing.

Healing has twin aspects: restoration now and empowerment for the future. It happens within and without, making body and spirit whole together. External healing is often a sign of inner healing; inner healing reveals itself through the body.

This liturgy invites you to ask the Divine for healing. Basically, healing restores a relationship with yourself, with others, and with the Holy One.

Centering Prayer

Light a candle. Put your body in a comfortable prayer position.

Prayer for Healing

O God! Grant me healing.

Healing in my eyes, healing in my ears;
Healing on my skin, healing in my blood;
Healing in my hands, healing on my face;
Healing in my bones, healing within me.

Source of Life! Grant me healing.

Healing in front of me, healing behind me;
Healing above me, healing below me;
Healing on my left, healing on my right.

Wisdom Sophia! Grant me healing.

Healing in my legs, healing in my feet;
Healing in my breasts (or where they used to be);
Healing in my ovaries (or where they used to be);
Healing in my womb (or where it used to be);
Healing on my tongue; healing in my lungs.

Spirit of Grace! Grant me healing.

Healing in front of me, healing behind me;
Healing above me, healing below me;
Healing in my body, healing in my soul.
Companion on the Journey! Grant me healing.

Reflect | Meditate | Journal

Hug yourself. Think of an image of healing: a waterfall, a sunrise, a sparkling ocean, a burning candle, a wishing well, salt water, a gentle rain, or another. Visualize a picture of your image. Take time to visualize your healing.

Take Action

- Write the word "heal" on a card. Just before you go to bed, focus your eyes on the word "heal," and concentrate your attention for five to ten minutes. Do this exercise nightly for at least two weeks. "Heal" will be with you in your thoughts as you proceed in your everyday life.
- Get a picture of your healing image and tape it in a place where you will see it during your day.
- Take a healing bath. Put a sacred symbol—prayer beads, rosary, Tibetan bowl, shells, or another—in or near the bath water. Add lavender bath oil or bath salts to the water. Play your favorite calming music. Light candles. Ease your body into the water and soak in the healing.

Learn More from These Resources

Neu, Diann L. *Seasons of Healing: Journaling and Resources.* Silver Spring, MD: WATERworks Press, 2010.

Oman, Maggie. *Prayers for Healing: 365 Blessings, Poems, & Meditations from Around the World.* San Francisco, CA: Conari Press, 1999.

47. November

Thanksgiving Meal of Gratitude

We return thanks to the Great Spirit,
and send greetings and thanks for all the gifts of Creation.

—Iroquois Prayer, Thanksgiving Address 2014 Ohenton Kariwahtekwen

Divine Wisdom calls her friends from every corner of Earth to gather at a meal in her name. "Come, eat my bread and drink the wine which I have prepared for you" (Prov 9:5).

Divine Wisdom gives her people daily bread. She sets her tables with many breads, including injera from Africa, tortillas from South America, rye bread from Europe, mochi from Asia, damper from Australia, corn bread from North America, and breads of every country. She provides many drinks, including water, wine, juice, and milk and honey. She offers plates of foods from every culture.

This liturgy invites you to gather your family and friends for a harvest meal of gratitude.

Preparation

Prepare a Thanksgiving feast. Put three candles on the dining table. Invite three people to light them.

Call to Gather

Welcome to our Thanksgiving Meal of Gratitude. There is so much that calls us to have a grateful attitude. Today we take time to say, "Thank You." Let us begin by lighting three candles of gratitude.

Lighting Candles of Gratitude

An Elder: I light this candle to say thank you to our family and friends, to Earth that grows our food, and to migrant workers who harvest it.

A Parent: I light this candle to thank those who have tried to keep us safe this year and to remember those who have suffered from natural disasters and human-made problems.

A Child: I light this candle to thank the prophets who have resisted and created new options for all.

To ensure that the lights remain a part of our journey long after the candles burn away, let us cup our hands over the flames and draw the heat toward our eyes three times.
Blessed is the light that guides us on the road to gratitude. With thanks we kindle the thanksgiving lights.

Iroquois Prayer *from Iroquois Thanksgiving Address 2014 Ohenton Kariwahtekwen, https://www.worldprayers.org/archive/prayers/celebrations/we_return_thanks.html)*

"We return thanks to our mother, the Earth, which sustains us.
We return thanks to the rivers and streams,
 which supply us with water.
We return thanks to all herbs,
 which furnish medicines for the cure of our diseases.
We return thanks to the corn, and to her sisters,
 the beans and squashes, which give us life.
We return thanks to the bushes and trees,
 which provide us with fruit.
We return thanks to the wind,
 which, moving the air, has banished diseases.
We return thanks to the moon and stars,
 which have given us their light when the sun was gone.
We return thanks to our grandfather He-no,
 who has given us rain.
We return thanks to the sun,
 that has looked upon the Earth with a beneficent eye.
Lastly, we return thanks to the Great Spirit,
 and send greetings and thanks for all the gifts of Creation."

Blessing Bread

One holds the bread and prays: Let us extend our hands outward and bless this bread in thanksgiving for life.

Blessed are you, Holy One of the Harvest, for giving us this day our daily bread, the bread of nourishment, the bread of peace, the bread of justice for all. Open our eyes to see the hunger of others. Thank you for promising and giving your people food for the journey, nourishment for the struggle, sustenance of every sort.

Response: (Sing to Lilies of the Field Amen)
We give thanks. *Danke. Gracias. Merci. Xiè-Xie.*

Blessing Drink

Another raises a glass and prays: Let us extend our hands outward and bless this drink in memory of our friends, children, students, parents, teachers, colleagues, and mentors who share their passion for life with the world.

Blessed are you, Holy One of Thanksgiving, for giving us this drink to quench our thirst. We thank you for the passion and joy of those we have known: young children, teenage dreamers, middle-aged visionaries, tireless prophets, and feisty elders. Let us share a Thanksgiving toast to life.

Response: We give thanks. *Danke. Gracias. Merci. Xiè-Xie.*

Blessing Food

Pick up the foods. Let us extend our hands outward and bless these foods in memory of those who sweat and toil for justice and those whose sweat and toil is the result of injustice.

Blessed are you, Holy One of Nourishment, for giving us Earth, water, air, and fire that combine to make this food. We thank you for the creative energy and labor of people we have known: cooks, homemakers, refugees, farmers, immigrants, gardeners; those whose muscles, minds, and hearts change the world.

Response: We give thanks. *Danke. Gracias. Merci. Xiè-Xie.*

Let Us Eat and Share

Who are the people and what are the things or events for which you are thankful? Let us share stories of gratitude with one another as we eat together.

Take Action

- Thank each person at the table for something.
- Work in a food pantry with others or serve food in a nearby shelter this month.

Learn More from These Resources

Neu, Diann L. "Feminist Eucharists at Wisdom's Many Tables." In *New Feminist Christianity*, edited by Mary E. Hunt and Diann L. Neu. Woodstock, VT: SkyLight Paths Publishing, 2010.

Weinstein, Miriam. *The Surprising Power of Family Meals: How Eating Together Makes Us Smarter, Stronger, Healthier, and Happier.* Hannover, NH: Steerforth Press, 2005.

Winter, Miriam Therese. *eucharist with a small e.* Maryknoll, NY: Orbis Books, 2005.

48. December

You Are Home

Come home to yourself, and be nourished.
Welcome home!

Home can be a source of joy and a cause for pain. Home is an important and meaningful place for many. Yet some are made homeless because economics favor a few, differences divide families, violence leaves scars, and some spaces are unsafe.

This liturgy invites you to your Home, that place within yourself where you can rest, take a deep breath, and be safe.

Preparation

Make yourself a cup of tea or drink of choice. Light a candle.

Centering Prayer

Take a minute. Think about what it means to be home for the holidays.

Listen to Words about Home

"Maybe journey is not so much a journey ahead, or a journey into space, but a journey into presence."

—Nelle Morton, The Journey Is Home *(Boston: Beacon Press, 1985)*

Come home to yourself, and be nourished. Welcome home!

"The ache for home lives in all of us, the safe place where we can go as we are."

—Maya Angelou, All God's Children Need Traveling Shoes *(New York: Random House, 1986)*

Come home to your friends, family, family of choice, and be supported. Welcome home!

"All I was doing was trying to get home from work."

—Rosa Parks, in Let My People Go! *by Robert J. Walker (Lanham, MD: Rowman & Littlefield, 2007)*

Come home to your community, and find hope. Welcome home!

Bless Your Home

For knowing that I am *home*, I am thankful!
For creating a *home* with others, I am thankful!
For having a *home* where people love me for who I am, I am thankful!
For welcoming others into my *home*, I am thankful!
For those who provide a *home* to people who do not have a *home*, I am thankful!

Reflect on Coming Home

What did you hear in the words about home? What does "coming home" mean for you?

Take Action at Home

- Welcome friends to your *home* for the holidays.
- Let go of any pain and hurt connected with *home*. Breathe out pain, breathe in healing.
- Be thankful for the spaces where you have felt at *home* and for the *homes* you have created.
- Volunteer at a local shelter.
- Educate yourself on why people are made homeless.

Learn More from These Resources

Cousteau, Philippe, and Deborah Hopkinson, et al. *Follow the Moon Home: A Tale of One Idea, Twenty Kids, and a Hundred Sea Turtles*. San Francisco, CA: Chronicle Books, 2016.

Kondō, Marie. *Spark Joy: An Illustrated Master Class on the Art of Organizing and Tidying Up*. New York: Ten Speed Press, 2016.

National Museum of African American History and Culture. *Sweet Home Café Cookbook: A Celebration of African American Cooking*. Washington, DC: Smithsonian Books, 2018.

section five

Ever-Flowing Streams

She studies, and disputes, and teaches, and thus she serves her Faith; for how could God, who gave her reason, want her ignorant?

—Sor Juana Inés de la Cruz, *Villancico*

To stand at the edge of the sea, to sense the ebb and flow of the tides, to feel the breath of a mist moving over a great salt marsh, to watch the flight of shore birds that have swept up and down the surf lines of the continents for untold thousands of years, to see the running of the old eels and the young shad to the sea, is to have knowledge of things that are as nearly enternal as any earthly life can be.

—Rachel Carson, *The Edge of the Sea*

All water has a perfect memory
and is forever trying to get back to where is was.

—Toni Morrison, "The Site of Memory"

49. Listen to the Cries for Justice

Be with us as we listen to the cries and act for justice.

People, Earth, animals, plants, water, air, the universe—all are crying for justice.

This liturgy challenges us to listen to why they are weeping and to take action when we see injustices.

Preparation

Gather thirteen candles, chimes, a pot of compost, a bowl of water, and a rain stick and place them on a table or space in the center of a circle.

Invoking the Spirits

Light a candle.
O Wisdom of the South, you who are Fire,
warm our hurting spirits and open us to stand with all who are crying.
Be with us as we listen to the cries and act for justice.

Sound chimes.
O Wisdom of the East, you who are Air,
empower us with your rising sun to breathe in and out again.
Be with us as we listen to the cries and act for justice.

Put compost into a pot.
O Wisdom of the North, you who are Earth,
strengthen us to move beyond what is cold and harsh in life.
Be with us as we listen to the cries and act for justice.

Pour water into a bowl.
O Wisdom of the West, you who are Water,
refresh us with waterfalls to heal the hurts.
Be with us as we listen to the cries and act for justice.

Lamentations for Justice

Play a rain stick to evoke weeping.
Question: Mother, why are you weeping?
Lament 1: I weep because I am an immigrant mother who is threatened with being deported and losing my children. Be with me.
Response: Mother, we see your tears and we stand with you.
Light a candle to honor the woman who is weeping.

Play a rain stick.
Question: Brother, why are you weeping?
Lament 2: I weep because I am a survivor of clergy sexual abuse. Be with me.
Response: Brother, we see your tears and we stand with you.
Light a candle.

Play a rain stick.
Question: Sister, why are you weeping?
Lament 3: I weep because my child died in the war. Be with me.
Response: Sister, we notice your tears and we struggle with you.
Light a candle.

Continue with the rain stick, question, lament, response, and candle lighting format for each lament.

Lament 4: I weep because my friend is experiencing homelessness. Be with me.
Lament 5: I weep because my sister is a survivor of human trafficking. Be with me.
Lament 6: I weep because I am living with cancer. Be with me.
Lament 7: I weep because my friend is a survivor of domestic violence. Be with me.
Continue with other laments.

Blessing with Water

All who cry, come to the water.
Get your hands wet, and bless yourself, especially your eyes, with this Source of Life.

Sending Forth

May we listen and take action when we notice injustice.
May all who are hurting be healed.
May we go forth accompanying one another in the struggles for justice.
Amen. Blessed be. May it be so.

Take Action

- Fast for a day or afternoon to be in solidarity with those who are crying for justice.
- Comfort those who are weeping by calling them, sending them a card, or taking them out for tea.
- Call your congressperson and request support for a particular justice issue.
- Read the newspaper and pray for someone whose story you read.

Learn More from These Resources

Brazal, Agnes M. *A Theology of Southeast Asia: Liberation-Postcolonial Ethics in the Philippines.* Maryknoll, NY: Orbis Books, 2019.

Domina, Lynn. *Devotions from HERstory: 31 Days with Women of Faith.* Valley Forge, PA: Judson Press, 2019.

Gafney, C. Wilda. *Womanist Midrash: Introduction to the Women of the Torah and the Throne.* Louisville, KY: Westminster John Knox Press, 2017.

Kilroe, Stephanie. *Anne Hope: The Struggle for Freedom.* London, UK: Darton, Longman and Todd, 2019.

Nutt, Maurice J. *Thea Bowman: Faithful and Free.* Collegeville, MN: Liturgical Press, 2019.

Peters, Rebecca Todd, and Grace Y. Kao, eds. *Encountering the Sacred: Feminist Reflections on Women's Lives.* New York: T&T Clark, 2019.

50. Pray with Us

Follow your own way of speaking to God sincerely, lovingly, confidently and simply, as your heart dictates.

—Jane de Chantal, *Letters of Spiritual Direction*

How do feminists pray? Let us count the many ways. Feminists who pray are searching for new names and understandings of God. We yearn to relate to the Divine, to one another, and to all creation without the distortions of patriarchy and kyriarchy. We are reclaiming women's traditions of prayer and creating renewed ways of praying.

This liturgy is an invitation to share insights and experiences about prayer. It uses traditional symbols of prayer and quotes from feminists about prayer to invite us to take our places in the stories of pray-ers.

Preparation

Gather symbols of prayer: a bell, a large bowl to create a well, candles. Fill the bowl with water and place it on a table in the center of a circle. Place candles, flowers, and shells around this well. Provide a cup and a paper with prayer quotes from the "Thoughts on Prayer" section of this liturgy for each participant.

Call to Prayer

One rings the bell three times and proclaims:

From generation to generation, our mothers, grandmothers, and ancestors heard bells that called them to prayer, and they prayed. Some of us still pray, often reluctantly. Many of us used to pray. A number of us don't or can't pray. Most of us have difficulty praying kyriarchal prayers. Some of us are reclaiming women's traditions of prayer. Others are creating new prayers.

Today we take our places in the stories of pray-ers. "Pray with us," they call. And we pray in the form of contemplation, song, and dance; reading, writing, and conversations; praise, petition, and thanksgiving; tears, cries for help, and lamentations; stillness, gazing, and waiting; fasting, feasting, and Eucharist; liturgies, meditations, and political actions.

Today we gather at Wisdom's Well to pray together and to share our experiences and struggles with prayer.

Song

"Prayer to Friends" by Carolyn McDade, from This Ancient Love *(Surtsey Publishing © 1988; renewed © 1991 Carolyn McDade). Used with permission.*

To this day I bring my life
Born of hope, born of sand
Yearning joy where now there's strife
All I have, all I am

Help me to see what I must see
Help me to be where I must be
Restless faith abide 'til all are free
Fill my life, turn my hand

Naming a Circle of Pray-ers

The bell-ringer continues:

The Japanese take off their shoes before entering a house, a sacred place. The people of the Hebrew Scriptures took off their sandals to stand on holy ground. Let us take off our shoes. *Pause.*

Today we walk on the holy ground of prayer. What wells up inside of you when you hear the word "prayer"? Let us speak our names and share a word or phrase about prayer.

Prayer

If some people are in wheelchairs, on walkers, use canes, or have mobility issues, invite them to the center of the circle. One gestures for others to stand, as they are able, hold hands, and move into the center, raising hands together. She prays:

Divine Wisdom, teach us to pray.

She gestures for all to continue holding hands, move outward, then return to the center, raising hands together for the second time. One person prays:

Divine Wisdom, Source of Life, be with us as we remember the prayers of our ancestors.

Continuing to hold hands, all move outward, then return to the center, raising hands together for the third time. One person prays:

Divine Wisdom, Source of Life, Font of Wisdom, encourage us to transform prayer. Amen. Blessed be. May it be so.

Thoughts on Prayer

Listen to women's thoughts on prayer. Our sung response after every third one is "Call to Prayer." *Different people read each quote, pausing after each.*

Song

"Call to Prayer" by Carolyn McDade, from This Ancient Love *(Surtsey Publishing © 1988; renewed © 1991 Carolyn McDade). Used with permission.*

For each part is a part of each other part.
We all are a part of one another.

"The life of prayer is so great and various there is something in it for everyone. It is like a garden which grows everything, from apples to potatoes."
—*Evelyn Underhill, in Lucy Menzies, ed.,* Collected Papers of Evelyn Underhill *(1946)*

"For prayer is the language of the heart—needing no measured voice, no spoken tone."
—*Grace Aguilar,* The Spirit of Judaism *(Philadelphia, PA: C. Sherman, 1842)*

"What we are doing when we pray as feminists in our respective traditions is something very radical in the literal sense of the word, that is, challenging our traditions at the very root. Sometimes we challenge by refusing, by using no words. Sometimes we challenge by creating new words that smash the old words. Both ways are powerful acts of resistance."
—*Marjorie Procter-Smith, in* Women at Worship, *ed. Marjorie Procter-Smith and Janet R. Walton (Louisville, KY: Westminster John Knox Press, 1993)*

Song
"Call to Prayer"

For each part is a part of each other part.
We all are a part of one another.

"As for prayer, don't burden yourself with making considerations; neither your mind or mine is good at that. Follow your own way of speaking to God sincerely, lovingly, confidently and simply, as your heart dictates."
—*Jane de Chantal,* Letters of Spiritual Direction *(1855)*

"To pray is to work, to work is to pray."
—*Ancient motto of the Benedictine Order*

"Prayer is essentially a process by which ideals are enabled to become operative in our lives. It may be more than this, but it is at least this."
—*Georgia Harkness,* The Recovery of Ideals *(1937)*

Song
"Call to Prayer"

For each part is a part of each other part.
We all are a part of one another.

"Prayer is the natural language of love."

—Joan Brown Campbell, in Jim Castelli, ed., How I Pray *(1994)*

"Prayer is naught else but a yearning of soul. . . . It draws down the great God into the little heart; it drives the hungry soul up to the plenitude of God; it brings together these two lovers, God and the soul, in a wondrous place where they speak much of love."

—Mechthild of Magdeburg (© 1250), in Lucy Menzies, ed., Mirrors of the Holy *(1928)*

"Absolutely unmixed attention is prayer."

—Simone Weil, Gravity and Grace *(1947)*

Song

"Call to Prayer"

For each part is a part of each other part.
We all are a part of one another.

"I don't know how I could survive the indifference and evil and violence rife in our nation and world, and the shallowness and pettiness of so much of Washington's self-important life, without these seeds of faith, prayer, and music that were planted in my youthful soul by parents and other elders."

—Marian Wright Edelman, Guide My Feet: Prayers and Meditations for Our Children *(Boston, MA: Beacon Press, 1995)*

"Pray inwardly, even if you do not enjoy it. It does good, though you feel nothing. Yes, even though you think you are doing nothing."

—Julian of Norwich, Revelations of Divine Love *(1670)*

"I betook myself to prayer and in every lonely place I found an altar."

—Elizabeth, bondswoman and minister, born in Maryland, 1766, from The Black Woman's Gumbo Ya-Ya: Quotations by Black Women, *ed. Terri L. Jewell (Berkeley, CA: The Crossing Press, 1993)*

Song

"Call to Prayer"

For each part is a part of each other part.
We all are a part of one another.

Meditation

Take a cup and come to Wisdom's Well. Dip it into the water and take a drink. Take the paper with women's thoughts on prayer that you just heard, find a place for quiet reflection, put your body into a prayer posture—sitting with hands open or with clenched fists, kneeling in a yoga position, lying down, whatever is your prayer posture—drink water as desired, and pray with the prayer thoughts.

Listen to what is going on when feminists pray. Listen to how a prayerful feminist lives. Listen to how you pray and live.

Read the words slowly. Take some deep breaths and sit quietly. Read the words again. Listen to the word or phrase that attracts your attention. Be comfortable with silent spaces between your thoughts.

Read the words once more. Be quiet. Be open to their effect on you.

When you hear the bell ring after ten minutes, come back to the circle.

Shared Prayer

The bell ringer sounds the bell three times to call people to the well.

Let us take a few minutes to share our reflections about prayer. What is going on when feminists pray? How does a prayerful feminist live? How do you pray and live? Share with us a glimpse of your prayerful reflections, then float a candle or flower, place a shell or pour water into the communal well.

Song
"Call to Prayer"

For each part is a part of each other part.
We all are a part of one another.

Prayers of the Faithful

Many around the world need us to pray with them or to pray for them this night. Let our response be, "Compassionate Mercy, hear our prayer."

A daughter sighs with resignation at the death of her mother.
Response: Compassionate Mercy, hear our prayer.
An aunt prays with her niece and nephew at bedtime. *Response.*
A friend knocks at the door to offer comfort during a time of despair. *Response.*
A single mother pleads for comfort and reassurance during moments of crisis. *Response.*
A woman cries in anger at a kyriarchal, abusive church. *Response.*
A despairing teenager laments in the face of physical violence. *Response.*
A previously unemployed woman offers a moment of thanks for finding a job. *Response.*
A mother cries for help when her daughter is pregnant unexpectedly. *Response.*
For whom else do we pray? *Response.*

Song
"Call to Prayer"

For each part is a part of each other part.
We all are a part of one another.

Blessing Bread, Milk, and Honey

Play instrumental music as the blessers set the table with bread, milk, and honey.

One blesser takes the bread into her hands and says:
Come! Pray with us. Touch this bread, or touch someone who is touching the bread, and remember feminist prayers. Blessed be this bread and blessed be those who pray.

Two blessers pray in turn:
Blessed are you, Wisdom Sophia,
for you promise your people food for the journey.
Blessed are you, Bread of Life,
for you send your people manna as they wander in the desert.

The blessers break the bread and invite each person to do the same and eat. The first blesser takes the cup of milk and honey into her hands and says:
Come! Pray with us. Touch this cup, or touch someone who is touching the cup, and remember feminist prayers. Blessed be this cup of milk and honey and blessed be those who pray.

The other two blessers pray in turn:
Blessed are you, Source of Life,
for you refresh us with a firm and daring spirit.
Blessed are you, Food for the Journey,
for even though we drink, you keep us thirsty for roots and wings.

The blessers drink from the cup and invite each person to do the same.

Blessing Prayerful People

Who is a prayerful person? How do we recognize one? We close, blessing several aspects of prayerful people.

A prayerful person laughs and enjoys life.
Response: Let us laugh and enjoy life.
A prayerful person resists all forms of domination.
Response: Let us resist all forms of domination.
A prayerful person notices signs of new life.
Response: Let us notice signs of new life.
A prayerful person gazes in awe at a colorful sunset.
Response: Let us gaze in awe at a colorful sunset.
A prayerful person pays attention to goodness.
Response: Let us pay attention to goodness.
A prayerful person sees things as they are.
Response: Let us see things as they are.
A prayerful person calls the best out of people.
Response: Let us call the best out of people.

A prayerful person lives deeply in touch with her own and the world's troubles.

Response: Let us live deeply in touch with our own and the world's troubles.

A prayerful person lets herself welcome a bold, daring, new adventure.

Response: Let us let ourselves welcome a bold, daring, new adventure.

A prayerful person . . . What else do we want to say about prayerful people? Tell us and we will respond.

Greeting of Peace

Let us honor ourselves and the prayerful people around us. Let us hold hands. First kiss your right hand, then kiss the hand of the person on your right. Next kiss your left hand and kiss the hand of the person on your left.

Sending Forth

Let us go forth as prayerful people.
May we fill our lives with profound meaning.
May we be alive to connections with creation, with one another, with the Divine.
May we bless the world with our prayers.
Amen. Blessed be. May it be so.

Song

"Gather Us, O God" by Monica Brown, from Holy Ground *(Sacramento, CA: Emmaus Ministries © 1991). Used with permission.*

Gather us, O God, Body, spirit, soul, and mind.
Gather us, O God, one in union now with you.

Take Action

- Pray using different prayer forms: prayer walks, pilgrimage, praying with icons, praying with scriptures, breath prayer, meditation, body prayer, labyrinth, prayer beads, guided imagination, praying with mandalas, dance, and others.
- Create a special place in your home where you can pray.

Learn More from These Resources

Black, Kathy, and Heather Murray Elkins. *Wising Up: Ritual Resources for Women of Faith in Their Journey of Aging.* Cleveland, OH: The Pilgrim Press, 2005.

Bourgeault, Cynthia. *Centering Prayer and Inner Awakening.* Lanham, MD: Cowley Publications, 2001.

Brown, Patricia D. *Paths to Prayer: Finding Your Own Way to the Presence of God.* San Francisco, CA: Jossey-Bass, 2003.

Furlong, Monica, ed. *Women Pray: Voices through the Ages, from Many Faiths, Cultures, and Traditions.* Woodstock, VT: SkyLight Paths Publishing, 2001.

Hayes, Diana L. *Trouble Don't Last Always: Soul Prayers*. Collegeville, MN: Liturgical Press, 1995.

Jeep, Elizabeth McMahon. *Blessings and Prayers through the Year: A Resource for School and Parish.* Chicago, IL: Liturgy Training Publications, 2004.

Kielbasa, Marilyn. *Prayer: Celebrating and Reflecting with Girls.* Winona, MN: Saint Mary's Press, 2002.

Neu, Diann L. *Women's Rites: Feminist Liturgies for Life's Journey.* Cleveland, OH: The Pilgrim Press, 2002.

Procter-Smith, Marjorie. *Praying with Our Eyes Open: Engendering Feminist Liturgical Prayer.* Nashville, TN: Abingdon Press, 1995.

Richardson, Jan L. *In the Sanctuary of Women: A Companion for Reflection and Prayer.* Nashville, TN: Upper Room Books, 2010.

———. *Sacred Journeys: A Woman's Book of Daily Prayer.* Nashville, TN: Upper Room Books, 1995.

Rose, Margaret, Jenny Te Paa, Jeanne Person, Abagail Nelson. *Lifting Women's Voices: Prayers to Change the World.* New York: Morehouse Publishing, 2009.

Rupp, Joyce. *Fragments of Your Ancient Name: 365 Glimpses of the Divine for Daily Meditation.* Notre Dame, IN: Sorin Books, 2011.

Rylant, Cynthia. *Give Me Grace: A Child's Daybook of Prayers.* New York: Simon & Schuster Books for Young Readers, 1999.

Steinkühler, Martina, and Barbara Nascimbeni. *Prayers for Young Children.* Translated by Laura Watkinson. Grand Rapids, MI: Eerdmans Books for Young Readers, 2018.

Ward, Hannah, Jennifer Wild, and Janet Morley, eds. *Celebrating Women.* London: SPCK, 1995.

Ward, Hannah, and Jennifer Wild, compilers. *Human Rites: Worship Resources for an Age of Change.* London: Mowbray, 1995.

Wiederkehr, Macrina. *Seven Sacred Pauses: Living Mindfully Through the Hours of the Day.* Notre Dame, IN: Sorin Books, 2008.

Winter, Miriam Therese. *WomanWitness: A Feminist Lectionary and Psalter, Women of the Hebrew Scriptures.* New York: Crossroad, 1992.

———. *WomanWord: A Feminist Lectionary and Psalter, Women of the New Testament.* New York: Crossroad, 1990.

Wisdom Commentary series, a feminist commentary on every book of the Bible: www.wisdomcommentary.org. Barbara Reid, general ed. Collegeville, MN: Liturgical Press, 2015– .

51. #MeToo: Reclaiming Our Voices in an Age of Violence

When someone is cruel, or acts like a bully, you don't stoop to their level—no, our motto is, when they go low, we go high.

—Michelle Obama, 2016 Democratic National Convention

The groundbreaking #MeToo, #ChurchToo, #NunsToo, #MosqueMeToo, Time's Up movements have become a worldwide phenomenon, giving voices a platform to speak out against sexual violence and harassment. They help survivors find ways to heal and connect with a community of advocates who work to interrupt sexual violence in their communities and assure survivors they are not alone.

This liturgy focuses on community healing for all. It raises up women who are resisting bullying, abusive rhetoric, harassment, and violence present in societies around the world.

Preparation

Put #MeToo posters around the room. Gather sprigs of rosemary, a stone, and a bowl of water. Place them and as many lit candles as you wish on a table or around the space.

Call to Gather

We gather for a liturgy of healing. We as individuals have been hurt; we have been betrayed; we have been abused; we have been scared. We as a people have been hurt; we have been betrayed; we have been abused. What happens to one of us affects all of us. We need healing. Our community needs healing. Our country needs healing. Everywhere needs healing.

We gather in the midst of the #MeToo, #ChurchToo, #MosqueMeToo, Time's Up movements to raise up women worldwide who are resisting bullying, abusive rhetoric, harassment, and violence present in our societies today.

We gather "Reclaiming Our Voices in an Age of Violence." We come together to challenge one another to speak out because only together can we create a world free from violence, abuse, and fear. We mourn those who have died because of domestic violence. We rage with those who have survived sexual abuse and are breaking silence to tell their stories. We pray for healing.

Naming Our Circle

Let us create our circle by speaking our name and saying, "I reclaim my voice in an age of violence."

Creating a Safe Space

To create a safe place here now let us take a candle, light it, and place it somewhere in the room. *Candles are powerful symbols for an evening liturgy. Evergreen branches or sprigs of herbs are effective for daytime or winter.*

Blessing the Light

Let us bless this light. Please say after me:
Blessed are you, Holy One of Justice, *Echo.*
for you empower us to kindle flames of healing. *Echo.*

Let us warm our hands over this healing fire. *Pause.*
Let us cup our hands over the flame and draw its healing energy to our eyes three times.
Let us open our hands outward and send healing energy to those who need it now.

Song

"Sanctuary" by Carrie Newcomer, from The Beautiful Not Yet *(Spotify | Apple Music© 2016), https://www.youtube.com/watch?v=HjOioWTVAl4. Used with permission.*

Chorus: Will you be my refuge
My haven in the storm,
Will you keep the embers warm
When my fire's all but gone?
Will you remember
And bring me sprigs of rosemary,
Be my sanctuary
'Til I can carry on
Carry on.
Carry on.

This one knocked me to the ground.
This one dropped me to my knees.
I should have seen it comin'
But it surprised me. *Chorus.*

In a state of true believers,
On streets called us and them,
It's gonna take some time
'Til the world feels safe again. *Chorus.*

You can rest here in Brown Chapel,
Or with a circle of friends,
A quiet grove of trees
Or between two bookends.

Will you be my refuge
My haven in the storm,
Will you keep the embers warm
When my fire's all but gone?
Will you remember
And bring me sprigs of rosemary,
Be my sanctuary
'Til I can carry on
Carry on.
Carry on.
Carry on.

Listen to Women's Words

Each reader puts rosemary into the water and then reads.

Tarana Burke, Originator of the #MeToo Movement

From Cassandra Santiago and Doug Criss, "An Activist, a Little Girl and the Heartbreaking Origin of 'Me Too,'" CNN, October 17, 2017

Tarana Burke, program director for Brooklyn-based Girls for Gender Equity, was a youth camp director when a young girl asked to speak to her privately.

"'For the next several minutes this child . . . struggled to tell me about her "stepdaddy" or rather her mother's boyfriend who was doing all sorts of monstrous things to her developing body. . . . I was horrified by her words, the emotions welling inside of me ran the gamut, and I listened until I literally could not take it anymore . . . which turned out to be less than five minutes. Then, right in the middle of her sharing her pain with me, I cut her off and immediately directed her to another female counselor who could "help her better."'

"Burke said she never forgot the look on the girl's face.

"'The shock of being rejected, the pain of opening a wound only to have it abruptly forced closed again—it was all on her face,' she wrote.

"'I couldn't help her release her shame, or impress upon her that nothing that happened to her was her fault. I could not find the strength to say out loud the words that were ringing in my head over and over again as she tried to tell me what she had endured.' . . .

"'I watched her walk away from me as she tried to recapture her secrets and tuck them back into their hiding place. I watched her put her mask back on and go back into the world like she was all alone and I couldn't even bring myself to whisper . . . me too.'

"That was the genesis of the movement—to help young women of color [and all women] who had survived sexual abuse, assault and exploitation.

"'On one side, it's a bold declarative statement that "I'm not ashamed" and "I'm not alone." On the other side, it's a statement from survivor to survivor that says "I see you, I hear you, I understand you and I'm here for you or I get it."'"

Response: We will be your refuge. Your haven in the storm. Carry on.

Malala Yousafzai, Pakistani Schoolgirl and Education Activist

From "The Full Text: Malala Yousafzai Delivers Defiant Riposte to Taliban Militants with Speech to the UN General Assembly," Independent, *July 12, 2013*

"I speak not for myself but for those without voice . . . those who have fought for their rights . . . their right to live in peace, their right to be treated with dignity, their right to equality of opportunity, their right to be educated."

Response: We will be your refuge. Your haven in the storm. Carry on.

Phu Nguyen, Freelance Writer

From "#MeToo Has Made Me Speak Up," Huffington Post, *October 16, 2017*

"I speak up today to stand with all women who have been sexually harassed, abused, exploited, and denigrated. I speak up to stand with all the women who are part of the #MeToo movement right now and always, who will no longer accept silence as the norm. I speak up for the women who don't have the privilege of a platform, like I do. I speak up for the men who want to be allies but who have been complicit in the silent assaults and harassment of girls and women. It's time for you to speak up with us, too. It's time for you to condemn the inappropriate, inexcusable, non-consensual sexual acts of abuse committed by your fellow men. It's time to start believing women when they speak up."

Response: We will be your refuge. Your haven in the storm. Carry on.

Katharine Viles, Sexual Assault Survivor

From "I'm a Sexual Assault Survivor: #MeToo Is Incredibly Isolating," The Washington Post, *October 20, 2017*

"Plenty of people talk about how brave it is to speak out, and they're right. It is brave to speak out, but that doesn't make you a coward if you don't. Silent or not, activist or not, we are worthy, and we will be just as worthy when #MeToo stops trending. I don't owe anyone my story, and neither do you."

Response: We will be your refuge. Your haven in the storm. Carry on.

Hillary Clinton, Former First Lady, Senator, and Secretary of State

From "Ask Hillary Clinton," Rookie, *November 2, 2016*

"Believe me, every strong woman you admire who has worked to make our world a fairer place has faced opposition along the way. It's usually a sign that you're doing something right. But—and this is a big but—when that disagreement crosses over into bullying or harassment, it's never OK. If it makes you feel scared or uncomfortable or unsafe, I hope you'll consider telling them directly to stop or asking someone you trust to step in. You should be able to go to school or use the internet or just live your life without fear of being bullied. . . . Don't let the haters get you down."

Response: We will be your refuge. Your haven in the storm. Carry on.

Lakshmi Puri, Acting Head of UN Women

From "It Is Time for Action to End Violence against Women," speech at the ACP-EU Parliamentary Assembly, UN Women, June 19, 2013

"It is time for action when up to 70 per cent of women in some countries face physical and/or sexual violence in their lifetime. When one in three girls in developing countries is likely to be married as a child bride; when some 140 million girls and women have suffered female genital mutilation; when millions of women and girls are trafficked in modern-day slavery; and when women's bodies are a battleground and rape is used as a tactic of war—it is time for action."

Response: We will be your refuge. Your haven in the storm. Carry on.

Michelle Obama, Former First Lady
From "Transcript: Read Michelle Obama's Full Speech from the 2016 DNC," The Washington Post, *July 26, 2016*

"When someone is cruel, or acts like a bully, you don't stoop to their level—no, our motto is, when they go low, we go high."

Response: We will be your refuge. Your haven in the storm. Carry on.

Reflection | Sharing

All of what these women have said and more happens to women as individuals and affects us as a community.

What are your thoughts after listening to the words of these women? How will you reclaim your voice and take action in this age of violence?

After a quiet time, let us share our thoughts and put rosemary into the water so that we may offer support and be a refuge for one another.

Response: We will be your refuge. Your haven in the storm. Carry on.

The Stone Ritual

One person picks up the stone and shows it to those gathered.

The stone ritual symbolizes a release from pain and a renewal of loving, healing energy. As we sit in this circle together, relax and focus on the stone. *Pause.* Let us pass the stone around the circle. As you receive the stone, hold it, imagine that you are pouring your pain into it, and then pass the stone to the next person.

When each person has filled the stone with pain, the leader puts the stone in a bowl of water, washes it, and dries it with a towel.

Let us pass the stone around the circle again. This time when you receive it, hold it, and fill it with loving energy. *When each person has filled the stone with loving energy, place it in the center of the circle.*

Let us reflect quietly on the stone, the drops of water, releasing and healing pain, and filling with loving energy.

After a quiet time, share what you would like to about this experience.

Blessing Our Voices

Let us bless our voices and reclaim our power.
Touch your ears, saying: Bless my ears, that I may hear the stories of women.
Touch your diaphragm, saying: Bless my diaphragm, that my breath may sustain me.
Touch your nose, saying: Bless my nose, that I may smell the scents of hope.
Touch your lungs, saying: Bless my lungs, that I may fill my body with courage.
Touch your vocal chords, saying: Bless my vocal chords, that I may speak loudly.
Touch your mouth, saying: Bless my mouth, that I may cry out for justice.
Touch your whole body, saying: Bless my body, that I may be safe and heal beyond pain.

Take Action

Let us put our prayers into action. Here are some possible ways:

- Reclaim your voice. Inspire. Interact. Ignite. Intervene. Impact.
- Learn more about domestic violence in the United States: https://www.cdc.gov/violenceprevention/intimatepartnerviolence/index.html.
- Almost half (47.5%) of American Indian/Alaska Native women, 45.1% of non-Hispanic Black women, 37.3% of non-Hispanic White women, 34.4% of Hispanic women, and 18.3% of Asian-Pacific Islander women experience sexual violence, physical violence, and/or stalking by an intimate partner in their lifetime (CDC, 2017).

Sending Forth

Let us go forth from this safe place filled with support for one another. When times are tough—and they will be—let us remember that this is a time when we are not alone.

Let us go forth healed by this water and rosemary and empowered by this community to speak out with love and boldness and break the silence.

Let us go forth to resist bullying, abusive rhetoric, harassment, and violence.

As we unite our voices and strength, may the God of love, mercy, and justice heal our hurts and help us work for a better world, free from fear and violence.

Amen. Blessed be. May it be so.

Song

"Guide My Voice," adapted from and sung to the tune of "Guide My Feet," African American spiritual.

Guide my voice as I speak my truth.
Guide my voice as I speak my truth.
Guide my voice as I speak my truth.
For I don't have to speak my truth
alone.

Hold my hand as I speak my truth.
Hold my hand as I speak my truth.
Hold my hand as I speak my truth.
For I don't have to speak my truth
alone.

Stand by me as I speak my truth.
Stand by me as I speak my truth.
Stand by me as I speak my truth.
For I don't have to speak my truth
alone.

Search my heart as I speak my truth.
Search my heart as I speak my truth.
Search my heart as I speak my truth.
For I don't have to speak my truth
alone.

Greeting of Peace

Let us greet one another with a word of hope and exchange sprigs of rosemary.

Learn More from These Resources

Adams, Carol J., and Marie M. Fortune, eds. *Violence against Women and Children: A Christian Theological Sourcebook.* New York: Continuum, 1995.

Brock, Rita Nakashima, and Rebecca Ann Parker. *Saving Paradise: How Christianity Traded Love of This World for Crucifixion and Empire.* Boston, MA: Beacon Press, 2008.

Cooper-White, Pamela. *The Cry of Tamar: Violence against Women and the Church's Response.* 2nd ed. Minneapolis, MN: Fortress Press, 2012.

Domestic Violence Awareness Project of the National Resource Center Against Domestic Violence. https://www.nrcdv.org/.

FaithTrust Institute provides faith communities and advocates the tools and knowledge they need to address the faith and cultural issues to abuse. (Includes sermon samples for preaching on sexual assault and abuse.) http://www.faithtrustinstitute.org/.

Fortune, Marie M. *Love Does No Harm: Sexual Ethics for the Rest of Us.* New York: Continuum, 1998.

Jones, Serene. *Trauma + Grace: Theology in a Ruptured World.* Louisville, KY: Westminster John Knox Press, 2009.

National Coalition Against Domestic Violence is the voice of victims and survivors. They are the catalyst for changing society to have zero tolerance for domestic violence. They do this by affecting public policy, increasing understanding of the impact of domestic violence, and providing programs and education that drive that change. https://ncadv.org/.

Our Stories Untold is open space to discuss sexualized violence within spiritual communities (especially in the Mennonite Church) though stories from all walks of life are welcome. Through a blog, it has evolved into a community for all who are and have been affected by abuse in their lives. http://www.ourstoriesuntold.com/.

Rape, Abuse and Incest National Network (RAINN) is the nation's largest anti–sexual violence organization. RAINN created and operates the Safe Helpline for the Department of Defense. In 2015, the online hotline expanded to offer services in Spanish at rainn.org/es. RAINN also carries out programs to prevent sexual violence, help victims, and ensure that rapists are brought to justice. https://www.rainn.org/. 1-800-656-HOPE (4673).

Sanders, Annemarie, ed. *However Long the Night: Making Meaning in a Time of Crisis—The Spiritual Journey of the Leadership Conference of Women Religious.* Silver Spring, MD: LCWR, 2018.

Spiritual Alliance to Stop Intimate Violence lifts up national and international interfaith leaders with decades of experience in providing tools for effective prevention and response to intimate violence within their own communities. http://saiv.org/.

52. Water Meditation for Wellness

To understand water is to understand the cosmos, the marvels of nature, and life itself.

—Masaru Emoto, *The Hidden Messages in Water*

Water is essential to life. This meditation uses the image of water to invite cleansing, clarity, and calmness. The meaning of water goes as deep as the deepest sea. It holds endless inspiration from dreams to intuition, magic to mystery.

This meditation invites you into a healthy and harmonious relationship with yourself. Then, centered and balanced, you can be well and stir waters.

Preparation

If you can, do this meditation in or near water. If you are with others, find a comfortable place—chair, fountain, pond, lake, ocean, wherever. If you are alone, perhaps soak in a hot tub or bath water. Play water music if you wish (search YouTube).

The Meditation

Begin to relax. Breathe in and out. Begin to enjoy the quiet and become more actively receptive. Close your eyes, and become aware of your breathing.

Gather your day together. . . . Breathe it to center . . . and *slowly* breathe it away. Be aware of your breathing . . . of breath traveling through your feet . . . legs . . . hips . . . hands . . . chest . . . arms . . . and out of the top of your head. Breathe all to center and be attuned to yourself.

Imagine you are walking through colorful woods, or running in a plush, green meadow, or strolling in the foothills of a mountain. Before you, see a flowing river, a lake, the ocean, any body of water. Walk over to this water. Create in your own mind the kind of water it is—water that's rapidly flowing, water that's gently meandering, water after a storm, water on a sunny day, water waiting for rain, water flowing after having been dammed up. Take a moment to become friends with your body of water. *Long pause.*

Look carefully now through the water to its bottom. Notice the various shaped rocks and pebbles it holds. *Pause.* Walk around and discover more closely these rocks and pebbles for a moment—notice their texture, color, shape, and size.

Now focus your attention on one of these rocks or pebbles. Imagine you are this rock or pebble. *Pause.* Feel the water washing over you, how it changes you on its journey—polishes you, cracks you open, chips off your roughness. Notice how you alter its path and how it alters yours . . . the changer and the changed—you are in continual dialogue. *Pause.*

Begin now to let go of your resting place and flow with the water. Let it carry you along—spilling over into waterfalls, bumping into the banks and other rocks, flowing through rough currents, stirring the water, and warming in the sun. Flow with this journey. *Long pause.*

Feel now the warmth of rays of sunlight dancing on the surface of your water. Welcome these rays; let them warm you with their wisdom. See in the enlightenment of these rays the face of a wise person, a person full of love and warmth and understanding for you.

Talk to your wise person about *(what is important for you now).* Feel free to share with this person your experiences . . . your resistances . . . your fears . . . your hopes . . . the choices or changes you may need to make . . . the strategies you need to develop. Take some time to communicate. *Long pause.*

Slowly begin to identify yourself with this ray of light. Take this ray of light inside of yourself. Be aware that the ray of light—the wise person—is always with you . . . and that you can get in touch with it and draw on its qualities whenever you choose.

Become aware of other rays of light touching the life around you—the other changing rocks . . . the meandering river bed . . . the drops of water filling up and spilling over becoming endless waterfalls . . . all are animated by the same life energy, all are part of the same planet . . . of the greater whole. Take a minute to experience this.

Slowly begin to be conscious of your breathing. Invite a word, phrase, or image to emerge in you to capture the experience that you had.

Begin now to bring yourself back to this room.

Now slowly begin to awaken your body. Stretch. Begin to move and become aware that you are in this room. Slowly begin to open your eyes, look around, and notice this space. Be present to yourself.

Drink some water!

Take some time to journal, draw, color, walk outside, dance, notice places of water.

Any time you pass water—a lake, pond, stream, river, a glass of water, a water bottle, a puddle, the ocean—send your love and gratitude to that water.

How to Create a Feminist Liturgy for Justice

Feminists worldwide are reshaping liturgies from their religious perspectives and in their own contexts. The liturgies we craft address the spiritual needs for justice from our own countries, cultures, religions, clans, tribes, neighborhoods, families, and communities. We are revisioning culture and religion to integrate the old with the new. We are bringing feminist concerns for justice to institutional religious services and prayers. We are reclaiming and redesigning traditional liturgies and symbols.

We are creating feminist liturgies for justice. We are stirring waters, drinking from the well, stepping into the pool, letting justice flow like water, and being well!

The art of creating feminist liturgies for justice can be learned. Some people have a natural talent for creating liturgies, others have traditional training, and some have both. Feminist liturgy making and writing guidelines are gleaned from the experiences of feminist liturgical communities, from the trials and errors of its practitioners, from traditional liturgical theory, and from cross-cultural ritual traditions.

Everyone can create meaningful liturgies that invite participants to pray for and address the justice issues of their neighborhood, community, state, nation, and world. Each can create out of their own traditions and include the family of humanity and the Divine Holy One (however one names the divine). Each liturgy can be unique and reflect a particular context.

From my fifty years of liturgy planning in Catholic, ecumenical, interfaith, and cross-cultural settings, including my thirty-five years at the Women's Alliance for Theology, Ethics, and Ritual (WATER), I have learned that, to create liturgies, you need inspiration, time, thought, and resources.

The guidelines that follow are intended to make the planning process more fruitful and/or give people courage to begin. This is the brainstorming method that I use and teach. This is the general structure of the liturgies in this book. To illustrate this, I will use the liturgy, "#MeToo: Reclaiming Our Voices in an Age of Violence," found in this book as number 51.

Think of the Feminist Liturgy That Your Community Needs

Be attentive to community events and global issues like International Women's Day or Breast Cancer Awareness month. You may want to raise up a woman like Sojourner Truth or Malala Yousafzai. Search with community members and talk about the needs of the group. (*We need to create a liturgy to reclaim our voices.*) Write down the major theme (*healing, reclaiming*) and give the liturgy a tentative name if you can (*Reclaim Our Voices*). Check out liturgies of the same theme that may already exist.

Focus the Theme

Think of what you want this liturgy to say, why you are creating it, and what you want to happen to people during and after it. Jot down your initial words, phrases, and ideas. (*#MeToo affects us all. We want to raise up women who are resisting bullying, abusive rhetoric, harassment. We want to reclaim our voices.*) You are brainstorming, so let the energy flow. You will be able to reject, use, alter, or combine your ideas later. You are creating the raw material for the liturgy.

Discover a Symbol That Will Visibly Carry the Message of the Liturgy

Symbols are key to successful liturgies. Reclaim symbols used by many traditions, such as oil, bread, salt, water, candles, and eggs. Try others, such as a variety of breads and drinks, shells, stones, ribbons, fans, bells, chimes, mirrors, herbs, fruits, milk and honey, birdcages, or balloons. Choose one symbol or several. Keep it simple (*#MeToo posters, sprigs of rosemary, a stone, candles, and a bowl of water*).

Identify Readings, Prayers, and Blessings That Make Your Message Concrete

What do you want them to say? Whose words do you want to hear—Scripture, poetry, quotes by women from international and cross-cultural settings? Should these be mimed, danced, read chorally, spoken with many voices? Do you need to write new prayers, blessings, or stories? Be sure to use language that is inclusive of gender, ethnicity, class, age, abilities, and lifestyles. (*In this liturgy we use quotes by women from different cultural backgrounds and different parts of the world to show that #MeToo is everywhere and affects us all.*)

Select Music That Conveys Your Message

Identify songs, chants, instrumental and taped music that support your theme. Note the mood and message to decide the appropriate place for each in your service. Use women's music whenever possible to educate others about it. (*In this liturgy we use "Sanctuary" by Carrie Newcomer and adapt the African American spiritual "Guide My Feet" using the words "guide my voice as I speak my truth."*)

Choose an Environment That Enhances the Theme of the Celebration

This could be outside near water, in a park or garden, in a special room, at someone's house, or in a religious space. Arrange the seating in a circle around a circular table, sometimes called an altar; circles connect to the cosmic flow of divine energy. Be attentive to color and coordinate with candles, cloths, symbols, and banners. Place the liturgical objects on a table, throughout the space, or decide to bring them into the liturgy at an appropriate time.

Share the Leadership for Various Parts of the Service with Several People

The liturgy belongs to the community; it brings to public expression the faith life of the community. Therefore, leadership is shared with different people initiating the various parts. Decide who will take leadership for each section. Give the leaders scripts and ideas to guide them in their parts, but encourage them to use their own words for introductions, blessings, and prayers.

Include Body Expression

Use prayer postures and gestures to embody the message of the liturgy. Move to music. Include dance/choreography that uses hand motions or bowing, and warm embraces at the time of peace sharing. Use dramatic gestures when interacting with the symbols, for example, pour the water like a waterfall. In the course of the liturgy, you may light a candle, wash your hands, break bread, drink from a cup, share herbs, plant bulbs, meditate, or pray with your arms crossed in front of your chest swaying side to side. Be aware that some bodies do not move easily and others cannot dance or gesture. Many bodies carry pain from physical and emotional abuse. Always ask permission for people to touch one another, even to hold hands. (*In this liturgy, we light candles, pass a stone around the circle, and bless our voices.*)

Be Attentive to Moments of Transition in the Liturgy

The liturgy works well when one section transitions smoothly into the next. This is done most effectively with music and gestures appealing to the senses, not by announcement.

Design the Order of the Liturgy

When the previous brainstorming is complete, it is time to create the order of the liturgy. I have discovered the following to be an effective structure for a liturgy. To illustrate this, I will continue to use examples from the liturgy, "#MeToo: Reclaiming Our Voices in an Age of Violence."

Preparation

Create the space and ambience to reflect the message of the liturgy. An example from "Reclaiming Our Voices": *Put #MeToo posters around the room. Gather sprigs of rosemary, a stone, and a bowl of water. Place them and as many lit candles as you wish on your table or around the space.*

Call to Gather

Welcome participants. Focus the liturgy, state why we are celebrating this theme, and invite people to gather. For example, from "Reclaiming Our Voices":

We gather for a liturgy of healing . . . Our community needs healing. Our country needs healing. Everywhere needs healing.

We gather in the midst of the #MeToo, #ChurchToo, #MosqueMeToo, and Time's Up movements to raise up women worldwide who are resisting bullying, abusive rhetoric, harassment, and violence present in our societies today.

We gather "Reclaiming Our Voices in an Age of Violence." We come together to challenge one another to speak out because only together can we create a world free from violence, abuse, and fear. We mourn those who have died because of domestic violence. We rage with those who have survived sexual abuse and are breaking silence to tell their stories. We pray for healing.

Naming the Circle

Invite participants to share their names, where they are from, and/or something that focuses the liturgy. For example, in "Reclaiming Our Voices" the gathered are invited to speak their names and say, "I reclaim my voice in an age of violence."

Music | Song | Chant

Be attentive to the mood you want to establish–quiet, festive, haunting, soothing. Music, songs, chants can be used in a variety of places in the liturgy. In "Reclaiming Our Voices" the song "Sanctuary" by Carrie Newcomer is sung after Creating a Safe Space and Blessing the Light, then the refrain "We will be your refuge. Your haven in the storm. Carry on" is used as a response throughout the liturgy. Songs and refrains can weave the liturgy together.

Prayer | Litany | Candle Lighting

Write or choose a prayer, litany, or candle lighting that could form a transition into the reading, be a general address to the Spirit for openness, or focus the theme of the liturgy. This is the "Blessing the Light" from "Reclaiming Our Voices."

Let us bless this light. Please say after me:
Blessed are you, Holy One of Justice, Echo.
for you empower us to kindle flames of healing. Echo.

Let us warm our hands over this healing fire. Pause. *Let us cup our hands over the flame and draw its healing energy to our eyes three times. Let us open our hands outward and send healing energy to those who need it now.*

Readings

Choose one or two readings that will be central to the liturgy. These can be Scripture passages, poems, stories, or excerpts from writings by women or justice leaders. If your group is Scripture focused, you will want to choose a scriptural text from *The Inclusive Bible* (Lanham, MD: Rowman & Littlefield Publishers, 2007). A sung or spoken refrain can be used to connect the readings and deepen the message. In the "Reclaiming Our Voices" section titled "Listen to Women's Words" excerpts from seven women around the world challenge us to reclaim our voices.

Reflection | Sharing

This is traditionally the homily, sermon, or preaching time. Since the divine speaks to everyone, the sharing is communal. Offer a few sentences that recap the message of the readings. Then pose one or two questions for reflection. Depending on the size of the group, form small groups or share in the whole gathering. The reflection from "Reclaiming Our Voices" follows:

All of what these women have said and more happens to women as individuals and affects us as a community.

What are your thoughts after listening to the words of these women? How will you reclaim your voice and take action in this age of violence?

After a quiet time, let us share our thoughts and put rosemary into the water so that we may offer support and be a refuge for one another.

Song Refrain

If people are meeting in groups, they need more than words from a human voice to gather them back as a whole. Singing a song refrain that has already been a part of the service invites attention and brings closure to this section. In "Reclaiming Our Voices" the Response *We will be your refuge. Your haven in the storm. Carry on* is sung after each woman's quote. You can also ring a bell or sound a gong.

Presentation of the Symbol

Name the symbol, touch it, show it to the group, and say why you are using it. In "Reclaiming Our Voices" the symbols of stones and water were presented in the Stone Ritual. The leader picks up the stone and shows it to those gathered, saying:

The stone ritual symbolizes a release from pain and a renewal of loving, healing energy. As we sit in this circle together, relax, and focus on the stone. Pause.

Interaction with the Symbol

The interaction with the symbol may come before or after the blessing. Give directions for interacting with the symbol: pass it around the circle, one person offers it to others, participants go to stations/centers to interact with it, several people start passing to different parts of the circle, groups of people come forward to drink water from the common well, and many other ways. Be specific so that people will feel comfortable. In "Reclaiming Our Voices" after presenting the stone, the leader continued:

Let us pass the stone around the circle. As you receive the stone, hold it, imagine that you are pouring your pain into it, and then pass the stone to the next person. (When each person has filled the stone with pain, the leader puts the stone in a bowl of water, washes it, and dries it with a towel.)

Let us pass the stone around the circle again. This time when you receive it, hold it, and fill it with loving energy. (When each person has filled the stone with loving energy, place it in the center of the circle.)

Let us reflect quietly on the stone, the drops of water, releasing and healing pain, and filling with loving energy. After a quiet time, share what you would like to about this experience.

Blessing the Symbol

Bless the symbol. For "Reclaiming Our Voices" the symbol we blessed was our voices.

Let us bless our voices and reclaim our power.
Touch your ears, saying: Bless my ears, that I may hear the stories of women.
Touch your diaphragm, saying: Bless my diaphragm, that my breath may sustain me.
Touch your nose, saying: Bless my nose, that I may smell the scents of hope.
Touch your lungs, saying: Bless my lungs, that I may fill my body with courage.
Touch your vocal chords, saying: Bless my vocal chords, that I may speak loudly.
Touch your mouth, saying: Bless my mouth, that I may cry out for justice.
Touch your whole body, saying: Bless my body, that I may be safe and heal beyond pain.

Take Action

Feminist liturgies bring together spirituality and justice. They challenge participants to take action for justice to make the world a better place for all creation. The Take Action section from "Reclaiming Our Voices" offers resources to inspire, interact, ignite, intervene, impact.

Let us put our prayers into action. Here are some possible ways:

- *Reclaim your voice. Inspire. Interact. Ignite. Intervene. Impact.*
- *Learn more about domestic violence statistics in the United States.*

Sending Forth

Pay careful attention to the closure. When the liturgy ends abruptly, people can be left with an unresolved feeling. The Sending Forth gathers up the message of the liturgy and challenges people to go forth to act on it. I usually offer this challenging closure in three sentences or three parts. To close "Reclaiming Our Voices," for example:

Let us go forth from this safe place filled with support for one another. When times are tough—and they will be—let us remember that this is a time when we are not alone.
Let us go forth healed by this water and rosemary and empowered by this community to speak out with love and boldness and break the silence.
Let us go forth to resist bullying, abusive rhetoric, harassment, and violence.
As we unite our voices and strength, may the God of love, mercy, and justice heal our hurts and help us work for a better world, free from fear and violence.
Amen. Blessed be. May it be so.

Greeting of Peace

I usually include a Greeting of Peace at the end of the liturgy to bring closure. People have created something together and want to bid farewell with handshakes, warm greetings, hugs, embraces, and/or by exchanging symbols used in the liturgy. Be mindful that many people have experienced abusive touch and do not want to be touched by others. Always ask and invite; do not assume. The Greeting of Peace in "Reclaiming Our Voices" was:

Let us greet one another with a word of hope and exchange sprigs of rosemary.

Song

Use a closing song that resonates with the message spoken in the Sending Forth. Sometimes it is good to use a song that invites a spiral or circle dance so people can sway and dance.

Learn More from These Resources

There are now many feminist resources that enhance and expand the theme for each liturgy. They can be books, websites, YouTube videos, organizations, articles, and more. Each liturgy offers an educational opportunity. After the liturgy, think about what went well, what worked, what could have been different or better. Then incorporate those changes the next time.

Many blessings, and enjoy your liturgies!

How to Start a Feminist Liturgy Group, Inclusive Eucharistic Community, or House Church

There is no magic formula, but we have had a significant amount of experience in animating and facilitating a variety of spirituality communities through the Women's Alliance for Theology, Ethics, and Ritual (WATER). We pass on the following in the hope that groups will start, grow, network, and, if necessary, end with minimal effort and maximal grace.

Groups gather for a range of reasons. Usually they are searching for a more inclusive liturgy and community, for sacrament and solidarity, for meaning and ministry.

What seems to work best is a combination of worship or prayer, meditation or reflection, with community-building such as a shared meal before or during the liturgy, or drinks and refreshments afterward. Formats vary, but liturgy and community are key since it is that combination that leads to effective networking for social change.

Groups work best when they are convened by a small core of people who share common beliefs and needs; for instance, a belief that women, LGBTQIA+ people, and others pushed to the margins are holy and called to be leaders of liturgy.

To get a group going, someone or several people need to take the lead, commit to starting a group, and follow through with the practical tasks of invitations through social media, phone calls, emails, and letters to make the first meeting happen.

Here are some guidelines to help:

1. Establish Basics

- Collaborate with other like-minded people who want to come together to worship in an inclusive way, in a feminist way.
- Choose key people who will take leadership in keeping the address list up to date, sending out the calendar, planning the liturgy, and hosting the gathering.
- Choose the space: a permanent one, an on-line one, or one that rotates from house to house.
- Seek guidance from local spiritual leaders and invite them to be part of the community.

2. Gather Members

- Think of the people you want to reach to participate.
- Invite people to gather for liturgy, and/or a meal, and/or a justice project.
- Seek religious group or organization sponsorship.
- Start a small group.
- Keep a manageable size.

3. Have Regular Meetings

- Plan a consistent, regular time for the liturgy. Decide to gather once a month, or every three weeks, or every week; agree on a specific day and time, for example, every Sunday at five o'clock in the afternoon.
- Decide on a specific routine: celebrate a liturgy planned by someone in the group, include a meal with the liturgy and invite each person to bring a food and drink.
- Pray together, eat together, and create a community.
- Engage in some common social justice outreach like working together in a soup kitchen one day a month.

4. If You Want to Become Legal

- Seek incorporation.
- Apply for a Federal Employer ID # (FEIN).
- Write bylaws.
- Decide on policies.
- Become a 501(c)(3) tax exempt group.

Index of Blessings and Prayers

Index of Readings and Authors

Maybe journey is not so much a journey ahead,	Nelle Morton	48. December
Miriam, as Moses' sister, could have been my great, great, great . . . great Aunt.	Marjorie Feldman	3. March
My cancer scare changed my life. I'm grateful for every new, healthy day I have.	Olivia Newton-John	22. October
My friends are my estate.	Emily Dickinson	32. August
My friends have made the story of my life.	Helen Keller	32. August
My mother told me two things constantly . . . to be a lady . . . to be independent.	Ruth Bader Ginsburg	29. May
My very sex, as I need not tell you, puts many obstacles in the way.	Catherine of Siena	4. April
My world turned upside down at seven o'clock on the morning of March 8	Susanna	22. October
NASA should embrace Mission to Planet Earth.	Sally Ride	17. May
Nobody sees a flower—really—it is so small it takes time—we haven't time—and to see takes time, like to have a friend takes time.	Georgia O'Keeffe	32. August
No tinsel of trumpets and flags will ultimately seduce women into the insanity of recklessly destroying life,	Olive Schreiner	33. September
O boundless charity! Just as you gave us yourself, wholly God and wholly human,	Catherine of Siena	4. April
O dearest daughter, this patience is a queen who stands guard upon the rock of courage.	Catherine of Siena	4. April
Oh Holy Spirit, come into my heart;	Catherine of Siena	4. April
Once upon a time there were three cups.	Diann L. Neu	37. January
One child, one teacher, one book, and one pen, can change the world.	Malala Yousafzai	19. July
O Nurturing, Nourishing, Mothering God,	Bridget Mary Meehan	5. May
Our soul must perform two duties.	Julian of Norwich	5. May
Our womanist work is to draw on the rugged endurance of black folks in America	Katie Geneva Cannon	26. February
Peace cannot exist without justice,	Rigoberta Menchú	33. September

Index of Songs and Songwriters

Acknowledgments

Profound and everlasting gratitude to the many people and communities around the world who have inspired, called forth, and participated in these feminist liturgies. These include local, national, and international groups: the WATER*ritual* community; Sisters against Sexism (SAS), the oldest US women-church base community; other women-church communities; house churches; women's religious communities; intentional eucharistic communities; the Providence community of St. Mary-of-the-Woods, Indiana; ecumenical and interfaith feminist groups; and justice organizations worldwide.

Gratitude, ever-flowing.

Mary E. Hunt, cofounder and codirector of the Women's Alliance for Theology, Ethics, and Ritual (WATER) for thirty-five years together of stirring waters, stepping into the pool, and doing pioneering work: using feminist religious values for religious and social change, challenging oppression so justice can flow, pushing boundaries that all may be well, and making friends around the world.

Gratitude, ever-flowing.

WATER colleagues who have helped bring these liturgies to life: Lauren Bennett, Emily Cohen, Clare Coker, Hannah Dorfman, Melissa Feito, Kali Huiyan Lo Ng, Cathy Jaskey, Heureuse Kaj, Cynthia Lapp, Charlotte Lim, Wendy Mallette, Mallory Naake, Emily Neufeld, Techika Rhodes, Annabeth Roeschley, Janaya Sachs, the late great Carol Scinto, Joe Scinto, Karis Slattery, Kate Stoltzfus, Kennedy Thedford, and Dana Tufariello.

Gratitude, ever-flowing.

Feminist liturgy colleagues whose creative and transformational works have inspired mine: Theresa Berger, Marcia Falk, Coralie Ling, Janet Morley, Marjorie Proctor-Smith, Susan K. Roll, Victoria Rue, Janet Walton, and Hannah Ward.

Gratitude, ever-flowing.

Feminist, womanist, feminista/mujerista, and Asian theologians whose challenging and prophetic life works have shaped my thoughts and liturgies: Rita Nakashima Brock, Mary Condren, Katie Geneva Canon, Mary Daly, Kelly Brown Douglas, Ivone Gebara, Mary E. Hunt, Ada Maria Isasi-Diáz, Kwok Pui Lan, Mercy Amba Odoyoye, Judith Plaskow, Rosemary Radford Ruether, Letty Russell, Elisabeth Schüssler Fiorenza, and Emilie Townes.

Gratitude, ever-flowing.

Musicians, songwriters, and authors who have generously granted copyright permission: Jann Aldredge-Clanton, Meg Ammons, Susan R. Beehler, Linda Bessom, Monica Brown, MariaElena Del Valle, Debbie Friedman estate, Jeremy Gallet, SP, David Lohman, Rose Mary Meyer, BVM, C. Murphy estate, Holly Near, Carrie Newcomer, Suzanne Noffke, OP, Fran Peavey estate, Jan Phillips, Kathy Sherman, CSJ, Marsie Silvestro, Sisters of Providence of St. Mary-of-the-Woods, Jean Stokan, The Collegeville Composers Group, Wailin' Jennys, Betty Wendelborn, Susan Werner, Cris Williamson, Alice Walker, and Miriam Therese Winter.

Gratitude, ever-flowing.

International friends who helped so graciously with translations: Fionnuala Bates, Carol P. Christ, Mary Condren, Donna Marie Fu, SP, Ivone Gebara, Diana Gomez de Molino, Ann-Cathrin Jarl, Herta Leistner, Tami Nguyen, Dolores Pomerleau, Veronica Schweyen, MM, and Cecilia Wadstein.

Gratitude, ever-flowing.

The Liturgical Press staff who produced *Stirring Waters: Feminist Liturgies for Justice* for all of us: Peter Dwyer, director; Shannon Chisholm, publisher, parish market; Stephanie Lancour, production editor; Colleen Stiller, production manager; and Michelle Verkuilen, associate publisher, parish market.

Gratitude, ever-flowing.

Every effort has been made to identify all the texts used in this book and to secure permission to publish and/or reprint. Anticipatory apologies for any errors or infringements.